World University Library

The World University Library is an international series
of books, each of which has been specially commissioned.
The authors are leading scientists and scholars from all over
the world who, in an age of increasing specialisation, see the
need for a broad, up-to-date presentation of their subject.
The aim is to provide authoritative introductory books for
university students which will be of interest also to the general
reader. The series is published in Britain, France, Germany,
Holland, Italy, Spain, Sweden and the United States.

Frontispiece. Plan of the Ka´ba at Mecca. A late
seventeenth-century faience tile from Iznik, Turkey.
Victoria and Albert Museum, London.

Francesco Gabrieli

Muhammad and the Conquests of Islam

**translated from the Italian by
Virginia Luling and Rosamund Linell**

World University Library

McGraw-Hill Book Company
New York Toronto

Contents

List of maps

1 Muhammad in history

The figure of the Arab Prophet, although it may be said, not altogether accurately, that he stands in the full light of history, is as difficult to grasp and evaluate in historical reality as are those other two great founders, Buddha and Jesus. As with them, between that reality and our judgment the distortion of legend is interposed, and in the case of Muhammad this is double, a tradition of exaltation and one of denigration. In the East, in his own community, the founder of Islam has indeed undergone a process of idealisation which, in its most extreme manifestation, has quite transformed his historical character; but in the West it early underwent a different transformation, appearing in medieval Christian apologetics and polemics in a no less tendentious and fantastic guise, until the more objective views of modern times intervened. And yet even in our own age, underneath the technical refinements and the assertions of objectivity, the old prejudices and passions can still sometimes be felt, often enough combined with new prejudices and passions. The following pages are intended to give some idea of all three processes; the double legend, eastern and western, and the modern historical view, in its growth and its principal versions.

The fact of Muhammad's humanity, which he himself had proclaimed, of his physical and moral dependence, even though entrusted with the highest of missions, cannot be said to have vanished entirely in the image which orthodox Islam has fashioned for itself of its founder. But naturally, alongside this substantial admission, veneration for the Prophet developed to the furthest possible degree every element, found in the Koran itself or more often drawn from pious legend, which would surround this human figure with supernatural events, qualities and capacities. We shall mention in due course the miracles with which Muslim piety has surrounded the conception, birth and infancy of the Prophet. This supernatural aura fades but does not wholly disappear with the beginning of his career as the inspired instrument of revelation, even if we discount the initial circumstances of his inspiration, where the open intervention of the supernatural is undoubtedly

Relief and ethnic distribution

based on the experiences and memories of Muhammad himself. The belief in his miraculous 'night journey' from Mecca to Jerusalem and thence to heaven, upon which so much of the Muslim eschatology was to be based, is founded on a few verses of the Koran which in fact can be interpreted as a description of a dream rather than of a physical journey. But there are other miraculous incidents without any direct warrant in the sacred book, with which tradition has embellished the Prophet's biography: sighings from trees, or animals uttering human voices in his presence, angelic apparitions, and even wonders or miracles personally performed by him, such as splitting the moon in two. A more historical tradition, however, preserves, on just this subject of miracles, the memory of Muhammad's rejection of anyone who demanded such supernatural feats, and his indication of the Koran as the one authentic miracle; but popular piety had no such hesitation in ascribing to him as well actions which by breaking the laws of nature (or rather, according to Muslim theology, interrupting their normal course by God's permission) placed him above common humanity. As for the Koran itself, its miraculous and inimitable character is deduced from the many passages in it in which the unbelievers are challenged to produce anything similar as something manifestly impossible. This belief which became the dogma, in the full sense of the word, of *i'jaz*, or inimitability of the sacred book, has had enormous influence both in the theological and the literary fields in Islamic civilisation. We mention it here simply as one element in the assertion of Muhammad's supernatural prerogatives; but it must be noted that the Islamic conception of the Koran as the direct word of God reduces the part played by the Prophet personally in the production of this miraculous text to that of simple mechanical transmission.

But the idealisation of the figure of the Prophet does not involve only the attribution of wonder-working powers. His human fallibility was admitted by Muhammad himself even in the revelation – there is a *sura* in the Koran (1xxx) in which Allah reproves him for having roughly sent away a poor blind man who asked for an explanation of the faith, while he was trying to ingratiate himself with the high and mighty of Mecca. But this recognition grew progressively dimmer, in contrast to the idea of the prophetic 'isma, the immunity, by divine protection, from error or fault; the privilege of all God's messengers, and especially of the seal of the prophets, Muhammad. His character appeared to later tradition and piety as the sum of all the moral virtues, of sweetness, patience and humility, of mercy, generosity, courage and solicitude for the humble, weak and suffering – by dint of adding to the genuine testimonies of the Prophet's life and character the fantasies of apologetics. This model of virtue, marked with the chrism of prophetic dignity, could not but possess special prerogatives in the life beyond the grave, such as the power to intercede with God; hence the figure of the Prophet as intercessor for the faithful, with its associated literature and liturgy. From this privileged position as an exceptional man which orthodoxy attributes to Muhammad develops the ever more markedly sacred conception of later Islam, culminating in the idea of the Prophet as a metaphysical and mystical primordial being, a sort of eon or Logos present *ab aeterno* in the divine mind. Such is the vision of mystics such as Ibn 'Arabi, who (certainly not without influence from parallel Christian ideas) hypostasise a 'Muhammadic reality' (*haqiqa muhammadiyya*), an intelligence and governing force of the world, as an emanation of the supreme Divinity. So the memory of the historical person of the Meccan merchant, and of the able and realistic head of state of Medina, is lost on the one hand in the speculations of a mysticism wholly foreign and unknown to him, while on the other it materialises in the most naive beliefs of popular piety. One last thin barrier, which neither the most subtle speculation nor the grossest superstition ever pierced, guarded the Prophet of pure monotheism from the sacrilegious assimilation to God Himself; but barring this last step, the idealisation of the man was carried, in his own community, to the furthest possible limits.

Muhammad, journeying in a caravan to Syria,
is served a meal by Christian monks.
A miniature painting from a Turkish
manuscript. University Library, Edinburgh.

The judgment of medieval Christianity

Over against the eastern legend, born of veneration and love,
stands that of the West, of opposite inspiration. The Christian
church, barely three centuries after her victory over pagan polytheism, saw rising out of Muhammad's teaching a rival faith,
which soon grew into a giant besieging her borders and snatching
from her territories where she had seemed securely rooted, among
them the birthplace of Christ Himself. The fundamental point to
bear in mind about the legend of Muhammad in the Christian
West is that the latter saw Islam as a heresy springing from her
own breast, through human malice and diabolic inspiration, and its
founder as an apostate, out of base motives, from his original
Christian faith.

This notion has its basis in a genuine historical fact; the part
which Christianity undoubtedly did play in the formation of
Muhammad's monotheism, and the contacts which he certainly
had as a young man with Christian circles in Syria and the desert,
to which the eastern legend has itself lent the precision of detailed
description. The character of the monk Bahira, who divined
Muhammad's prophetic mission, appears already in the *Sira*,
the Muslim biography of the Prophet; and whatever kernel
of truth it contains passed through Byzantine channels to the
Christian West, and served, together with the much more certainly
historical figure of the Christian Waraqa, Khadija's cousin, to
represent the supposed Christian origins of the Prophet of Islam.
From these slender foundations in fact, and what the eastern
legend represented as fact, sprang the hostile western legend which
D'Ancona described in his classic study. We find it in various
versions, inconsistent in their content, but entirely consistent in
their spirit of vituperation and hatred, in the writings of chroniclers,
apologists, hagiographers, and encyclopedists of the Latin Middle
Ages; Guibert of Nogent and Hildebert of Tours in the eleventh
century, Peter the Venerable in the twelfth, Jacques de Vitry,
Martinus Polonus, Vincent of Beauvais and Jacobus a Varagine in

ددی ودخی مجیره أيندی يا مخد سنك شربتك شرابك ندر

ددی حضرت رسول ایندی بنوم شربتم سُوذ دُر شرابم صودور

اکرسُوذ وارسه کتورک واکرسُود یوعیسه صوکتورک ددی مجیر

بوردی سُود کتورد یلرصو حاضر ایلدیلر فلان جماعت خمر حبلر

the thirteenth, up to Brunetto Latini and his imitators, and Dante and his commentators.

The essential of the legend is the attribution of Muhammad's preaching to the false indoctrination of a malicious and embittered apostate, the aforementioned Bahira, who in Byzantium and the West was later known as Serge, who is a Christian monk, a bishop, or even a cardinal, moved by hatred and delusion to tear with schism the bosom of the church. Muhammad (*Mathomus*, *Mamutius*, *Machometus*) is nothing but the instrument of his revenge. Subject to epileptic fits (a tendentious misinterpretation of the trances which must have accompanied his early revelations), he proclaimed while in this condition a law of utter sexual license and blasphemous denial of the divinity of Christ, supporting his pretended mission with puerile conjuring tricks. Thus he is said to have trained a cow or a bull-calf to kneel before him, and it appeared at his call carrying the alleged sacred book between its horns; or a dove was trained, this time to fly to the ear of the pseudo-prophet, attracted by a grain of millet which he had put there for it to peck at. The base heresy spread, given the advantage by its immoral teaching (it was Muhammad's relatively easy-going position on sexual relations – which in fact he intended to regulate and restrain – to which Christian rigorism and asceticism reacted most strongly). But divine retribution was not slow to overtake the foul heresiarch, who ended by being torn to pieces by pigs, while going apart to perform a natural function. So he fell headlong into hell, where Dante was to see him among the sowers of scandal and schism, obscenely displayed in a tableau of unsurpassed plebeian realism. But the evil weed, once sown, did not die with him but grew to become the *flagellum dei* both in the East and the West.

In this, the more common version of the legend, the Prophet of Islam is, as we have seen, egged on to his nefarious work by a perjured Christian mentor; in another version, however, the deluded and vengeful cleric is identified with Muhammad himself. Muhammad is the bishop, or even cardinal, known in Christendom as either Pelagius or Nicholas, who, refused or cheated of the pontifical dignity he coveted, let loose schism and ended torn in pieces by the pigs.

This grotesque fiction, the product of ignorance, fantasy and *odium theologicum*, is the answer of the Christian Middle Ages to the idealising attitude of Islam towards its Prophet. It is not surprising, therefore, that Muslim apologetics produced a work with the significant title 'The sword unsheathed against the insulters of God's Prophet', or that even today the twenty-eighth canto of Dante's Inferno is expurgated or omitted in translations of the Divine Comedy intended for Muslim countries. This medieval travesty, and the state of mind which inspired it, have been gradually modified with the passing of the centuries; more enlightened Christian apologists have abandoned the frontal attack on Islam and make use of points of contact rather than opposition, in particular avoiding polemic against Muhammad personally. But the old prejudices have continued even into modern times, even among twentieth-century Catholic scholars like Père Lammens, whose extremely learned studies on the *Sira* yet burn with the uncontrollable repulsion of medieval apologetics towards the Prophet and his works. Such, then, was Muhammad for the Latin Middle Ages; a false Prophet of the lusts of the flesh, preacher of a vile heresy, and render of the seamless garment of the universal Church.

Muhammad reassessed

The Middle Ages were a distant memory for western civilisation when a new valuation of the Prophet of Islam began to dawn. The European Enlightenment was in many ways open to a more balanced judgment of this kind, free from *odium theologicum*, though not equally so from rationalist prejudices. The first half of the eighteenth century saw the attention of the West turned with fresh eyes, half curious, half benevolent, towards the Muslim world and its Prophet, whose religion seemed to some to compare

Christ on a donkey and Muhammad on camelback, riding together. From Rashid ud-Din's 'Universal History' of 1307. University Library, Edinburgh.

favourably with Christianity. In 1730 there appeared a life of Muhammad, in French, by De Boulainvilliers; and in 1734 the English translation of the Koran by Sale, which was to hold the field in Europe for many years. Biographer and translator agree in presenting Muhammad in the eighteenth-century style, as a sage and lawgiver in the same category as Theseus or Numa Pompilius, who introduced a religion conformable to reason instead of the abstruse dogmas of Judaism or Christianity. This benevolent judgment is echoed by Savary, the first French translator of the Koran, who relied largely on Sale. But other voices, from the very heart of the Enlightenment and prompted by the same rationalistic principles, were raised to contradict it. It was Voltaire himself who, in his tragedy *Mahomet* (1742) and the later

Essai sur les Moeurs took up arms against contemporary admirers of the Prophet in the name of their own eighteenth-century ideals of humanity and rationality. The author of the battle-cry *décrasons l'infame!* was not led away like some other men of the period, by the desire to contrast Christianity with a more natural, non-dogmatic religion; his reading of the Koran, with its preposterous disorder, its monotonous repetitions, its minute juridical and ritual precepts, horrified him, and his knowledge – broadly correct – of Muhammad's political and private career outraged his moral sense. A man who made war on his own city, who massacred enemies and abducted women in the name of an incomprehensible Book could not, in Voltaire's view, lay claim to true greatness.

While the Enlightenment exalted the Prophet on the one hand as a non-Christian secular legislator, and on the other condemned him as a blood-stained traitor, the Romantic epoch attempted, with Carlyle, to reach the obscure depths of Muhammad's religious consciousness, taking as its premiss his complete sincerity. Starting from much the same historical materials as the men of the Enlightenment, but principally from his own concept of the Hero as religious founder, through his mystical contact with the absolute and the mission which this imposes upon him, the Scottish writer was the first in the West to present the founder of Islam in a heroic light, as the inspired awakener of the dormant energy of his people. For Carlyle, Muhammad is the spark fallen from heaven to set alight the apparently 'unnoticeable sand' of the Arabian desert; to gather together the poor bedouin tribes into a unity of irresistible power; 'lo! the sand proves explosive powder, blazes heaven-high from Delhi to Grenada!' This is a poetic and emotional vision rather than a historical one, overflowing with the ingenuous idealism of the Romantics, but it has the undeniable merit of having overcome the sometimes equally ingenuous, excessively abstract and moralistic approach of the Enlightenment, and of having drawn attention to the intimate personal drama which (as no-one today would deny) underlies all the religious experience and the political actions of the Prophet of Islam.

Carlyle's spirited chapter on the Hero Muhammad dates from about 1840. During the second half of the nineteenth century, oriental history and philology began to provide a more secure basis for the understanding of the man and his work. In 1860 appeared the first edition of Nöldeke's *Geschichte des Qorans*, a fundamental reconstruction of the genesis and formation of the sacred Book. In 1858 and 1860 came out respectively the Arabic text and the translation of the *Sira* of Ibn Ishaq, the canonical biography of Muhammad, edited by Wüstenfeld and Weil. With these materials A. Sprenger was able to publish in 1861–5 his work *Das Leben und die Lehre Mohammeds*, the first scientific biography of the Prophet written in the West, and the first of a long series of biographical and evaluative studies which has continued up to the present day. We can do no more here than point to the principal phases of this *Leben Muhammads Forschung*, and its most significant and eminent representatives.

Sprenger's work, more learned and laborious than profound, is a typical product of the positivist epoch, with its accurate sifting of material, its setting of Muhammad, as far as the knowledge of the time allowed, in the general historical situation of Arabia and Asia as it was before him, with its patient discussion of numerous points of detail. What it lacks is a principle of historical interpretation, a guiding idea, a thesis. All these are to be found in the work of the first more or less systematic biographers to succeed Sprenger, H. Grimme and H. Lammens. For the former (*Mohammed*, 1892–5), the message of the founder of Islam was pre-eminently social in its nature and origin. What impelled the obscure Meccan orphan to preach his subversive message was not so much theological problems as indignation at the unequal division of wealth and desire for a more just human society. 'Proletarians of Arabia, arise!' was, according to this theory, the gist and purpose of the message which Gabriel breathed into the sensitive soul of Muhammad on Mount Hira. This social thesis of Grimme's, even though more or less consciously revived by modern Marxist interpretations of Islam, and though certainly containing elements of truth, is as a whole unacceptable, and diametrically opposed to the deeper modern investigations of the religious phenomenon. No less unacceptable is the spirit of obsolete religious prejudice in which, as we have already noted, Lammens treated Muhammad, with his family and *milieu*, in a series of brilliant and learned studies (though without ever producing a single connected biography). While demolishing on the one hand the reliability of Muslim tradition, he nevertheless accepted as much of it as suited his thesis, and presented the origins of Islam as a compound of mystification and tyrannous imposition. Muhammad was for him the 'false Prophet' as he had been for the men of medieval Europe, except that their prejudice was supported by a bulwark of childish fables, whereas the twentieth-century historian founded and fed his on a direct and thorough knowledge of the original Muslim sources, but all interpreted with the same hostile animus. His conclusion, inevitably, was that Islam was an error of History, a deviation from the order of divine Providence, a *pessima corruptio optimi* of the newly-planted Christian faith.

Lammens, however, is an isolated and anachronistic voice as against the modern consensus of historical judgment on Muhammad, which, without doctrinal prejudice, sees the Prophet against the background of his own people and time, stressing one aspect of his message or another, but assuming beyond discussion its fundamental sincerity. At the beginning of the present century, Leone Caetani and the Danish writer Frants Buhl, starting from different historical principles, both paid tribute to the exceptional figure of the Arabian Prophet, and not only to his political genius but to the genuine nature of his religious inspiration and to the high level (in relation to his time and *milieu*) of his moral character. Caetani, in *Annali dell'Islam* and *Studi di Storia Orientale* (1914), although inclined to allow great weight to economic and social factors, rejects with sound historical judgment Grimme's extreme thesis; he assigns a frankly religious inspiration the central place in Muhammad's life's work, and without concealing his human faults concludes with a favourable verdict on his honesty and disinterestedness, his desire for good, and the prodigious results achieved in one lifetime. Buhl, in his ample biography (1903, German edition 1930), the longest published before those of Montgomery Watt and Gaudefroy-Demombynes, underlines both his human failings and his human sincerity, measuring his greatness by the endurance of his work and by the fascination – almost entirely lost to us – that he was able to exercise over his contemporaries. This last argument is found in one form or another in all the modern western biographies of the Prophet, from Caetani to Andrae: the authors see among the circle surrounding him personalities, perhaps morally more congenial to us, whom the Prophet was able – and certainly not by vulgar conjuring tricks – to bind to himself in life and death; a vivid witness to a superiority otherwise difficult to appreciate.

The Prophet's gradual rise in the esteem of occidental scholarship has been going on steadily during recent decades, at a pace which one may not altogether approve, but which it is impossible to ignore. A Lutheran bishop, Andrae, who in the second and third decades of the century pioneered a more subtle historico-religious approach to the connections between Muhammad's message and Syrio-Byzantine Christianity, and was the author of a classic study of the figure of the Prophet in the faith and doctrine of his own community, concludes his biography of Muhammad (1932) by acknowledging his exceptional qualities, though with a caveat against attempting to draw any parallels with 'the high and unmatchable figure we meet in the Gospels'. A Catholic scholar, M. Guidi, though without attempting any such parallel, is inclined to allow the founder of Islam a providential role, as 'the one way of winning souls too far removed from the truth, sunk in the horror of the grossest idolatry, to the acknowledgment of divine supremacy, and the affirmation of a system of just rewards and punishments, and of homage to the one true God of all humanity.' But Guidi reaches this concluding justification, which stands Lammens' hostile prejudice on its head, to the greater glory of pure monotheism (a position also taken by other well-known religious thinkers of our time, such as L. Massignon), only after an impas-

sioned analysis of Muhammad's personality and life's work which
for him is characterised by a 'genius of compromise' – compromise
between the traditional values of Arabia, which he himself felt
strongly, and the higher concept of monotheism, which reached
him chiefly from Christianity.

The most recent of those to write Muhammad's biography without religious *parti-pris* (we must exclude on this account another
contemporary biographer, of great erudition but strict Islamic
orthodoxy, M. Hamidullah) are the Frenchman Gaudefroy-
Demombynes (*Mahomet*) and the Scotsman Montgomery Watt,
whose volumes *Muhammad at Mecca*, *Muhammad at Medina*, and
Muhammad Prophet and Statesman, together with various separate
studies of great penetration, all published between 1950 and 1960,
represent Western scholarship's last word to date on the Prophet
of Islam. Watt deserves credit for his methodical revaluation of
Islamic tradition, which he has retrieved from the hypercritical
scepticism of Lammens and Caetani, and used, by a critical evaluation of the material it provides, to reconstruct certain passages in
the Prophet's life which the sceptical tradition left blank; and for
having used Andrae's comparative research combined with sociological principles to explain the success of Muhammad's message.
In his judgment of the man himself, Watt has gone beyond any of
his western predecessors in his unqualified admiration, which
personally we are unable to endorse. Admittedly the ethical standard by which the Prophet should be judged is not that of the Gospels but of the Arabia of his time; the fact remains that even in the
Arabia of his time some virtues were known and valued which
in his struggle Muhammad subordinated to political and personal
considerations. Watt's portrait of him, minimising or denying his
'alleged moral failures', seems too close to the Muslim *'isma*
to be acceptable to a Christian of whatever denomination, or
indeed to any modern moral consciousness. At all events, this
extreme case shows how far the West has come from the hatred of
the Middle Ages, towards a more just and sympathetic appreciation
of the Prophet of Islam.

The modern view of a paradox

After all this critical study, certain points at least may today be taken as settled. Above all, there is Muhammad's absolute sincerity in feeling himself the recipient of a special contact with the divine, and the transmitter of a message which was, in the beginning at least, infinitely higher than any ambition or interest of his own. A second point is the dependence of this message for its monotheistic content on the two great religions of the Near East historically prior to that of the Arabian Prophet and the precondition of its existence, though he soon came to consider them as completed, perfected and superseded by his own faith. This faith presented itself to him from the first as the special revelation of God to the Arab people; a national embodiment, so to speak, of the monotheistic principle. Here it seems to us that those writers such as Guidi are correct who insist on this quality of rootedness in Muhammad; he had a profound feeling for the historical and pseudo-historical traditions of his people, and in order to replace the polytheism which flourished all around him, he created an imaginary proto-historical religion of Arabia, connected with the figure of the patriarch Abraham, and restored in renewed power by himself, the last of a whole line of prophets. Even while he swept the pagan pantheon uncompromisingly away, he kept all the time a filial respect for the ancestral sanctuary of Mecca, which he placed at the very centre of his new faith and his (up to a point) purified rite. To the triumph of these ideas, which he continued to develop and elaborate as time went on, he devoted all his energies; as a religious soul, as one who knew and could win the hearts of his fellow-men, as a leader and master sealed with a divine privilege. When persuasion alone failed, force sustained and supplemented it in what was to him a perfectly natural way; the work of the visionary *hanif* of Mecca was continued in that of the head of state of Medina, and neither he nor his contemporaries felt that profound hiatus which so disturbs our European consciences. 'The rationalisation of inspiration' is a phrase which has been used of his Medinese period, postulating a process of which it is most unlikely that the protagonist himself had any clear consciousness. We may accept, at least, that in performing or tolerating those acts in his political career and in his private life which we find the most perplexing and repugnant, he sincerely believed himself always to be obeying a divine command or permission. From our own point of view, this is equivalent to saying that his originally very high conception of Divinity became distinctly lower and more human, to a degree which strikes us as unsatisfactory, but which satisfied him, and the men about him, whose leader and model he was.

Our aim here is to evaluate, not so much the phenomenon of Islam, as that of its founder. The two, however, are at first indissolubly linked and, though the fortunes of his religion were to take it so far beyond the limits of his own earthly pilgrimage, yet at the fountainhead of the great river of Islam there remains the complex, difficult, sometimes mysterious figure of its originator. The mystery, for us, seems often to lie precisely in the disproportion between his undoubtedly outstanding but far from superhuman character, and the immense extent and duration of the movement he started. It lies also in those paradoxes and contradictions in him which resist all rational explanation; an Arab to the marrow of his bones, he repudiated the faith of his city and people, to impose upon them and adapt for their benefit a different faith of frankly foreign origin. A patient, merciful, humane man, he was capable of the greatest cruelties and treacheries. Always ready for reconciliation and compromise, he was unshakeably firm in the intuition which was the centre of his life, the uncontaminated *tawhid*, the proclamation of the divine unity. Knowing well the dangers and moral corruption that spring from the desire for material wealth, he modified this initial ascetic tendency into a limited acceptance of the value of such goods, and indeed did not hesitate to claim (not, in our opinion, for purely political reasons) a particularly large share of certain such goods as the prerogative of the Prophet.

The *shahada*, the formula of the faith of Islam, expressed in the two principles 'There is no God but God, and Muhammad is the

Prophet of God' is the symbol of the, for a Muslim, indissoluble unity of his faith in Allah, and in the person and dignity of the Prophet. With a judgment which may be quite unhistorical, but which springs from the very fibres of an entirely different religious and philosophical tradition, one might regret that Muhammad did not feel himself to be demeaning that vision of the One God to which he had attained (whether at a single bound or by a slow, painful ascent) by claiming for his own person a privileged position as the means of access to Him. But, according to all the ideas of the Semitic peoples, of the Arabs, and of Muhammad himself, this initiate could not imagine any contact with God as possible to others except through himself, as messenger, delegate, apostle. He considered himself, without any shadow of sacrilegious dissimulation, *rasul Allah*, and such he has been for thirteen centuries to the generations who have lived and still live by his faith.

In world history, he stands out by virtue of the movement which began with him, and whose end is far from being in sight; a movement whose first effect was to rescue the Arabs from their poor and obscure life as children of the desert, and to throw them forward, to conquer an empire and to change the face of the world.

2 Arabia before Muhammad

It is impossible to deal with Muhammad and his achievement without first learning something about the land, the people, the society and the national tradition into which he was born, and which he partly revolutionised or altered profoundly, and partly retained and consolidated. It is therefore necessary by way of an introduction to the history of the Arabian Prophet and of the universal victory of his people and his faith to have a look at the characteristics and at the events of pre-Islamic Arabia.

Arab tribalism and the historical background

The Arabian Peninsula, cut off from the rest of the ancient world by the wedge of desert jutting into the arc of the Fertile Crescent, was to the monarchies of the East and later to the Greeks and Romans a somewhat inaccessible territory the direct domination of which was never contemplated, and the restless population of which was to be kept at bay or at most to be recruited for other wars. The desert Arabs were thus by turns frontier raiders or mercenaries for Assyrian kings or Greek overlords, and as such were occasionally mentioned in the inscriptions and the texts of the period. Yet, beside this poor nomadic Arab way of life, biblical and classical tradition knew of more advanced and civilised Arab states in the south of the Peninsula; there was the kingdom of the Queen of Sheba, a guest and a friend of Solomon, and the Homeritae or Himyarite kings of *Arabia Felix*, the owners of fabled wealth (Horace's *beatae gazae* and *plenae Arabum domus*). These two contrasting pictures reflect exactly the dual historical, geographic, economic and sociological aspects of ancient Arabia: the prevalent nomadism in the rudimentary conditions of the north and the sedentary and advanced agricultural states of the south, which for a millennium and a half gave to southern Arabia its own physiognomy, quite distinct from that of Arabia Deserta. Let us say immediately that the personality and achievements of Muhammad, though they grew out of a small urban centre, are bound up with and are to be understood in relation to the tradition and history of this primitive and nomadic Arabia Deserta even more than in relation to the southern Arabian civilisation which was anyway in full decadence and almost extinct at the time of the Prophet.

The ancient south Arabian states which flourished from the tenth and the ninth centuries BC to the first centuries AD were the Minaeans in north Yemen; the Sabaeans, with Maryab (modern Marib) against whom the expedition of Aelius Gallus under the emperor Augustus fought in vain; and the Himyarites, with whom the aged south Arabian civilisation finally declined and disappeared. Occupied at the beginning of the sixth century AD by Christian Abyssinia and then for a short while by Sasanid Persia, the Yemen in Muhammad's day preserved little more than the memory of its ancient glory and autonomous past, and merged with the rest of the Peninsula in the faith of Islam. But in its golden age it represented as against the low economic and social level of the rest of Arabia, a factor for stability, for economic prosperity and for superior social and religious life, all based on the cultivation and marketing of spices and aromatics (the famous 'perfumes of Arabia'). Organised into patrician monarchic states with a pantheon of astral deities and a strong priesthood, and gifted with fairly advanced agricultural techniques and craftsmanship, southern Arabia contrasted vividly with the poor and anarchic north. The memory of that Yemenite civilisation survives in its own epigraphic evidence (written in a language and an alphabet different from that of the northern Arabs) and in the references made to them by classical writers, Greco-Latin and Syrian, even more than in the legendary and confused traditions of the later Arabic literature.

The desert, nomadism and the tribal bond are the essential features of the most ancient and authentic Arab way of life. The first represents the premiss of the natural world which conditions the life of this and other related peoples to such an extent that an old theory currently being rehabilitated sees within the Arabian Peninsula the common matrix of all the Semitic peoples. Whether native or immigrant into the Peninsula from time immemorial, the Arabs introduced the domestic use of the camel comparatively late (probably at the end of the second millennium BC) and with this precious means of communication and alimentation, they were able to survive the very harsh climatic and environmental conditions with a way of life which remained until very recently essentially the same. The view that Arabia became progressively more arid relates to a period earlier than the one we are discussing. Nomadism based on a pastoral economy and the periodic change of site in search of the thin pasture remains the basic feature of the ancient way of life, and a root word which is surely Arabic, *badw*, adjective *badawi* with *badawiyyin* for plural, has supplied the term for describing this phenomenon in a particular sense even outside the Arab world. The Arabs have been and are 'bedouin' par excellence. This is not to say that the Arabs of central and northern Arabia have not also known settled periods and above all that 'semi-nomadism' which is today opposed to pure nomadism as the intermediate stage between it and the settled life. Outside the Peninsula proper, the settled Arab states of antiquity were the kingdom of the Nabataeans, which the emperor Trajan incorporated in the Provincia Arabia in AD 106, and that of Palmyra, famous for the luxury of Odenathus and Zenobia, somewhat confused echoes of which are heard in the later Arabic traditions. There were settled agricultural and trading communities in the peninsula proper in the fertile oases of the northern Hijaz: Dedan, today al-'Ola, already the centre of the little kingdom of the Lihyan; Wadi l-Qura, Fadak, Khaybar, Taima', all of which are connected with the spread of primitive Islam during the Prophet's lifetime. In central Hijaz, the two small towns of Mecca and Yathrib (later to be known as Medina) and the even smaller Ta'if were destined to be inscribed even more deeply into the records of the origins of Islam. But such urban nuclei (strictly speaking only the two principal centres of Hijaz deserve the name) and every other minor settlement engaged in continual contact and traffic with the prevalent bedouin element, both nomadic and semi-

nomadic, which formed the real reserve and the demographic mass of the Peninsula and which always influenced the life of the settled south Arabian states. When trying to analyse the economic and social life of the pre-Islamic northern and central Peninsula, one has to consider first of all this bedouin Arab way of life; it constitutes the framework of the *Jahiliyya* i.e. the period of Arab paganism which is so vividly transmitted, although in somewhat romantic colours, in the historical and antiquarian traditions of the first two centuries of Islam. It is also the most important factor in the 'rebedouinisation of Arabia' which, according to some scholars, took place between the fourth and the sixth centuries AD after the disappearance of the kingdoms of the Nabataeans and of Palmyra in the north and the complete decline of the south Arabian states. During those centuries cultivated areas returned to the desert and the Arab people, notwithstanding their contacts with higher forms of civilisation, reverted to primitive barbarism.

The tribal bond, the only solid and accepted social structure in that environment and that stage, is the essence, the symbol almost of these primitive living conditions of Arabia in the centuries immediately preceding Muhammad. With the exceptions that we have seen for the older period and those we shall see for later periods, bedouin society is entirely dependent on the principle of tribal solidarity and authority; it is organised in flexible and varied genealogical groups which the later Arab tradition mistakenly represented as rigid and clear-cut. The tribe is the self-sufficient cell of the embryonic political and social life; it is the only structure to which the individualistic and anarchically inclined mentality of the bedouin will in the nature of things submit; it guarantees support for him in the *bellum omnium contra omnes* which is the natural law of the desert; thanks to the collective solidarity in property disputes and blood feuds, it offers him personal protection; it also satisfies his vanity and desire for glory with its genealogical and martial traditions. Within its democratic and patriarchal structure, the tribe acknowledges a freely elected head (*sayyid, shaikh*) with limited authority confined particularly to advice and guidance and not usually extending to the conduct of war. The affairs of common interest are discussed and decided by the assembly of the entire tribe where great prestige is attached to the wisdom of old age, prowess in war and to eloquence and skill in poetry. Hospitality, protection of the weak, bravery in the unceasing skirmishes and raids, facility for aphorism and rhyme, are qualities universally respected. Outside the tribe to which one belongs either by direct blood relationship or by affiliation and alliance (*wala'*, *tahaluf*) there is no possible existence except the precarious one of rebel or outlaw, as the poet Shanfara sang. The collective consciousness of ancient bedouin Arabia revolted with all its strength against the alternative to the tribal bond, namely the 'kingdom' (*mulk*), that is, the tribal and supertribal tyranny of one man; witness the very short-lived attempts at personal leadership which we shall mention later.

Historical traditions

Besides the inscriptions and the references made to them by Greek and Syrian authors, two kinds of native sources give information about the life and the affairs of these pagan Arabs, both nomad and settled, and even manage to throw some light on the south Arabian policy itself. The first source is that of the ancient historical and pseudo-historical tradition preserved in Arab historiography of the Muslim period; the second is pre-Islamic poetry or what passes as such. In order to discuss the first, which is in any case strongly bound up with the second, we would say that from the works of Muslim antiquarians and literary historians, as well as from the exegesis of the Koran, it is easy to extract a whole historical and genealogical framework of early Islamic history which seems highly questionable to critical investigation. Useful historical elements are mixed here with others of an undoubtedly legendary nature variously interwoven among themselves; while it is certain that the Koran, where it alludes to or develops this early Arab history, draws on an existing heritage of native traditions and legends, it is no less certain that these were later amplified and formulated with precision in order to buttress Koranic exegesis itself. This native tradition validated and almost canonised in the sacred Book speaks of peoples of the earliest antiquity (the legendary 'Ad, the historical Thamud, the Amalekites) who would have inhabited the Peninsula from the beginning, and whose disappearance is attributed in the Koran to their sacrilegious disobedience of the precepts of the Prophet of God; of vast structures and buildings of these peoples of furthest antiquity, such as the mythical Iram of the Columns falling into ruins after the extermination of their builders. Coming to a less legendary period, the whole of the subsequent history of Arabia is based on the division of the race into the two great branches of Adnan and of Qahtan, which became respectively the original ancestors of the northern and of the southern Arabs. The story of these last, who (according to some) would be the purest Arabs, should reflect exactly the events of the reigns and of south Arabian polity which are now known to us straight from their inscriptions. But in fact however, although there is an unquestionable link between real epigraphic testimony and literary tradition, the reconstruction of names and of dynasties which results from this latter does not coincide in fact with epigraphic and archaeological evidence and appears to be very much the child of fantasy and of arbitrary learned arrangement and reconstruction. The series of Tubba' (such is the name which north Arabian tradition gives to the Yemenite rulers) diverges too much with regard to names and chronological successions from what we can reconstruct today through more direct evidence, as to allow us to rely confidently on that Islamic research and historiography. And finally we discussed above the so-called 'south Arabian saga', a transformation in a fantastic sense, a mixture of pseudo-history and poetry, of the surviving vague memories of the independent polity of the south and of its agricultural prosperity and of the breach in the fourth or fifth century AD of a great hydraulic barrage (the Marib Dam) which had catastrophic results for the Yemenite economy and society. But another historically certain event is mirrored by that learned reconstruction and that legend, namely the migration northwards of southern ethnic elements and their intermingling with the language and the primitive culture of the northern Arabs. Many stories and legends of the latter have for heroes tribes and characters of undoubtedly southern origin, and we may say in conclusion that the really valid dividing line between north and south is not so much genealogical as sometimes sociological and economic: the north with its nomadic tendencies as against the agricultural and settled south, the raiding bedouin as against the cultivator and the artisan.

If native tradition seems here so little worthy of attention for the history of southern Arabia (although some modern scholars such as M. Guidi tend to give it more credit than we have done here), it is no more historically useful and, above all, chronologically useful for northern and central Arabia, the domain of the desert and of nomadism. It is true that the desert as such has no history, it merely presents us with man's monotonous fight for survival against adverse conditions; but to its periphery were attached less rudimentary political and social groupings, the affairs of which it is partly possible to reconstruct, and in the heart of the desert itself poetical fantasy sometimes transforms into epic the incessant monotony of inter-tribal contests and raids. A good deal of what has finally reached us through the work of scholars and anti-quarians about these battles, stylised into a particular literary genre (the *ayyam al-'arab* or the battles of the Arabs), clearly carries the imprint of that fictional and fantastic exaggeration in which the real story seems to evaporate. From a sociological and ethico-political point of view, what can be extracted from that tradition concerning the affairs of the pagan northern Arabs is precisely the efforts to replace the particularist tribal anarchy by more solid units based on the rule of one kin-group or one head, acting as an absolute ruler or a 'king' and their subsequent failure; such is the historical substratum which seems to emerge for instance from the stories about the fratricidal war of al-Basus, which was triggered off by the efforts to establish absolute rule made by the Taghlibi chief Kulaib, fallen victim to his pride and ambition. A similar and more certain case is that of the southern tribe of Kinda, of which the kin-group of Akil al-Murar tried for a couple of generations, between the end of the fifth and the beginning of the sixth century, to exercise its own patched-up monarchic power over various other tribes, and whose attempt at hegemony succumbed to the surging centrifugal forces fed by bedouin particularism. Besides these cases where the faint traces of an historical development are buried in exuberant anecdote and poetry, the life of these Arabs of the desert went on in the same century-long misery, of skirmishes and raids, panegyric and tribal vendettas, intent on snatching from a cruel nature a difficult sustenance while cherishing its own primitive ethical ideal of generosity and the warrior virtues. Such hatred of tyranny and such exaltation of the strength of the individual had its counterpart in the constant fratricidal war which consumed the pre-Islamic tribes whether nomadic or settled (the long internal feud between the two tribes of Medina, the Aus and the Khazraj is typical), thus helping to the rise, almost *extrema ratio*, of new forces and ideals which made for mediation and arbitration.

While it was not possible before Muhammad to found in the heart of the Arab Peninsula a political power superior to the egalitarian tribal order, this was realised on the northern periphery of the desert with the formation of two small Arab states who were the clients of two neighbouring empires, Byzantium and Persia. Neither of these traditional rivals of the Near East had an interest in attempting the direct conquest of that patch of sand, but they both favoured the emergence on their own frontier of buffer states which would be their own vassals and which would hold at bay the anarchic turbulence of the desert: these were the Ghassanids for Byzantium and the Lakhmids of al-Hira for Sasanid Persia. The Ghassanids, southern in origin like their Lakhmid rivals, supplanted the Daja'ima at the beginning of the sixth century as phylarchs or tribal chiefs on the frontiers under the protection of Byzantium, and throughout the century represented in that zone an outpost and a medium of communication between pure Arab life of the desert and Byzantine Syria. Semi-nomadic as they still were, they had various centres of residence but no capital. The Ghassanids professed monophysite Christianity, and in the eyes of their own people they seemed, because of the hated monarchic principle which they followed, a sorry mixture of pure Arabism, Hellenism and Christianity. Their dynastic and chronological sequence, beginning with the great Harith ibn Jabala who carried high the fortunes of the race to his less distinguished successor Jabala ibn Ayham who fought on the side of the Byzantines against the Muslims at the Yarmuk, and later became Muslim but returned finally to the faith of his fathers and ended obscurely among the Byzantines, is well noted in the Arab and the Byzantine traditions which are in full agreement here, and more solidly attested than that of the Yemenite dynasties. This is also the case with the Ghassanids' rivals, the Lakhmids of al-Hira on the Euphrates, who gravitated within the orbit of Ctesiphon, and showed elements of Iranian culture just as the Ghassanids were of Greco-Christian culture. Surrounded by a Christian society, the 'Ibadites of al-Hira, the Lakhmids remained pagan much longer, occasionally massacring monks and nuns, and it was only with their last sovereign Nu'man III that they embraced Nestorian Christianity. Throughout the sixth century, which was the golden age of both dynasties, they fought savagely in the cause of the empires whose vassals they were, as well as in their own feuds and vendettas: Arab tradition, here embroidering on an undoubtedly historical basis, knows many famous battles in which the Ghassanids and the Lakhmids clashed (one celebrated instance is the battle of Halima of around 554, which marked a great Ghassanid victory and the death of the Lakhmid leader Mundhir III). The personalities of all the principal dynasties of the two branches were the subjects of laudatory poems by the poets of the desert. The political importance of these small frontier monarchies consists in their having offered to the Arabs a model for these countless local emirates into which, after the golden age of the caliphate, the Islamic community came to be fragmented; culturally, however, for their countrymen of the Peninsula they formed a link with the material and spiritual characteristics of two superior civilisations.

The great struggle between Persia and Byzantium, both of whom were to succumb completely to a force unleashed from the arid desert, had repercussions in Arabia beyond the endemic guerilla warfare of their little vassal states. The Koran itself echoes the Byzantine defeat of 613–4 which ended with the loss of Damascus and Jerusalem, thus probably marking the end of the Ghassanid power, as well as their recapture by Heraclius fifteen years later. Since the previous century the peninsula had known the interventions of foreigners who were divided according to the politico-religious antagonism of the two colossi of the Near East. When in the first half of the fifth century Aksumite Ethiopia had intervened to support the Yemenite Christians and annexed South Arabia as a province, it was to Sasanid Persia that the local aristocracy turned for its liberation, and the Yemen became for a short while a Persian outpost in the Red Sea. A few years earlier, in the fateful 'Year of the Elephant' – the year 570 connected in tradition with the birth of the future Prophet – Abraha, an Aksumite commander, practically independent governor of the Yemen, undertook an attack from the south against Mecca which some have interpreted as a move against Persia with Byzantine connivance. Less than a century later, victorious Islam was to overthrow all these alignments and to change radically the political and religious map of the Near East: but until its new history matured and exploded the Arabian Peninsula was internationally a marginal and subsidiary factor within the political game of the great contemporary powers in the Near East.

The cultural legacy of pagan Arabia

Against this background and under these rudimentary conditions of economic and social life, the existence of the Arab people in its pre-Islamic state was crystallised for centuries: herdsmen and raiders, mercenaries paid by bigger states or guerilla fighters and plunderers for their own benefit or for the benefit of the tribe; merchants, caravan guides, or more rarely, in particular areas, farmers and artisans. With this poor material life, which Islam did not change greatly inside the Peninsula, there went a spiritual life which was also poor and rudimentary, but of which some features, given an artistic expression, have been transmitted with exceptional vigour.

Even before Muhammad, the Arabs had a clear consciousness of their own ethnic individuality and contrasted themselves with the non-Arabs or Barbar ('*Ajam*); this consciousness was expressed in an elaborate genealogical system which was undoubtedly systematised later by the Muslim scholars, but which mirrors all the same the ancient self awareness of the race. Proud of their anarchic freedom they contrasted it, as we have seen, with the border 'kingdoms', and even a minor encounter with the latter resulting in victory for the sons of the desert as was for instance the case with the battle of Dhu Qar between the bedouin Bakr and the Persian forces at the beginning of the seventh century, became in their eyes a symbol of national glory. Such an awareness of ethnic and cultural identity linked to a radical dislike for any larger political bond, which is not without a certain similarity to classical Greece, expressed itself in a lasting fashion in the poetry which constitutes the best evidence which has reached us for the material and spiritual life of the pagan era. Even more than in the early centuries, grave doubts have today been expressed about the authenticity of pre-Islamic Arab poetry, which, according to some extreme views, was but a gigantic fraud perpetrated by bards and scholars of the first two centuries of Islam. We find such radical scepticism unacceptable: in spite of the uncertainties and corruptions of the tradition and the proven existence of isolated forgeries, we consider the heritage of ancient poetry of the Jahiliyya taken as a whole as the authentic voice of that age. A voice no doubt to be heard and to be judged with discrimination; a document the genuine primitive form of which is difficult to reconstruct in many cases and which appears in an already rigid stylisation of motifs and images, of language and of style, but which it is not possible, all things considered, to ignore or to underestimate in its artistic and particularly its documentary importance. We must remember that this poetry which the Arabs were to call the 'archives' of the race is consonant with the historical and pseudo-historical tradition concerning the more ancient affairs of pagan Arabia and with the corresponding features of biblical, Byzantino-Iranian and south Arabian traditions, though it remains still uncertain how much this poetry was influenced by these traditions and how much it has itself inspired and promoted them. Stylised and one-sided as it sometimes likes to be, it does above all express eloquently the soul of that people before the new faith came to mould it again in its depth: a people individualistic and proud of soul, patient and bold in natural adversity and in the fight for life with its own kin, caring little for an after-life, committing the survival of its name rather to the memory of noble deeds and the faithful adherence to the ethical code of the desert. It is with reason that we may talk of a rudimentary 'tribal humanism' among these ancient Arabs, which Islam was to fight and to disown violently in order to replace it by its theocentric and transcendental vision of life. It is useful to add that this secular Arab humanism, attacked and soon abandoned by the new generations of Muslims, maintained itself into the Muslim era, gradually waning, however, except in the realm of poetry where its imprint was too strongly marked for it wholly to disappear. Poetry after Muhammad sang, indeed, the glories of the new faith, but where the conquests and politico-religious struggle within the new Muslim community were concerned, it did so in a rather fragmented and desultory fashion. Its mainstay always continued the forms and the feeling of the pre-Islamic era, abandoning only the more specifically pagan features: it continued the poem of praise (*madih*) and of invective (*hija'*), love poetry (*nasib*, which started as a compulsory conventional prelude to every poetical composition and then developed as an autonomous form on its own) and the elegy for the dead (*ritha'*), the poetry of glorification (*fakhr*), the descriptive (*wasf*), the gnomic; in short, all the motifs which the poetic art of the pre-Islamic Arabs had already inaugurated, considering them as a classical and unsurpassable model. If such a rooted belief in the superiority of pre-Islamic art proved harmful to the subsequent development of poetry in the Muslim era, yet it confirms the importance of that more ancient production as the authentic expression of the primitive Arab way of life, and justifies its use to document the pre-Islamic vision of life, a vision at the same time materialistic and idealistic, with a gloomy and at times heroic awareness of the human condition.

Paganism, Judaism and Christianity

To complete this sketch of Arabia before Muhammad, we must refer briefly to the religion, in the strict sense, of the pre-Islamic Arabs, leaving out the cults of southern Arabia, and confining ourselves to the desert and urban areas of the north and of the Hijaz, where the word of the Meccan Prophet grew deep roots. The religion of the greater part of these Arabs (reconstructed in part only, with the help of the work of Muslim antiquarians and of the fragmentary evidence of pagan poetry) is an elementary polydaemonism with elements of fetishism and animalism. The Arabs worshipped a varied pantheon of divinities none of which had ever assumed any human form, and not one of whom had ever been able to rise above the others to produce monotheism. Some of these divinities, as in southern Arabia and in general in the whole Semitic area, were astral; such is al-Lat (the *Alilat* of Herodotus) a sun goddess, and al-'Uzza (the 'Most High') originally personifying the planet Venus; while contrary to the situation in southern Arabia there was no lunar god. Other deities personify abstract ideas, like Manat the goddess of fate and of death, and Wadd the god of love; others have an exclusively local importance such as the various idols of the Ka'ba in Mecca. The revered Hubal towered above them all. The name and perhaps the concept itself of Allah (the god, God), destined to take in Islam the place of all the other gods, does not seem to have been unknown in that pagan pantheon although it took a long time for it to assume the prominence it was to have later: according to some it would seem to have been originally no more than an addition to the names of individual gods (for example to the Meccan Hubal) later assuming a proper physiognomy and supplanting the name to which it was affixed. But other scholars, whether under the influence of the theory of primitive monotheism or because of the evidence provided by the ancient Arabs themselves, saw in it a vague and supreme god of fate prominent already in the pagan era standing above the lesser but more concrete and earthier deities; some of these were in fact connected with him and the three famous goddesses, al-Lat, Manat and al-'Uzza, were retained in Mecca as daughters of Allah. Besides these true and genuine gods, Arab paganism populated the deserts with a crowd of genii (*jinn*), benevolent and malignant, themselves supranatural intermediaries between the deity and man, which Islam has also absorbed and subordinated to Allah equally with man.

All these divinities were worshipped by the Arabs as idols in the form of sacred stones, rocks, trees, crude anthropomorphic or animal shapes the cult of some of which had a merely local importance, and that of others having a larger intertribal diffusion. Their sanctuaries sometimes confined within a simple sacred zone (*haram*) surrounding the idol and entrusted to custodians (*sadana*), to sorcerers and diviners rather than to real and genuine priests, were the objects of pious visits, of sessions of divination and of pilgrimage; among these the Meccan Ka'ba stood out as of pan-Arab importance. We know of sacrifices (even human ones in the more ancient period), of oblations and votive offerings; few real and genuine rites except in Mecca where the rite of pagan pilgrimage, circumambulations, stone-throwing for averting the evil eye, are still clearly apparent through their later Islamic garb. We have before us a primitive stage of religion (according to some even more primitive for the nomads than for the settled) of a very low ethical level, of a minimal or non-existent intellectual content. It is possible, as some assert, that at Mecca the local gods and cults were defended in the face of the Islamic revolution by a pious feeling for the national religion as well as for economic and political interests. Everywhere else they disappeared without a fight before the youthful force of Islam or as if their real hold on the soul of the sceptic and religiously lukewarm bedouin had been, even before Islam, rather limited.

If this Arabian paganism was without a future, as much cannot be said of the two great monotheistic religions which before Muhammad had already taken a firm foothold in the Peninsula and which together were to contribute to the creation of the new faith. As a result of the diaspora and the proselytisation subsequent to the final destruction of Jerusalem in the second century, Judaism had found an entrance both in the Yemen and in the Hijaz: in the former it even became the official religion of the last Himyarite king (Yusuf Ashab called in Arab tradition Dhu Nuwas) who persecuted the Najran Christians, thus inviting the subsequent Abyssinian intervention. In the Hijaz, Jewish colonists were to be found as much in Medina as in the oases of the north (Fadak, Khaybar, Wadi l-Qura); they were agriculturalists, craftsmen and particularly goldsmiths. It is correct to assume that there were everywhere judaicised Arab elements who shared the language and the culture common to their pagan countrymen and were only distinguished for their synagogal worship and the hierarchy of rabbis and learned men with whom Muhammad was to have an unhappy experience. The pitiful end of this Arabian Judaism, eradicated with a relentless harshness by Islam, must not make one forget either its important influence on the origins of Islam or the modest intellectual and moral level which it attained; as far as we know it contributed little or nothing to the religious and cultural development of post-biblical Judaism, and could only die with dignity and loyalty in the Peninsula while continuing abroad, in the vast areas of the conquest, its economic, religious and cultural connections with the new polity of Islam.

The characteristics and the fate of Christianity in Arabia to which, according to some historians, would belong the larger part of the dogmatic, ethical and spiritual influences in general over the new faith, were altogether different. Spread in the first centuries of our era by the monophysite and the Nestorian missionaries, Christianity was the faith of the Ghassanids of Syria (officially however only at the end of the dynasty) as well as of the Lakhmids of Hira, and in the desert it won over wholly or in part some large and small tribes such as the Kalb, the Tanukh, the Taghlib, the Hanifa, as well as isolated urban groups and individual anchorites. The figure of the Christian hermit whose solitary light shines through the darkness of the desert is often mentioned in pre-Islamic poetry together with other features of the Christian cult, the churches and the icons, the processions and the wine which passed from its sacrificial use to a more profane use in ordinary consumption and commerce. If one had to judge only by such poetical testimonies, Christianity would have exhausted its strength in the Arabian Peninsula merely in the picturesque formality of ritual; however, this poetical stylisation does not exclude more profound and deeper spiritual values, which were to well up again through another channel in the heart of Islam itself, fertilised by Christianity. The superior Christian ethic shone, in fact, through many aspects of Islamic spirituality and the modest intellectual level of that Christian community of Arabia was to be made up for by unknown treasures of devotion and piety which aroused the admiration of Muhammad himself. In a decisive Koranic verse about the later relations of Islam to Christianity, he was to call the Christians 'the nearer and the more benevolent' towards the new faith. Persecutions of Christian groups as such, unlike that of the Jews, were unknown at the beginning of Islam and if the ban against the infidels sanctioned by Muhammad at the end of his career and applied by the Caliph Umar drove the Christians out of the Peninsula, the disappearance from Arabia of Christianity did not have the tragic and cruel aspects held by that of Judaism. In spite of the stumbling block represented by the Trinity and by Christology, Islam was always to feel vaguely that Christianity was a brotherly and cognate faith.

The religious panorama of pre-Islamic Arabia will be completed with the mention of the *Hanif*, a phenomenon to which the sympathy of the modern historians has perhaps attributed more widespread diffusion and more importance than it had had in reality but which cannot in any case be ignored. *Hanif* (from the Syriac word *hanpa*, originally 'pagan heretic', and then 'religious dissident') was the name given by the Arabs to the individual religious men whose monotheistic faith was not identified either with Judaism or with Christianity and who later were either to adhere to Islam or to disappear in its triumphant rise. Leading a life of ascetic purity, they assiduously meditated on the monotheistic solutions of the eternal questions which the majority of the bedouin in Arabia overlooked or accepted with a fatalistic resignation. These *Hanifs* moreover did certainly have a share in the gestation of the new faith and one of them at least, Waraqa ibn Naufal, was a neighbour of the young Muhammad and had direct contact with him. But the God whom they sought and worshipped in secret assumed exactly with Muhammad the firm and rigorous aspect of the Allah of Islam, who then absorbed and developed that uncertain monotheistic aspiration. Arabia after Muhammad became and remained, officially at least, one hundred per cent Muslim.

Such, in brief, is the Jahiliyya background of Arab paganism, later supplanted and destroyed by Islam. Whoever approaches it with a romantic sympathy for the popular and primitive and with a taste for its austere and manly poetry, its acute gnomic sentences, the colourful wealth of its narrative, its knights, its heroes, its bards of the desert, in short those germs of 'tribal humanism' of which we spoke, may unduly overestimate its positive values which are certainly not lacking, and ignore its undoubted political, social and religious backwardness. Such a romantic consideration cannot however ignore the fundamental fact that Islam, drawing its energies from the soil of pagan Arabism but enriching it with decisive elements foreign to it, put an end to a period which which was called, with reason, 'barbarism' (this is better than 'Age of Ignorance' which is the translation usually given to the term '*Jahiliyya*'), and put the Arabs on the road to civilisation with a new and lofty concept of the divine, a society and a state shaped by it. The pagan prelude contributed more than one element distinguishable even today but it was fused by the genius of Muhammad and by the later history of Islam into an altogether new complex, the total novelty which Islam represented for so much of the world.

3 Muhammad in Mecca

The future prophet of Arabia was born at Mecca, in what year is not certain, but tradition makes it coincide with the 'year of the elephant', that is, of the unsuccessful expedition of Abraha the Abyssinian against the sanctuary of the Hijaz in 570 or shortly before. As in the case of the authenticity of pre-Islamic poetry, so in that of the sources for Muhammad's biography, there runs through Western scholarship a current of radical scepticism which considers nearly everything that Islamic tradition tells us, in particular of the early life of its Prophet, pure hagiography, and ultimately retains the Koran itself as the only reliable source. This scepticism is opposed by some of Muhammad's most recent biographers, who, while admitting that our knowledge, especially of his origins and early life, contains gaps, uncertainties and pious legends, consider tradition on the whole trustworthy and worth using, with critical discrimination, in its main outline and in many details.

Discounting the aura of pious legend which surrounds the birth and even the conception of the Prophet with premonitory signs (the light that shone from his young father Abdullah as he was on his way to marry the future mother of Muhammad, Amina; the earthquake and the quenching of the sacred fire in the Persian palace of Ctesiphon on the night of the Prophet's birth, and so on), there is no doubt that Muhammad (this seems to have been his actual name from birth, an unusual one but not unknown in pre-Islamic times) was of modest but not ignoble origin. He saw the light, at about the above-mentioned date, in the tribe of Quraish, which had for some generations had the control and guardianship of the shrine at Mecca, and the sub-tribe or clan of the Hashimites, a branch of the tribe which though it may have come down in the world was still respected and important. Abdullah, his father, died before his birth, possibly while away from his native city on a trade journey. When the child was six years old he lost his mother also, and was entrusted to the care, first of his paternal grandfather, 'Abd al-Muttalib, and later of his uncle Abu Talib, both of whom seem to have looked after the little boy with affectionate care. In spite of this, the sadness of an orphaned childhood and youth surrounded Muhammad's early years, and a touching record of it remains in an early verse of the Koran (XCIII, 6–8):

Did He not find thee an orphan, and shelter thee? Did He not find thee erring, and guide thee? Did He not find thee needy, and suffice thee?

These few authentic words give us more insight into the Prophet's unhappy youth than any hagiographic embellishments.

The urban nucleus in which he was born was famous throughout Arabia for its sanctuary, the Ka'ba, with the revered meteorite, the Black Stone, embedded in it, and its associated group of pagan divinities (the three goddesses, al-Lat, Manat and al-'Uzza surrounding the illdefined Allah, and a crowd of minor idols); but the real source of Mecca's prosperity, which while taking advantage of this religious primacy nevertheless came to extend much more widely, was trade: the bi-annual caravans which every winter and summer left Mecca for Syria and with which all the propertied men of the city were associated. The whole economic and social life of Mecca, which has been well described as a 'mercantile republic' governed by a council of the chief citizens, was based on this constant movement and trade, in which Muhammad himself, as a young man, certainly took part. The result was an emphasis on economic interest as the chief factor in the life of society, a concentration on and cult of riches which gradually pushed into the shade the ethical values by which the bedouin still lived and which the poets praised, and producing, in the last analysis, that social disequilibrium and discontent which it would be as false to consider, as some have done, the essential motive power behind Muhammad's work, as to ignore or undervalue it among the impulses which inspired him. The young Muhammad knew poverty, though not destitution; he saw the traditional national cults reduced to crude idolatrous ritual, and material interest become the mainspring of life for his contemporaries – grasping merchants for whom a man's worth was measured by his possessions. Though without, probably, reaching the height of special esteem and repu-

tation which tradition attributes to him by anticipation already in his youth, he took part in a modest way in the political and social life of his city, witnessing the outbreak and the settlement of external wars and internal feuds, and above all accumulating, in his journeys with the caravans, experiences and contacts which were later, after a long period of gestation, to have a decisive influence on his personal crisis. He crossed the desert, where he had already lived for a time as a boy, several times; he probably visited Syria and the rich Byzanto-Arabic city of Damascus; he had conversations (if without the accompanying miracles of the legends) with Christian monks and hermits. Something of a religious universe higher and more complex than his native polytheism impressed itself early on his mind and imagination, later to grow and ripen. His true vocation indeed came late, when he was about forty. Before that time, the young Hashimite had earned his living by his shrewdness and reliability as a dealer in the caravan trade, on his own account and still more on that of others. His good management of the wealth entrusted to him had won him first the esteem and then the affection of a rich Meccan widow, Khadija, some years older than himself, who had finally offered herself to him in marriage. This woman, no longer in her first youth, the first to take a permanent place in his life, remains the most sympathetic feminine figure in the Prophet's biography, among her many successors. Dying some time before the *Hijra*, she did not see the triumph of Islam, but she saw and encouraged its beginnings, and for as long as she lived she alone held the heart, the affection and the respect of the young Prophet as his vocation grew up within him. The slow maturation of the religious unrest in Muhammad's soul naturally escapes any attempt at precise dating. One thing is certain: that in about 610 (if we accept the traditional dating which makes him forty years old when his prophetic vocation began) there exploded within him a crisis, of which a sufficiently clear and reliable tradition has been preserved. During one of the occasions when he retired to pray and meditate in a cave on Mount Hira, outside Mecca, there appeared to him repeatedly a supernatural being (the same whom he afterwards named the Angel Gabriel), who commanded him to 'recite' a sacred text, in praise and gratitude to God the creator: this was the first of those revelations the full number of which, continuing for a good twenty years, almost to the end of his life, formed the sacred Book of Muhammad's new faith, the Koran (literally 'reading', or rather 'ritual recitation'). In this, the earliest, and the following short, ecstatic revelations which are found today at the end of the Koran (as it was later collected and arranged), are expressed in an enthusiastic and lyrical rather than a logical form the fundamental outlines of Muhammad's religious vision: one single omnipotent God (for whom the name Allah was the natural choice, not a new one to the pagan Arabs but filled with a new content and raised far above any polytheistic conception), author and ruler of creation, lord of the life of man, giver of blessing and chastisement, stern judge of the day of doom – the terrible end of the world – and the resurrection of the dead which was to follow. As he awaits this apocalyptic conclusion, the duty of man is to acknowledge and worship the one supreme divinity and to lead an honest and pious life according to His precepts, avoiding lies, prevarication, and violence. All in all, a simple, unilinear creed in which emotional theology, eschatology and moral effort are the dominant elements, against an as yet very elementary background of law and ritual. The lonely aspiration of the *hanif* towards a pure monotheism, concentrated entirely on the consciousness and adoration of the one God, seemed to gain its most moving and effective authority from these first experiences and revelations of the Meccan Prophet – for such Muhammad felt and proclaimed himself to be from the beginning: messenger and transmitter to his people of the new word of God.

In obedience to the express command of heaven, Muhammad began to preach these ideas in the milieu closest to him, and then gradually throughout the whole city. The first converts of the new faith (which he named 'Islam', i.e. 'abandonment' and consecration of man to the will of Allah) were, first of all his wife Khadija, whose cousin Waraqa, a *hanif* who later became a Christian, certainly exercised an important influence over Muhammad's religious thought; then the prophet's own young cousin, 'Ali, his freedman and adopted son, Zaid; and his faithful friend Abu Bakr. This first tiny group of believers grew with the passage of time, welcoming into its ranks men of different origins, for the most part young, with minds open to new experiences and ideas, and members of the less powerful and solitary tribal groups (the term *mustad'afin*, which the Koran itself applies to these first followers should perhaps be understood in this sense rather than as simply the poor, the proletariat). Contrary to certain modern interpretations, Islam was not primarily a social protest, a revolution of the economically depressed classes against the rich, since some of its most ardent supporters were men of large or moderate means – the Prophet himself, to begin with; but rather a call, encouraged by social discontent and disequilibrium but essentially spiritual and religious in nature, to substitute for the rule of force, the worship of money and the loyalties of the tribe, a transcendent faith in the relation between man and God, and an equality of believers in this relationship. In this sense and in this sense only is it correct to speak of Islam as a movement towards democracy; the resistance to it put up by the Meccan mercantile oligarchy is to be explained, not merely as the repugnance of rich men towards being dispossessed, but by a combination of many different motives.

Indeed it was not long before Muhammad's preaching, and the young community which was gathering about him, encountered hostility, mild at first, then more and more fixed and stubborn, from the ruling circles of the city. This resistance arose partly from the normal distrust of anything new, especially when proclaimed by an as yet relatively obscure person like the Hashimite preacher; partly from the undoubted interest of the rich in maintaining a status quo threatened by the new teaching which set up generosity and brotherly charity against the fixed privilege of wealth; and partly from the less egotistic fear that the city might fall from its position of economic and commercial leader of the Hijaz and centre for pagan pilgrimage – in spite of the fact that Muhammad had included in his earliest revelations hints of loyal solidarity with the political and commercial interests of his native city (the '*sura* of the elephant', which celebrates the rout of the sacrilegious Abraha, who attacked the Meccan sanctuary; the '*sura* of the Quraysh' with its reference to the concord of the city in its commercial enterprises and its call for gratitude towards 'the Lord of this House'). But on more specifically religious grounds also, Muhammad's violent attack on polytheism, one of whose shrines was precisely the Ka'ba of Mecca, could not leave indifferent those who were sincerely attached to their ancestral customs, to a tradition which the new doctrine branded as impious, idolatrous filth, proposing in its place beliefs, like that in the resurrection and the future life, which were repugnant to the empirical materialism of the great merchants of Quraysh. 'What, when we are bones and broken bits, shall we really be raised up again?' these fellow citizens asked Muhammad sceptically, unconsciously allying themselves with the scepticism of the younger generation of today, newly escaped from the iron hold of Islam – but between these two scepticisms lie thirteen centuries of unshaken faith, a faith which then, in the Mecca of the second decade of the seventh century, had its stormy beginnings.

In the Meccan *suras* of the Koran it is possible to follow step by step the impassioned polemic of the Prophet against this opposition – part mistrust, part mockery, part obstinate rejection. All his simple dialectic is employed in defending himself (or rather, according to Muslim ideas, in having God defend him, since it is God Himself who speaks in the first person in the Koran), against the accusations of being a madman, a fortune-teller, a poet; in hammering constantly on the marvels of nature as proof of the divine omnipotence, on the fate of ancient Arabian peoples exterminated by God for their unbelief, on the rewards and punishments waiting in the next world for the faithful and for infidels. For a moment Muhammad considered making terms with the ancestral beliefs, venturing on the way of compromise and admitting the existence, even if subordinate to Allah, of the three

Muhammad replacing the Black Stone in
the Ka´ba. Miniature painting from Rashid ud-Din's
'Universal History'. University Library, Edinburgh.

Meccan goddesses, al-Lat, Manat and al-'Uzza – 'the noble helpers and intercessors' as some Koranic verses called them – but this instant of weakness was quickly overcome, the compromising verses declared the inspiration of Satan and expunged from the Revelation, and the *tawhid*, the proclamation of the absolute unity of God reaffirmed in all its rigour. From the 'house of al-Arqam' (a young and wealthy convert) where Muhammad had his headquarters during that time, the new gospel went on to spread, in those first difficult years, throughout the hostile city.

While the men to whom the future belonged – Abu Bakr, 'Umar, 'Uthman, came one by one to array themselves under the command of Islam, the oligarchy of city notables were beginning to feel it not merely as a disagreeable novelty but as a danger, and passed from mockery to persecution. In the terrible history of the world's religious persecutions, those suffered by the young Islam in fact seem singularly mild, and with all its willingness to amplify, Islamic tradition only records a few isolated cases of believers who died after maltreatment by pagans. For the most part it is merely a matter of scoffing, irritations and annoyances, like the thorns which a pagan woman is said to have scattered on the ground where the Prophet was passing. (He repaid her with an explicit promise of hell, included in the Revelation for her benefit.) Within individual families the penetration of the new faith gave rise to intimate domestic dramas, as in the case of the still pagan 'Umar, who after using violence against his own sister passed to a sudden repentance and became one of the Prophet's most zealous and active companions. The Meccan oligarchs were restrained from violence against Muhammad himself by the law of clan solidarity which pervaded the whole of Arab society, bedouin or sedentary, and made his clansmen automatically close their ranks in defence of their fellow, even if they did not agree with or believe him. Thus Muhammad was protected by the solidarity of all the Hashimites, from his uncle Abu Talib, who nevertheless remained a pagan, to his other uncle the convinced pagan Abu Lahab (the husband of the woman who scattered the thorns) who yet hesitated to withhold his protection from his innovating nephew at least up to a certain moment. This moment arrived when, in about 616, the pagan opposition decided on a boycott of the whole Hashimite clan – relying on the same law of clan solidarity – excluding it from the city commerce and all other forms of contact with the citizens. Then Abu Lahab, perhaps on the pretext of other blood-ties, dissociated himself from the Hashimites, and when, after the short-lived boycott had ended and Abu Talib was dead, he in his turn became acknowledged head of the clan, he eventually withdrew his protection from his nephew Muhammad, who found himself forced to look elsewhere for some equivalent protective alliance.

But even before these last events, Islam had reached out beyond Mecca and even the Hijaz, with the emigration in about 615 of a group of the faithful to Abyssinia, a forerunner of the great *Hijra* of seven years later. The times of Abraha and his elephant were past; now Christian Abyssinia could be thought of by the Prophet as a suitable country for the faithful to take refuge in, and perhaps also for propaganda and political penetration. About eighty Meccan Muslims, on Muhammad's advice, crossed the Red Sea and were received kindly by the Axumite Negus, in whose presence one of them, according to tradition, spoke words which reflect the young Islam's consciousness of its religious, ethical and social superiority over the paganism it was fighting:

O King, we were a barbarous and idolatrous people, stained with horrible crimes, careless of the bonds of kinship and of our duties to our neighbours; among us the stronger devoured the weaker, until God raised up from among us a Messenger, whom we have acknowledged as a man of clear speech, just, faithful and honest. He has summoned us to know and worship the one God and to put away the idols of stone which our fathers, and we ourselves, adored in His place. He has exhorted us to be truthful and loyal, to care for our kinsmen and neighbours, to abstain from forbidden actions, from the shedding of blood, from lying, from consuming the goods of orphans, from slandering virtuous women. He has admonished us to adore God without putting other gods beside Him, and to observe the commandments of prayer and almsgiving and fasting. And we have put our faith in him and followed him, and for this our people persecutes us.

A pilgrimage to Mecca showing the Great Mosque
and the Ka´ba. A late eighteenth-century
Turkish painting. Topkapi Museum, Istanbul.

Was it only the persecution, generally bloodless but in the long run exasperating, which induced this Muslim nucleus to emigrate? There have been many imaginative conjectures as to other possible concurrent motives, including even internal divisions in the little Muslim community, remedied by the Prophet's sending away the dissidents. What is certain is that some of these emigrants returned not many years afterwards, in time to join, in 622, in the great *Hijra* to Medina; others only arrived later, in 628, in Medina itself, which had meanwhile become the capital of the Muslim State. Abyssinia was certainly not for the moment a suitable mission field, and Islam penetrated it only much later and then only partly; but the memory of the asylum given to the first community lasted long and was recalled in every age, including the most recent ones, in which an Afro-Asian solidarity has asserted itself against common enemies.

The years between 615 and 620 must have been the most difficult for Muhammad. During this time came the death of the faithful Khadija, who had stood boldly by her husband's side, encouraging him and confirming him in his mission, and that of his uncle Abu Talib, who although he remained a pagan had fulfilled faithfully the duty of protection which the bonds of kinship imposed upon him. The Meccan opposition, led by the Makhzumite Abu Jahl and later by the Umayyad Abu Sufyan, did not slacken. The Prophet began to search for support outside his native city, and made a first attempt with Ta'if, the Hijaz city south-east of Mecca, the seat of the Thaqif tribe. But the Thaqif lost their chance of becoming the Helpers of Islam, and Muhammad had to withdraw amid the jeers and stones of the street urchins, egged on by the chief citizens of the town. The only compensation, a wholly non-material one, is said to have been the conversion to Islam of a troop of jinns, who during this unfortunate expedition had lent their ears more favourably than men to the Prophet's preaching, and had accepted the new faith.

Other ears, however, were about to become open to his call, and new prospects to his cause. Muhammad made contact during the pilgrimage of 620 with six men from Medina, of the tribe of Khazraj, who showed themselves more receptive to his preaching than the Thaqif or the Meccan oligarchs. This first seed bore fruit, and at the next year's pilgrimage five out of the six returned, with seven of their fellow-citizens, among whom were some of the Aus, the other large tribal group of Medina. Between these twelve and the Prophet little honoured in his own country was held a secret meeting on the mountain pass of al-'Aqaba between Mina and Mecca, and the twelve swore to Muhammad 'not to associate any other god with Allah, not to steal or commit forni- cation, not to kill their children (referring to the barbarous pagan custom of disposing of female children at birth), not to make false accusations, not to disobey him in anything that was lawful.' This was the first oath of al-'Aqaba, the 'pledge of the women', as tradition calls it, under the influence of a later passage of the Koran which speaks of women who pledged themselves to the Prophet in similar terms. But those who swore at al-'Aqaba were certainly men, and this has led some to doubt, wrongly, the historicity of this first meeting of 621, as distinct from the second, the definitive one. The 'second 'Aqaba' in fact took place the following year, after Muhammad had sent to Medina, with this first group of followers, a catechist to instruct and guide them in the new faith. In June 622 a troop of seventy-five Medinese, among them two women, arrived with the other pilgrims in Mecca and assembled at a nocturnal rendezvous with the Prophet in the same place, at al-'Aqaba. Tradition places at Muhammad's side at this decisive moment his uncle al-'Abbas, he too still a pagan but said, like Abu Talib before him, to have helped his nephew out of anxiety for his personal safety; quite probably this is a case of the later honouring of this subsequently sainted figure, the founder of the dynasty of the Abbasid Caliphs, whereas in reality Muhammad had to seek protection outside his own Hashimite clan. In any case the 'pledge of the women' of the previous year was followed this time by the 'pledge of war' – the undertaking by these Medinese to recognise the Prophet and to defend him, even in arms, as they would their own wives and children. With this second oath of al-'Aqaba the young Muslim community ceased to be an un-armed and persecuted minority and took on the military character which it was to display from then on, both in the near and in the far distant future.

What impulses drove these Medinese to entrust their fate and that of their city to the still controversial and despised prophet from Mecca? There can be no reasonable doubt that the earliest of them especially were moved primarily by the religious essence of his message; however, to understand his rapid success in these new and, to him, strange surroundings (though he had ties of kinship with Medina on his mother's side) it is necessary to bear in mind the disturbed political and social situation of this second urban centre of the Hijaz – based, unlike the mercantile city of Mecca, on an agricultural and artisan economy, and inhabited by a mixed population of Arabs and Jews. The pagan Arab element consisted of the two rival tribes, the Aus and the Khazraj, who held the dominant position in the city, but for the last few decades had been bleeding to death in fratricidal feuds; the Jewish one – Jewish by religion, that is, for they too were probably Arab by race – of strong minority groups who had themselves once been at the head of the city and though they had lost political supremacy still carried great weight in the economic and social life of Medina. These Jewish nuclei, which constituted one of Muhammad's most difficult problems once he had reached Medina, had no part at all in his invitation; this came from elements among the Aus and Khazraj together, who probably saw in him not only a relig-ious leader but a possible arbitrator and mediator in their internal conflicts. Indeed the preoccupation of the Medinese converts at al-'Aqaba seems to have been lest Muhammad, once he had made use of their support to gain the upper hand over his own countrymen, would abandon them to their discords. Muhammad reassured them with the famous words:

Your cause in strife is my cause; your remission for blood that has been shed is my remission; you are with me and I with you.

Words which neither love for his native city nor the final triumph of his cause ever made him forget; from that moment the pagan Yathrib became the Muslim 'City of the Prophet', his home and later his burial place.

Once his fate had been joined to that of the Medinese by the pact of al-'Aqaba, the decision must immediately have matured in the Prophet's mind to transfer himself and his small community of fellow citizens thither. So in the course of the summer of 622, between the oath-taking at al-'Aqaba and the final departure of Muhammad himself, there began little by little the *Hijra*, the secession or abandoning of their native city by the Muslims of Mecca. The word does not carry any meaning of 'flight', as it is often mistranslated; in Arabic it simply means a departure, a separation from former dwelling places and neighbours such as was common in bedouin society. In fact, however, there is a suggestion of flight in the gradualness and secrecy of the emigration (although the Meccans do not seem to have offered any hindrance or obstacle to it), and, at the end, in the circumstances of Muhammad's own departure. His life, which up till then had never been seriously threatened, probably was so at this critical moment, when the Meccans considered getting rid of this dangerous agitator in their midst, who now had become by his connections with the Medinese a trouble-maker in the city's external relations as well. A plot to assassinate Muhammad was in fact made – even if not, as tradition has it, on the advice of the devil in disguise – at a meeting of the chief citizens' council of Mecca; a band of young men, belonging to different clans (so as to divide and in effect cancel out the common legal responsibility borne by kinsmen as a group in a case of bloodshed) were to seize him in his bed and kill him. But Muhammad was, miraculously or otherwise, warned of the plot and escaped – according to some accounts leaving in his place his cousin 'Ali, whom the conspirators, noticing the substitution, dared not touch. Accompanied perhaps by this same 'Ali, certainly by Abu Bakr, the Prophet left his native city secretly within a few days; pursued at first by his enemies he hid himself in a cave with his companion, over the mouth of which a pious spider is said to have spun her web to deceive the pursuers and send them in the wrong direction. So by short stages and avoiding the more frequented roads he rejoined his followers in Medina, where he arrived at the end of September, 622. (The mistake sometimes made of dating the *Hijra* from the July is a result of the fact that the lunar year in which it took place begins in July.) His safe arrival in the outer suburb of Quba was greeted with jubilation by both Meccan emigrants and Medinese converts to the new faith (known as the Ansar or 'Helpers'); from there he soon moved to settle in a new house especially built for him nearer the centre of the city. So began both the official era of Islam and the decisive period in the life of its founder.

Looking back over the period that was now coming to an end, the far-off youth and the stormy first decade of his preaching in his native city, we find it wrapped, certainly, in pious legends, full of obscurities and questions destined to remain for ever unanswered, but not so much so as to prevent the essential outlines of this personality, this life, from emerging clearly enough. After an unhappy, orphaned boyhood and a hard-working youth, Muhammad attained his great religious experience after long and patient travail, all knowledge of which is lost to us, but whose sincerity and depth of feeling are obvious to any unprejudiced mind. His condemnation of his ancestral polytheism did not prevent his at first feeling solidarity with the traditions, institutions and festivals of his native city – and indeed we shall see them, after his passionate attack, taken up again by him and inserted, but with new meaning, into his vision of Arabian and human history. Finding himself up against an increasingly rigid opposition from the ruling class of Mecca, he carried on his struggle with passionate and impetuous fervour, with unshakeable faith in the truth of his message and its religious and ethical superiority to a primitive idolatrous cult and the interests attached to it. He knew, too, how to win to himself, with no other means of attraction, at that time, than the undoubted fascination of his own personality and the intrinsic nobility of his faith, the noblest spirits among his fellow citizens, who were destined to become the organizers of the future Islamic state and empire. But no hint of any such future development was apparent during the Meccan period, when the Koran, the faithful mirror of Muhammad's thought, shows him wholly engaged in clarifying to himself and to others the fundamental religious themes of his creed: the dependence of man on the one God and his responsibility towards Him, the impending threat of the last judgment, and the ethical duties which follow from this within the human community. His own status as Messenger is affirmed energetically from the first, but as one implying duties rather than rights, a position of humility, patience, and fidelity at all costs to his mission. The dignity and privilege of the Prophet, his distance from the mass of the faithful, his political power over men and his compromises with their passions and his own – all this was to belong to the new Medinese period now about to begin, when the religious reformer would become at once political head, war leader and legislator. And while in this role also Muhammad was to show exceptional qualities and gifts, the religious purity of the original message of Mecca was to become fatally blurred, just as the panting lyrical impulse of the oldest Koranic *suras* which express that first contact with the Numinous was to give place to the long, prosaic administrative provisions of the Medinese *suras*, with their human, all too human background. And yet the basic genuineness of his first inspiration was never altogether lost in Muhammad, and it is for this reason that the source and secret of all his later work, as religious and social reformer and maker of history, must be looked for in this earliest period of his mission. Among the arid rocks of Mecca the flower first blossomed that in Medina was to bear such an unsuspected wealth of fruit.

4 Triumph in Medina

The Medinese period is that of the gradual rise and the final total victory of Muhammad's cause, which in his own city had not succeeded, during more than a decade of struggle, in conquering the pagan opposition. But this victory and his position of absolute theocratic power as Prophet and head of his own new-founded state were only reached slowly, by surmounting difficulties and eliminating by degrees adversaries open and secret, in open conflict with Mecca and in a close and subtle game of political intrigue with the factions and groups in Medina itself. On his first arrival at the time of the *Hijra* Muhammad was far from being the unchallenged arbitrator he was to become in future, though tradition tends to present him in the light of that future from this time on. To begin with he was merely the chief of his fellow-emigrants, the *muhajirun*, and of those Medinese who had accepted his faith and had sworn fidelity to him at al-'Aqaba. Certainly, the propaganda of more than a year had won over a good number of the pagans in Medina to Islam, besides the group which had met at 'Aqaba, but that by September 622 the whole population of Medina should have been converted is out of the question. There were certainly pagan groups and individuals left, later to be absorbed gradually by the new faith, though it is difficult to assess their numbers or trace their fate with any precision (these people, still unbelievers or else tepid and vacillating in their loyalty to Islam, are referred to in the Koran by the term *munafiqun*, generally translated as 'hypocrites'). There was also the tightly-knit Jewish community, subdivided into three principal tribal groups, the Banu Qainuqa', the Banu Nadir and the Banu Quraiza, with their sub-tribes and lesser groups; and there were a few stubborn individual opponents like Abu 'Amir ar-Rahib, a sort of Medinese *hanif*, who, dissatisfied whether for religious or political reasons with Muhammad's work, made a *Hijra* of his own in reverse, and left with a group of followers for Mecca. Between these opposed forces the Prophet showed himself able to make his way gradually, with a sense of timing, a shrewd judgment of men and situations, a mixture of astuteness, suppleness and energy, which for the first time demonstrated the political genius which from then on took its place beside his religious inspiration as a directing principle of his work and life.

The situation at the beginning of the Medinese period, and the Prophet's prudent and far-seeing tactics in developing it to his advantage, are mirrored for us in a precious and undoubtedly authentic document which has come down to us, the 'charter' or pact which Muhammad made with the whole population of Medina shortly after his arrival (the oath of al-'Aqaba bound to him only the Muslims of the city). In this document, of outstanding historical, legal and linguistic importance, the Prophet declared the population of Medina as an entirety – believers, pagans and Jews – to be one single community, and made an effort to regulate relations between its various elements, advising the retention of certain traditional principles of the pagan era, such as the collective responsibility of the tribal group in cases of ransom or bloodshed, along with the new reality which he had come to bring. The Meccan immigrants formed, at least to begin with, a first self-sufficient and solitary group; this was followed by the various Medinese groups, with equal rights and duties, and the Jews of Medina also, though only in so far as they were allied with and incorporated into the Arab groups. The polytheists of Mecca appear as the common enemy, to which the composite community of Yathrib stands opposed, whether for religious or merely political reasons. The Prophet is named discreetly once or twice as mediator and judge of unspecified disputes and uncertainties, never, yet, as the one undisputed authority to whom all owe unconditional obedience. Such indeed must have been Muhammad's original position in Medina, before assiduous preaching and the growth of proselytism, the fidelity of his followers and above all the success of his arms, had raised his authority and prestige high enough to make him the absolute head of the Islamic State of Medina, while the population of the latter, in consequence of the events we are about to describe, ended by becoming exclusively Muslim.

The year after the *Hijra* was spent by Muhammad consolidating

The Great Mosque (or Mosque of
the Prophet) at Medina. From a Dutch
print by C. Philips Jacobé, 1774.

and trying out the new position; seeing his Meccan companions settled in the brotherly hospitality of the Medinese 'Helpers',
dealing with a quantity of practical problems, and at the same time
clarifying and developing the dogmatic and ritual content of his
faith, especially through his contact with the Jews of Medina.
It had been clear to him from the beginning that the message of
the uniqueness of God which had been entrusted to him coincided
with that, known only vaguely to him, preached by the two older
religions which had taken root in Arabia and the Hijaz especially,
Christianity and Judaism. In the case of the former an insuperable
difficulty at once appeared, the concept of Christ as the Son of
God, and of the Trinity, which Muhammad rejected with all his
energy. In the case of Judaism no such obstacle existed, and the
refusal of his message by the Jews of Medina, whom at one time
he had considered as potential allies and converts to Islam, must
have seemed all the more strange and painful to the Arab Prophet.
Enclosed in their religious exclusiveness, always ready to lay
mocking emphasis on the confused and fragmentary notions
which he showed himself to have of their faith, trained by their
Rabbis in apologetic debate and logic-chopping, the Jews constituted Muhammad's greatest disillusionment in his new surroundings, with decisive consequences for the development of the new
faith and for the state of mind of the disappointed Prophet towards
these unforeseen adversaries. Disowned and rejected by Judaism,
he was led to accentuate the Arab character of his message,
declaring that the Jews had falsified and corrupted their own
Scriptures, and perverted the true monotheism which their common
ancestor Abraham had once introduced into Arabia and which
he, Muhammad, was to restore and reform. The clearest manifestation, almost a symbol of this change of attitude, was the alteration
of the *qibla*, the orientation of prayer, which Muhammad changed
from Jerusalem to Mecca precisely in these early days in Medina.
That Jerusalem which had once shone like a beacon of holiness in
the imagination of the Prophet of the one true God, so much so
that he had on one occasion felt himself miraculously transported

there in a nocturnal journey or vision, to ascend from thence to heaven; that Jerusalem now lost its religious primacy in favour of his native city, still idolatrous and hostile, but which Islam claimed for its own as the site of the primitive 'Abrahamic' monotheism of Arabia, goal of prayer and of future pilgrimages freed from the taint of idolatry. At the same time, in the political and social field, the fate of the Jews of Medina was marked out; from then on Islam was simply to tolerate them while waiting for any suitable opportunity to exile or exterminate them.

Meanwhile the *bai'at al-harb*, the oath of war at the 'second 'Aqaba', and the associated divine permission given to Muhammad to resort to arms if necessary, began to bear their first fruit as Islam moved from words to deeds, and sometimes bloody deeds. The raids on caravans from the Hijaz, which the Prophet began to organise from Medina in 623, followed the age-old custom of pagan Arab society and so aroused no scruples or outrage. Both were aroused, however, when one of these predatory expeditions, prompted chiefly by the simple necessity of providing food and provisions for overcrowded Medina, led to a treacherous attack, at Nakhla (between Mecca and Ta'if), where a caravan was set upon by a small band of Medinese Muslims during the sacred month of *Rajab*. It was this breaking of a truce, held sacred since time immemorial which produced reactions of outrage in Mecca and uneasiness in Medina. But then their minds were set at rest by a revelation, one of the first of many which were to be sent from then on to resolve concrete dilemmas, the difficulties of the moment, by a message from the Divinity. Through the mouth of Muhammad, Allah declared that it was indeed a grave matter to have violated the truce of the sacred month, but that misbelief and opposition to the true faith were graver. Although from motives of psychological expediency and perhaps also from personal conviction, he could not deny the sacredness of the ancient pagan ban of *Rajab*, Muhammad countered it with what seems to us an evasion, but was enough to quieten the scruples of his followers. The essential point was that blood had begun to flow on the way of Islam, with approval and soon with open encouragement from the Divinity; and this is a fact which, whatever the reaction of our own religious and moral consciousness at the instinctive comparison with the spread of early Christianity, was to condition the entire later evolution and diffusion of the religion of Muhammad.

The incident at Nakhla had been a mere exchange of blows, but necessity, and perhaps also the desire for a definite show-down with pagan Mecca, led Muhammad to launch attacks on a larger scale. When, in March 624, he attacked a big Meccan caravan on its way back from Palestine, a force of about a thousand of his fellow-citizens with his old enemy Abu Jahl in command rushed from Mecca to its defence. The caravan, under the able leadership of Abu Sufyan, escaped the Muslim intercepting force, but a clash between the latter and the Meccan party was inevitable. It took place at Badr, a place to the south-west of Medina, on the caravan route between Mecca and Syria, and the result, in spite of their inferior numbers, was total victory for the Muslims. Emigrants and 'Helpers' here fought side by side, sealing with their blood the substitution of the common tie of faith for the old tribal bonds. Muhammad, who did not fight in person, but followed the encounter praying and at one point threw a handful of earth towards the enemy, felt and proclaimed that God had intervened directly in the battle. As a verse from the Koran has it (VIII, 17):

It was not you who slew them at Badr, but God slew them; thou did not throw dust against them, but God threw it!

With hardly a dozen dead among the Muslims and a few dozen among the Meccans, among whom was Abu Jahl himself, in an encounter which in military terms was hardly more than a brawl, Islam had received its victorious baptism of fire, had inflicted a scorching blow on the pagans of Mecca, and had become conscious of its own striking power, which was destined in the years and decades that followed to grow into an irresistible avalanche. The victory of Badr was also the occasion for the revelation of the first law on the division of booty; one fifth was reserved 'for God, for the Messenger and his kin, for orphans and the poor, for strangers'; in practice, that is, for the Prophet himself and after him for the public treasury of the Islamic empire. Some pagan prisoners were ransomed, but others were killed, and among these was Muhammad's old enemy, Nadr ibn al-Harith, who at Mecca had competed successfully with him, countering his pious biblical tales with the beautiful fantasies of Persian epic, destined one day to be sung by the Muslim Firdawsi.

These enemies, slain, or captured weapon in hand, were not the only ones to prove at the cost of their lives the strength of victorious Islam. The months after Badr were marked by other episodes of politico-religious hatred which apologists of the Prophet would do better to pass over, for instance the assassination, which he approved if he did not actually instigate it, of his Medinese enemy Ka'b ibn al-Ashraf; but politically more important was the expulsion from Medina of the first of the three Jewish tribes, the Banu Qainuqa'. Taking advantage of a trivial incident, Muhammad besieged them in their fortresses, forced them to surrender, and drove them out of the town.

In vain the leader of the 'hypocrites', 'Abdallah ibn Ubayy, interceded for them; but some of their fellow-Jews of the other two Medinese tribes were to have reason before long to envy their fate.

The counter-attack from Mecca

While Medina was rejoicing over the victory at Badr and enjoying the fruits of success, at Mecca consternation spread. Abu Sufyan, who from that moment was the *de facto* leader of the Meccan citizenry, forbade mourning the fallen for the time being and began immediately to think of organising a counter-attack. The poets, among whom was that Ka'b ibn al-Ashraf who was to pay with his life for his opposition to Islam, whetted the desire for revenge with their laments. Exactly a year after Badr, in March 625, the punitive expedition set out for Medina, with a nucleus of Meccan troops reinforced by contingents from their bedouin allies. On reaching the oasis of Medina they encountered the Muslims near the hill of Uhud, to the north of the city, and battle was joined. The Muslims were on the point of getting the upper hand when they were attacked on their flank by Khalid ibn al-Walid (the future great general of the conquests, who was already showing his gifts as a strategist) and driven back in disorder up the slope of the hill. Muhammad himself was knocked down and bruised in the rout, which could have ended in total disaster if the Meccans had pushed their advantage to the limit. But they did not, and Abu Sufyan retired, satisfied with having taught the enemy a hard lesson. Many of the Muslims had fallen, among them the Prophet's uncle Hamza, later to be venerated by Muslim piety as one of the first and greatest martyrs of the faith.

But even this reverse only showed the Prophet's rising fortunes more plainly. What might have been a mortal blow to the young Medinese community remained no more than a momentary setback; the Prophet whose life had been in danger, was safe, and revelation intervened immediately to explain the defeat and soften it with reprimands and exhortations.

When you were going up, not twisting about for any one, and the Messenger was calling you in your rear; so He rewarded you with grief on grief . . . Then He sent down upon you, after grief, security . . . Those of you who turned away the day the two hosts encountered – Satan made them slip . . . but God has pardoned them; God is All-forgiving, All-clement . . . O believer, be patient, and vie you in patience; fear God; haply so you will prosper.

Koran, III 147–9, 200

The lowered morale of the Muslims was raised a few months later by a punitive action against the remaining Jews of Medina; this time it was the turn of the Banu Nadir; they also were besieged in their quarter on a trivial pretext and banished, leaving their arms and their well-cultivated palm trees. Of the three major Jewish tribes of Medina there now remained only the Banu

Quraiza, who at the next opportunity were to pay the dearest price.

The opportunity came two years later, in the Spring of 627, in the shape of the last military expedition of Mecca against its rebel son. At the end of March 627 (March is Muhammad's month of destiny throughout this Medinese decade), the Meccans, still under the command of Abu Sufyan, attacked Medina in force; this time there was a veritable confederation of the Prophet's enemies (*al-Ahzab*, the confederates, as the Koran calls them), gathering around Mecca contingents from different bedouin tribes such as the Ghatafan and the Sulaim. From the beginning, the bedouin had been spectators of the conflict between Mecca and Medina, but as it grew more serious they began to be involved in one way or another, joining either the cause of the Prophet or that of his enemies, and sometimes manoeuvring between the two parties. Now an army which with both Meccans and bedouin consisted of about ten thousand men attacked the city of the Prophet. However, a rough entrenchment which Muhammad had dug was enough to protect its northern, more gently sloping and open approach, (on all the other sides lava blocks prevented cavalry action) and to stop the attackers, and after a few weeks of inefficient blockade, with a few skirmishes on the part of the archers, the pagans retreated. Their absolute lack of the will or capacity to mount an effective attack, in spite of the great concentration of forces they were able to put in motion, gives the measure of the military and moral crisis which was already developing in Mecca, and which only grew more serious in the next few years.

The epilogue of the 'war of the ditch', as the episode of the siege is known in Muslim tradition, brought to a dramatic conclusion Muhammad's relations with the remaining Jews of Mecca, the Banu Quraiza, who were now in their turn to suffer the reaction to the good or ill fortune of the Muslims. During the siege these unbelievers had constituted a potential fifth column at the Prophet's back, and while externally at least they remained neutral, they certainly hoped for his defeat and were in contact with the enemy. Hardly was the emergency over, therefore, than Muhammad decided to rid himself of them, and prepared to besiege them as he had the other two tribes. The Banu Quraiza put up only a feeble defence, although through the indiscretion of an emissary of Muhammad himself (who repented later) they must have had a plain warning of the fate which awaited them. When in spite of this they surrendered, pressure was put on Muhammad by the Aus, one of the two tribes of the Helpers who had been allied to the Quraiza, to treat them mercifully; Muhammad responded by referring the decision to one of his companions, himself of the Aus tribe, who was suffering from a wound got during the siege; the sentence was death for the men and slavery for the women and children. Weak in their defence, the Quraiza faced death with courage and dignity; six hundred men died in this brutal massacre.

This dark episode, which Muslim tradition, it must be said, takes quite calmly, has provoked lively discussion among western biographers of Muhammad, with caustic accusations on the one hand and legalistic excuses on the other. In reply to the horror of Christian and modern sentiment at the unnecessary slaughter (though indeed the twentieth century should have become hardened to atrocities) it has been argued that these things took place in an Arabia whose ethic was neither Christian nor modern, and where the only restraint against the extermination of an enemy would be the thought of the revenge or blood-money which it would entail. By liquidating the Quraiza without leaving any survivors and ensuring, by the expedient of delegating the decision, the support of the Aus in the extermination of their former allies, Muhammad was able to exclude any considerations of the kind, and act as the pitiless rule of war in his times permitted. For our part, we do not care to submit the bloody course of history to legalistic disputes as to guilt or innocence; we merely note that *haqn ad-dima*, the avoidance of bloodshed, was a virtue not unknown even in pagan Arabia, and one which the Prophet of Islam himself showed on other occasions, if perhaps from political motives rather than from innate gentleness. In this case he was ruthless, with the approval of his conscience and of his God, for the two were one;

The birth of the Prophet Muhammad.
From Rashid ud-Din's 'Universal History'.
University Library, Edinburgh.

we can only record the fact, while reaffirming our consciousness as Christians and civilised men, that this God, or at least this aspect of Him, is not ours.

It would be unfair, however, to see Muhammad's activities during these years as lit only by the glint of weapons. Though the organisation of warfare, both offensive and defensive, certainly took first place among his responsibilities, he had others at the same time; the organisation of his community, the legislation connected with it, the endless problems, legal, ritual and social, which the Prophet was called upon to solve either by his personal judgment or by the aid of the divine revelation. During this time the foundations were being laid for the whole edifice of Muslim society, in the verses of the Koran and in the canonical sayings, the *hadith* (i.e., decisions and remarks attributed to the Prophet and reflecting his 'custom' or way of life, *sunna*, which have a normative value second only to that of the Koran for all good Muslims). Along the lines of that simple, unilinear dogma which had already largely been established at Mecca, and through the increasing power and authority of the Prophet to pronounce laws accepted as valid by the whole community (laws which for the Muslim have their origin in God Himself), the new religion and the new state were beginning to take on their final shape. He gave decisions on family and penal law and laws of inheritance, modifying and adding to pagan custom; the cult was given fixed and articulated form with such fundamental institutions as the canonical prayers, and the obligations of alms, fasting and pilgrimage. Above all he taught, with understandable emphasis, the duty of the holy war against pagans and unbelievers generally. More and more Islam was moving out of the realm of the interior life, in which it had its origins and to which it had originally been addressed, into that of the exterior world; to the regulation of actions and behaviour, business and even mere social convention, on a diversity of levels which appear strange and incongruous to the outsider, but were not so to that generation, nor to the many later generations of Islam. As regards the biography of Muhammad himself, we must not omit some mention of his many marriage ties – all of them subsequent to the *Hijra*, and to that with Khadija. There was the young 'A'isha, daughter of Abu Bakr and destined to be his favourite wife, and the more mature beauty Zainab, repudiated by his adopted son Zaid ibn Haritha, and married by Muhammad by special divine permission. The question of the matrimonial and sexual life of Muhammad is another on which much has been written, not all of it intelligent. There is no doubt that, as both ancient and modern apologists insist, some of his many marriages (a good dozen, as against the four wives allowed an ordinary believer) were political in their object and nature; but there is also the unimpeachable Islamic tradition which attributes to the Prophet the praise of women and perfumes as the dearest to his heart of all the good things of this world (of the attractions of money and material goods, on the other hand, he was much less sensible.) In the case of the Zainab episode, for example, the most devoted exponent of the political alliance theory would find himself in some difficulty. From all these unions, with legitimate wives and with slave concubines (these were freely permitted both by pre-Islamic custom and by Islamic law), Muhammad never had the happiness of seeing a full-grown son; his one boy died in infancy, and of his daughters only Fatima, Khadija's daughter, later married to 'Ali, was to have any importance in the later history of the Prophet's family and of the Muslim community.

The struggle with Mecca, after the unsuccessful siege of the 'war of the ditch', moved into a new and surprising phase with the episode of Hudaybiya, which shows us a pliable, opportunist Muhammad, open to negotiation and compromise. In March 628 the Prophet with his companions set out unexpectedly towards their native city with the explicit intention of performing there the holy visit (*'umra*), distinct from the true pilgrimage but no less indicative of the importance and sanctity which he always attributed to the Ka'ba, his ancestral sanctuary, whose foundation was held to go back to the patriarch Abraham. The Quraish, disturbed, assembled to confront this unwanted pilgrim. And, incredibly, at

Hudaybiya at the edge of the sacred ground of Mecca, the Prophet halted his armed advance and stooped to bargain with his enemies, to the astonishment and discomfiture of his own companions. The negotiations led to an agreement, by the terms of which the Muslims withdraw for the time being, and the Meccans undertook to vacate the city in the following year to allow them to make the pilgrimage. A ten years' truce was declared between the two cities. Meccan fugitives to Medina were in future to be sent back (with no reciprocal obligation on the other side), and both parties were to be free to contract alliances with any tribes or individuals they might wish. The whole treaty, which was conceived in terms of mutual equality (although with some incivilities and points of protocol humiliating to the Prophet, who accepted them without batting an eyelid) certainly seemed out of keeping with the rising fortunes of the leader of the Medinese state, and it took all his authority and prestige to restrain his companions' discontent, and extract from them a second oath of loyalty (the 'bai'a of the consent', or 'of the tree', after the place where it was sworn), and to lead them back with nothing accomplished to Medina. This episode will serve to give the measure of the Prophet's tactical ability, of the absolute obedience he was able to command from his followers, and of the situation, by now seriously weakened, of the Quraysh. The pact of Hudaybiya was faithfully kept, at least as far as the next year's pilgrimage was concerned, and the Prophet was able to complete it in peace with his companions. For the first time in seven years he set foot again in his native city, as the dreaded leader of a community of foreigners. A few months later he was to enter it again as a conqueror.

Between the compromise of Hudaybiya and the final collapse of Mecca, we can see the power and authority of Muhammad growing irresistibly both within and without the Hijaz. Already a few months after Hudaybiya he had led his followers to the conquest of the fertile oasis of Khaybar, north of Medina, until then held and cultivated by Jews. The outcome of the expedition was that the Jews continued to cultivate it, but as tenants of the

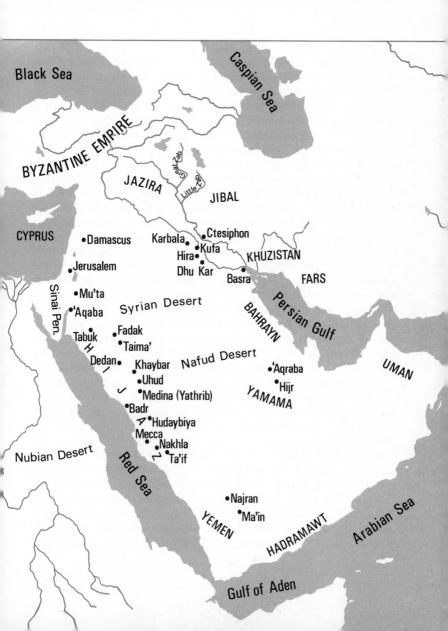

new Muslim proprietors, to whom they had to give half of their
harvest. This completed the liquidation of all the political and
economic power of the Jews in the Hijaz, pending the total expulsion of all Jews and Christians from Arabia under Caliph 'Umar.
It was during this same period that Muhammad sent embassies to
the rulers of the states bordering on Arabia (the Byzantine Emper-
or, the King of Persia, the Governor of Egypt, etc.) inviting them
to become converted to Islam, the fame of which had by now passed
the boundaries of the Peninsula. Although the letters from the
Prophet and the replies to them which tradition has preserved are
of very dubious authenticity, the fact of this correspondence, of
which there is no doubt, shows how the new faith was taking on
that universalism which was to characterise it from then on, and
anticipates developments which were to appear during the period
of the conquests. On the military plane, these first attempts were
not, for the time being, very fortunate; a Muslim force which had
advanced as far as Mu'ta, in Transjordania, in 629, was beaten
and driven back, probably by other Arabs employed by the
Byzantines as auxiliaries, and its leader Zaid ibn Haritha (whom we
have already mentioned several times) killed. But this reverse made
little difference to the now irresistible advance of Islam in Arabia
itself; in Mecca the anti-Muslim resistance was crumbling, and
the more clever men whom the Meccans still had to rely on
(such as Khalid ibn al-Walid and 'Amr ibn al-'As) were one by
one going over to Muhammad. The last, or one of the last, to join
the side of the victor was Abu Sufyan, for long the moving spirit
of the anti-Muhammad party. At the eleventh hour, taking advantage of the tie of kinship he had contracted with the Prophet, who
had married his daughter, Umm Habiba, the capable Meccan chief-
tain managed to get himself pardoned and welcomed by his son-in-
law. Thirty years later, one of his sons was to be the Commander of
the faithful at Damascus, the head of the whole Muslim Empire.

At the end of 629, an attack made on, and provoked by, one
of the tribes allied to Muhammad, provided him with a convenient
pretext to declare the truce of Hudaybiya null and void. At the

beginning of January an army of ten thousand men with the
Prophet at their head marched on Mecca, where Abu Sufyan
(on the strength of an understanding with Medina which, according
to some, had been secretly reached long before) contrived a triumphal entry for the erstwhile fugitive, with scarcely a blow struck.
The conquest of the holy city was practically bloodless, carried out
under the sign of pardon and magnanimity. The Prophet, surrounded by his exultant followers, rode his camel seven times round the
Ka'ba, proclaimed a solemn ban on all the customs, privileges and
duties of the *Jahiliyya*, and ordered the sanctuary to be cleansed of
all the litter of idolatry. Except for a very few executions of old
personal enemies and attackers of the Prophet, there was a general
amnesty, in accordance with the policy of the 'gaining of hearts',
which Muhammad now began to apply. By January 630, paganism
may be said to have been eradicated in his city for ever. Among
the bedouin the situation was different; many tribes who had been
neutral up to that time felt that the moment had now come to

join the winning side, and sent embassies (*wufud*) to the Prophet to negotiate their acceptance of Islam and the associated tributary obligations. But for some others, the Hawazin for instance, enemies of the Quraish, the victory of Islam meant imminent danger, which they determined to meet with force. At the end of the very month of his victorious entry into Mecca, Muhammad left it again to meet the fierce bedouin tribe in the field. The battle of Hunayn marked their total defeat, and with it the defeat of paganism throughout the Hijaz. In the distribution of the booty, preference was given to those 'whose hearts were to be won over', most of them Meccan Muslims only lately converted, and here also Muhammad succeeded in overcoming by his personal charm and authority, the obvious discontent of his old Medinese companions. Then, true to the old compact made at al-'Aqaba, he returned to Medina.

Muhammad's last conquests and death

Less than a year and a half were left him to consolidate and organise the fruits of victory. Central, and to a lesser extent eastern Arabia had been won for Islam; the Yemen, too, formerly in the hands of the Persians but now practically autonomous, received his envoy, and ended its glorious history as a separate region by embracing the new faith. Towards the North, the way of the future, Muhammad himself led an expedition whose object is not very clear – perhaps an attempt at revenge for Mu'ta. They reached Tabuk, but turned back without having accomplished anything, exhausted by the heat, and in the midst of recriminations and also, it seems, the beginnings of religious discords, which were energetically uncovered and stamped out by the Prophet.

He visited Mecca for the last time in March 632, in his 'pilgrim-age of farewell'. Here there sounded the solemn words of what is held the final revelation, in which Allah proclaimed to the faithful:

Today I have perfected your religion for you, and I have completed My blessing upon you, and I have approved Islam for your religion.

Koran, v, 5

Beyond and above all legal and ritual casuistries, or the petty personal concerns to which the revelation had sometimes been reduced in these later years, Muhammad's inspiration returned to its religious fountainhead; but now it was no longer simply the concern of one individual, or of a small conventicle of believers, but the faith of an *umma*, a collectivity, which now included the virgin strength of the two greatest cities in Arabia and of many desert tribes, ready to loose them towards new destinies. Did the Prophet, as his own day drew to its end, foresee these destinies? We shall attempt, in discussing the great conquests, to shed some light on this question, but it is difficult to reach any certainty on this point.

He returned once more to Medina; already worn out, he died there peacefully on 8 June 632, after an illness of a few days. All those great figures were present who were to fill the history of the succeeding years; Abu Bakr, 'Umar and 'Ali, Abu 'Ubaida and Khalid ibn al-Walid, the future Caliphs and generals of the conquests. But his end was a quiet and solitary one, in the arms of his beloved 'A'isha, to whose apartment he had ordered them to carry him when his illness became serious. But more important than any outward details concerning this death are the last words, which an almost certainly reliable tradition puts in the mouth of the dying man; the mention of the 'high companion of paradise' – the same who had appeared to him more than twenty years before in the cave of Mount Hira. He named no successor or representative; only his community's will to survive produced one. And on the modest site of his home, where his tomb was made, there grew up afterwards the Mosque of the Prophet, second only to the Ka'ba in the veneration of Muslims down the centuries. The seed was sown.

Let us look back for a moment, as we did with the Meccan period, over this Medinese phase of the Prophet's life, as a whole. Unlike the former, it emerges in the full light of history, and the quality and quantity of the relevant traditions is enough to satisfy, taken together, any reasonable scepticism. Certain points may have been embroidered by legend, or rather by bias in favour of the Prophet (though indeed acts are reported of him which seemed not at all reprehensible to his contemporaries, while our own moral sensibility reacts otherwise); or, even more often, in favour of subsequent political and religious positions, *ad maiorem gloriam* of persons and families who later attained power and honour in the Islamic world. On the whole, however, we may repeat that we have a picture of the character and work of Muhammad in Medina which is sufficiently reliable, coherent and honest. We have to deal no longer with a rejected and persecuted prophet, inspired by pure religious zeal; but with a very able ruler, judge and captain, exceptionally gifted in politics and diplomacy, yet always impelled by that first inspiration. His rise, within Medina itself, from the position of the refugee leader of a small group of followers, to that of the loved and dreaded ruler of the whole city, and then of his own state, must win the admiration even of those who are unable to admire certain individual actions in his public or private life. The magnanimity he showed in his hour of triumph contrasts with the occasional harshness or duplicity which is all too plain, whatever his panegyrists may say, in the course of his struggle. It was a struggle, after all, with no quarter, for a cause to which he had devoted his life, and which, taken as a whole, can be seen to be the raising, through faith and the whole way of life which hinged upon it, of his entire people; his fellow-citizens of Mecca, the Helpers of Medina, and after them the restless and religiously refractory bedouin tribes. As we pointed out in the preceding chapter, one should not draw too sharp a dividing line between the Muhammad of Mecca and of Medina; the later was, in the new conditions in which he found himself, the continuation and development of the former, and their common denominator was an unconquerable faith, sometimes obscured but never quenched by human frailties; for he himself always felt and proclaimed himself to be a man and nothing more, though one honoured by God with a special mission. He himself would have approved the memorable words in which his first successor, Abu Bakr, announced his death to his followers:

O men, whosoever worshipped Muhammad, know that he is dead; whosoever worshipped Muhammad's God, know that He is alive and immortal.

5 Islam and the Arab-Muslim state

Between the obscure history of the Arabs before Muhammad and their miraculous expansion after him stands the great fact of Islam, the faith which he preached to and imposed on his people, and which they in their turn carried to other, varied and distant peoples. For the latter as for the former, Islam was to become the pattern of life itself and to determine all their subsequent history. It is not the purpose of this book to trace that history, even for the Arab people, beyond its initial phase in which their new faith led them to their extraordinary conquests; but before narrating these *gesta Dei per Arabes* we must begin by briefly outlining the nature of the new faith, and describing the internal evolution of the Islamic state and community in its earliest period after the death of the Prophet. This evolution is indeed closely linked with the phenomenon of the conquests; its action soon occupied a theatre wider than Arabia alone, and some of the factors in it were the reactions of the Arabs to the new situation created by their diaspora and their contacts with subject peoples. Just as certain of the aspects and results of the conquests are unintelligible without some knowledge of the internal evolution of the Arab – Islamic community, so also the latter is often conditioned by the former. In this brief outline, therefore, we shall necessarily have to refer from time to time to facts which will be treated adequately only in the following chapters; but our intention is that this chapter as a whole should provide a background against which the great adventures of the Arabs outside Arabia may be seen enacted.

The Muslim faith is summed up in a lapidary double formula: 'There is no God but Allah; Muhammad is the Prophet of Allah.' The whole of Islam, all its rich centuries-long development, is contained *in nuce* in this double affirmation. An absolute, uncompromising monotheism, for which *shirk* – the association of any emanation or offspring with God – is the depth of impiety. The most coherent and rigorous form of Muslim theology – though it was finally rejected by orthodoxy – went so far as to declare it an offence to true monotheism to consider the divine attributes (justice, power, mercy, etc.) as separable from the divine essence.

Muslim monotheism set out to surpass even that of the Jews in rigour, accusing them of the pollution of polytheism on account of their supposed teaching that Esdras was the son of God. All the more understandable is that stiffening of incomprehension and negation when faced with the Christian Trinity, which was to determine the agelong antagonism of the two faiths in three continents. As for the dignity of Muhammad as the apostle of Allah, the apostle of the Arabs, the 'seal of the prophets', this is canonised in the *shahada*, the formula of belief quoted above, and is the indesociable historical complement of the first dogma. No honest exposition of Islam, past or present, can ignore or evade this point.

Under the aegis of the one God, creator and judge, and with the Prophet of the revelation as its model, the life of the Muslim believer unfolds from the cradle to the grave. Through the faith he is made capable of eternal salvation, through the cult he is in docile contact every day with the divine, and the good works inculcated by the Koran yield, like a sure capital investment, the joys of paradise. The sacred Law, the *Shari'a*, which includes both juridical and ritual prescriptions, wraps a man in a close and elastic net of precepts of various degrees of obligation or recommendation, which looked at from the outside may appear oppressive, but has not been so to the many generations of Muslims. Of the ritual obligations we need only mention here the five basic ones, the so-called *arkan al-islam*, which for thirteen centuries have been the fixed points in the life of the believer. The first of these is the profession of faith (*shahada*) already quoted, the recitation of which before two witnesses is enough to make one legally a Muslim. The second – in practice the first and most obvious in daily life – is the canonical prayer (*salat*) repeated five times a day at fixed hours, and consisting of a certain number of formulae and bodily movements (standing, prostration, genuflection) minutely regulated by the Law. One of the five, that of midday, on Friday, is the canonical public prayer which gives such a characteristic aspect to Muslim society even today. The third principle, now out of use almost everywhere, but practised for a long time and especially in the early days of Islam, is the legal alms (*zakat*) owed by every believer to the state out of certain goods and products, and destined for specified objects of charity or social assistance. The fourth basic institution of Islam is the fast of *Ramadan*, from dawn till sunset, still known and practised today in every country which has preserved or revived the tradition of the Islamic faith, as one of its essentials. Fifth and last is the pilgrimage, the Islamic adaptation of the ancient pagan rite, which every believer who is physically and financially able is bound to perform at least once in his lifetime, and which to this day unites every year, at the beginning of the month *Dhu l-hijja*, multitudes of the faithful from all parts of the Islamic world, at the Meccan sanctuary and the sacred places surrounding it ('Arafa, Muzdalifa, Mina), keeping up an uninterrupted continuity of ritual from the very first Muslim generations.

The religious duty of the *jihad*, the holy war against the infidels, is not formally reckoned among these 'pillars of Islam', but in practice it may be considered a supplement to them, supported as it is by imperious passages from the Koran, for example:

... fight in the way of God with those who fight with you ... and slay them wherever you come upon them, and expel them from where they expelled you. (II, 186–7)

We have seen how it became an integral part of the Prophet's own activity as soon as he found himself at Medina at the head of a bold warrior community. We shall see further how after his death the precept found its application, immediately in suppressing the secession of Arabia (*ridda*), and later in the whole manner of the conquests, though these were determined by other factors also. From the heroic age of its beginnings up to the time when Islam launched its last attacks on the Christian West, the *jihad* was the basis, the justification in theory, the religious ideal and inspiration of the Muslim dynamic. Today in its pure state it is no more than a memory, in part replaced by other principles and slogans guiding the actions of the Islamic peoples, such as the struggle against colonialism and the real or imagined imperialism of Europe or America.

Conquests of the early seventh century

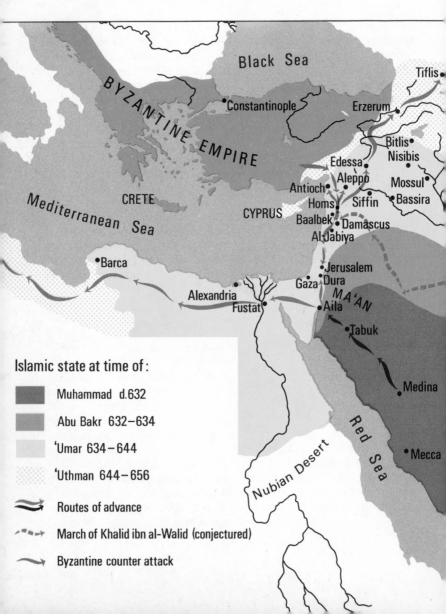

Black Sea

BYZANTINE EMPIRE

• Constantinople

Tiflis

Erzerum

Bitlis •
Nisibis

Edessa
Aleppo
Antioch •
Homs
Siffin
Baalbek • Damascus
Al-Jabiya

Mossul •
Bassira

Mediterranean Sea

CRETE

CYPRUS

Jerusalem
Gaza
Dura
MA'AN

• Barca

Alexandria
Fustat

Aila
• Tabuk

• Medina

Red Sea

Nubian Desert

• Mecca

Islamic state at time of :

Muhammad d.632

Abu Bakr 632–634

'Umar 634–644

'Uthman 644–656

Routes of advance

March of Khalid ibn al-Walid (conjectured)

Byzantine counter attack

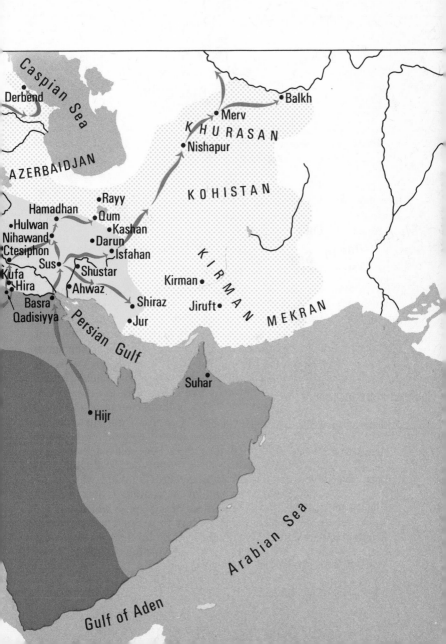

Caspian Sea

Derbend

Balkh

Merv

K H U R A S A N

Nishapur

AZERBAIDJAN

K O H I S T A N

Rayy

Qum

Hamadhan

Kashan

Hulwan

Darun

Nihawand

Isfahan

Ctesiphon

K I R M A N

Sus

Shustar

Kufa

Kirman

Hira

Ahwaz

Basra

Shiraz

Jiruft

M E K R A N

Qadisiyya

Jur

Persian Gulf

Suhar

Hijr

Arabian Sea

Gulf of Aden

Such, in outline, is the heritage of dogma, ritual and law which the first Muslim generations drew from the Koran and from the 'custom' (*sunna*) of their Prophet, and later developed by means of the two basic principles of 'consensus' (*ijma'*) and 'analogy' (*qiyas*). These principles, along with the former two sources, constitute the 'foundations of the law' (*usul al-fiqh*). The Islamic civilisation of the early centuries witnessed the development and deepening of these rudimentary guiding lines of the community. Our only concern here, however, is to record how this community was organised and governed immediately after the loss of its Prophet and legislator, and what internal changes it underwent during the time when externally it was overflowing in the impetus of conquest.

The caliphate succession

Muhammad had died without designating a successor. During the disturbance and uncertainty of the moment, while the Ansar of Medina were trying to put up a candidate of their own, the will of the earliest Companions, especially 'Umar, prevailed: that the government of the young community ought to remain in the hands of the Quraysh, the Prophet's own tribe. And 'Umar's was the decisive action in imposing, almost by surprise, the acknowledgment of the elderly and authoritative Abu Bakr as 'deputy' or 'representative' of Muhammad. This is the meaning of the word *khalifa*, which in the West became 'Caliph', from then on the title of the Muslim head of state; the alternative name *Imam*, which occurs quite often, in this case signifies 'one placed before', a chief or leader, and has taken on a more specifically religious significance. The question of whether the Caliphate was, as an institution, more religious or secular in character, has been in modern times in the West the subject of a dispute which has led to gross errors, and, in reaction against them, to a certain wilful blindness. The idea, already current in the Middle Ages and often repeated in more recent times, that the Muslim Caliphate is the equivalent of the Catholic Papacy, is nonsense; Muslim orthodoxy knows no priesthood, and since the death of the Prophet allows no dogmatic authority or sacramental character to his successors. The Caliph was the guardian and protector of the faith, not its interpreter or promulgator; even if in the course of the centuries individual Caliphs have shown themselves to favour, and even to support by force, certain theological positions as against others. But the juridical and dogmatic evolution of Islam in fact took place entirely among the doctors, and any proposal to entrust to the Caliph even so much as the codification of varying juridical norms, remained an isolated impulse. As guardian and administrator of the sacred Law, on the other hand, the ruler of Islam had very wide, indeed all but absolute powers, over all that area where the Law did not itself establish unequivocal norms; the government of the peoples and territories over which Islam came to hold sway, the administration of the state within the boundaries of the rough principles laid down by the Koran and the 'custom' of the Prophet, the nomination of governors and judges, the declaration of war or the conclusion of peace (in theory merely truce) with the infidel world. The powers, in fact, of what we, following the occidental distinction between sacred and profane, would call a secular sovereign – and it is from this point of view that some have assimilated the Caliph to the figure of the Emperor in medieval Christendom rather than that of the Pope. But the much deeper interpenetration of sacred and profane in the Orient, the fact that the Islamic state was at the same time a religious community (or more precisely a religious community which had become a state), the Caliph's position as direct successor to the venerated Head and Founder of the state, the community and above all the faith of Islam – all this surrounded him with the aura of a dignity which was far beyond that of a mere political leader, and which was only further emphasised by the fierce internal struggles which we are now to describe. While the legitimism of the followers of 'Ali and the Hashimites in general certainly insisted on the right of Muhammad's descendants by blood to his inheritance (and their conception of the Caliphate or Imamate attributed to it frankly religious and even sacred powers), even among the most orthodox the supreme magistrature of Islam acquired and retained the prestige of a much more than merely secular institution. Under the Abbasids especially (from 750 on) the 'blessed dynasty' was thought of as invested with a religious character which modified, in practice if not in theory, the original non-sacred character of the institution, and gave it the unmistakable aspect of a 'spiritual power'. And it was precisely this spiritual power and prestige which remained as its sole surviving prerogative when, from the second half of the ninth century on, its material power was progressively lost, usurped by pretorians and foreign 'protectors'. In this sense, and in this sense only, the idea of the Caliphate as a spiritual authority is not, at least as regards this later period, so erroneous or divorced from historical fact as it might seem from the point of view of a purely institutional analysis.

During the earlier period with which we are concerned, however, the fullness of executive power coincided, in the persons of the first Caliphs, with the aura of religious prestige inherent in their position as the immediate successors of the Prophet. Throughout the period of the conquests it was they who ruled the Muslim community, at first from Mecca, later from Damascus. The foundation and growth of the Arab-Muslim state in its earliest period is the work of the individual Caliphs and of the ruling elite which they headed, on the still white-hot metal of the Prophet's heritage, of the expanding Arab community, and of the new peoples and cultures with which it was coming into contact. The first 'representative' of the Prophet was Abu Bakr, a pious and upright follower of Islam from its very beginning, the father of Muhammad's favourite wife 'A'isha, who ruled the young community of the believers for barely two years. The chief problems with which he had to deal were the suppression of the revolt of Arabia (the *ridda*), and the tumultuous beginnings of the conquests, which arose almost uninterruptedly out of the former. His faithful and authoritative counsellor was the same man who had forced through his election as Caliph, and whom he in his turn, when dying, nominated as his successor. This second Caliph, 'Umar ibn al-Khattab, as we shall see, during the decade of his Caliphate (634–44) directed from Medina the full flood of conquest, and at the same time laid the foundations of what was to become the classical Islamic state of the first centuries. His work, even when we discount certain later developments which posterity has attributed to him, remains decisive for the future of the state and community of Muhammad. In particular, the institution of the *diwan* is held to be derived from him; the list, that is, of Muslims fighting on the ever-widening frontiers (and also of kinsmen of the Prophet, and the old Companions) who received a fixed allowance from the public treasury, though they were forbidden to acquire or possess personally any land in the conquered territories. The type of rule imposed on the latter, which varied according to whether they were acquired by force (*'anwatan*) or by capitulation (*sulhan*), is also traditionally attributed to 'Umar's decisions, which are held to have provided the starting point for all the subsequent developments in agrarian and fiscal problems in the Islamic state. Lands conquered by force became the property of the state, which, however, left their former owners the use of them, on condition of their paying tribute, as tenants of the victors, as it were. In those which the Muslims had gained through capitulation, the actual ownership of the inhabitants was confirmed in return for tribute. In addition, 'Umar established a domain actually owned by the state, on the lands of the Byzantine and Sasanid monarchs and other abandoned estates, which he thus removed from the cupidity of individuals. In all his actions, in fact, or those attributed to him, there is a visible effort to maintain the agricultural prosperity of the conquered area by keeping it as a going concern and making as few innovations as possible; and a distrust of the abilities of the conquerers as settlers. The great Caliph showed clearly his firm determination to subordinate individual, egocentric interests to those of the collective, which he directed with patriarchal simplicity and indefatigable energy.

'Umar died before his time, assassinated out of a private grudge (some have suspected also a conspiracy of wider interests), and before dying he nominated a group of six authoritative Companions, who were to choose a successor from among themselves. The man chosen was 'Uthman, of the Umayyad family, a gentle and pious man, but a member of that Meccan aristocracy which with his kinsman Abu Sufyan had so long resisted Muhammad. And it was upon them that he relied during his Caliphate (644–56), giving posts of authority and wealth to his kinsmen, and offending and outraging the party of the old Companions, and of the pious, who saw in the rising fortunes of the Umayyads something like a resurgence of defeated paganism. 'Umar's ban on possessing land outside Arabia was evaded by means of private concessions, particularly in Iraq; and so began the growth of a class of big landowners and capitalists, and the consequent class-hatred. The payments from the central fund did not always reach those entitled to them, through increasing financial difficulties; for the spectacular pace of the conquests, and the flow of wealth they brought into the state coffers, had begun to slacken. All this complex of social and economic factors, as well as religious ones, resulted in profound discontent with the Caliph, and this was exploited as well by men with motives of personal enmity or ambition, especially the Prophet's son-in-law 'Ali, already three times disappointed in his aspirations to the Caliphate. In the Spring of 656 there were signs of rebellion, and from many different places groups of malcontents converged on Medina. A series of misunderstandings, or acts of provocation, embittered the already tense situation, and finally the Caliph was besieged in his own house. Before relief forces called in from Syria could intervene, the malefactors broke into 'Uthman's simple home, and killed the old man while at his prayers (June, 656); this was the ill-omened *yawm ad-dar*, the day of the attack on the house, which began the period of discord and civil war in Islam. 'Uthman had been murdered in the absence, and possibly with the tacit consent, of 'Ali, who immediately took the opportunity to have himself proclaimed Caliph, and this at once raised the moral problem of his position, and of the legitimacy or otherwise of the assassination. The Umayyad governor of Syria, Mu'awiya, rose in rebellion to claim vengeance for his kinsman, and, when 'Ali neither could nor wished to punish those directly responsible, contested the legitimacy of 'Ali's own power. The latter had already had to fight the opposition of his former allies, Talha and az-Zubair, who had the support of Muhammad's widow 'A'isha; and had defeated them in the 'battle of the camel'. Next, he marched against Mu'awiya and met him, with his army, on the upper Euphrates near Siffin in July 657. This battle, which ended indecisively, marked the first rupture, not only political but religious, in the Muslim community. 'Ali had almost gained the victory when he was checked by a ruse of Mu'awiya who was advised, it seems, by the subtle 'Amr ibn al-'As; he had his troops raise leaves from the Koran on their lances, thus appealing to the sacred Book to settle the conflict. Compelled by his followers to accept, against his own will, this suspension of hostilities, 'Ali later found himself being admonished by the same Muslim zealots to recognise the error, or rather sin, which he and they had committed in referring to human arbitration – for this was the understanding he had arrived at in the negotiations held with Mu'awiya after the armistice – a question whose decision belonged to God alone – meaning that the Koran already laid down the obligation to fight the rebel, and this was what Mu'awiya was. 'Ali refused this demand, from a mixture of motives: fidelity to his given word, pride, reluctance to associate himself with the *volte face* of these fanatics, besides political considerations partly lost to us. He thus broke with this section of his former supporters, who from that moment became his bitterest enemies. These men, from then on known as Kharijites (seceders, or rather 'insurgents', 'rebels') under the watchword 'to God alone belongs judgment' abandoned 'Ali's camp, formed a party of their own, and started one of the most violent and bloody dissident movements of ancient Islam. From then on, 'Ali had to fight on two fronts, against these (whom he soon afterwards endowed with the halo of martyrdom

Musicians and hunter, a floor fresco from
the Umayyad palace of Qasr el-Hayr al-Gharbi,
south-west of Palmyra in Syria. The palace was built
by the Caliph Hisham during his reign 724–44.
Fresco in the National Museum, Damascus.

97

when he slaughtered many of them at Nahrawan near Kufa, in July 658), and against Mu'awiya, who was conducting his political and military campaign with great ability, assisted by capable advisers.

The chronology and the nature of the events which followed the battle of Siffin are among the most disputed points in the history of Muslim origins. The sources speak of two meetings during the years 657–8, at Dumat al-Jandal and at Adhruh, at which plenipotentiaries from both sides (according to the agreement of Siffin) are said to have discussed a whole series of knotty problems: the lawfulness or otherwise of the killing of 'Uthman, and of Mu'awiya's demand for vengeance, the legitimacy of 'Ali's claim and his suitability for the Caliphate, and finally the candidature for the Caliphate of Mu'awiya himself. The times and manner of conducting these discussions, of which the existing accounts are contradictory and bristling with improbabilities, remain obscure. The one certain thing is their conclusion. 'Ali was finally disqualified by his own representative, who, it seems, was tricked by the greater cunning of his adversary 'Amr ibn al-'As, who himself declared Mu'awiya worthy of the Caliphate. 'Ali naturally refused to submit to this dubious verdict, and from Kufa, where he had been in residence for some time (having left Medina, whose position was by now not central enough), he attempted to carry on the struggle in arms. But Fortune had turned her back on him for good; one by one the provinces of the newly-won empire slipped from his authority, won by force or cunning to the cause of his rival. His *coup de grace* came, after a few years of painful inaction, from the Kharijite terrorists, who had started on the career of bloody activism which was to trouble the Muslim world for a century. The last of the 'orthodox' Caliphs fell, stabbed to death by a Kharijite assassin, in the mosque of Kufa in January 661; Mu'awiya meanwhile escaped a similar attempt on himself, and remained undisputed master of the field. The elective Caliphate of the first decades was now to be replaced by a leadership hereditary on the Umayyad dynasty, whose founder was Mu'awiya.

The Muslim community emerged from this first crisis severely tested. Instead of the single block which it had formed under the first three Caliphs, it was already splitting into three factions, who were to fight one another throughout the Umayyad period and after; an orthodox majority, who accepted the new Caliph and later the new dynastic state with burning loyalty or at least with pious repugnance for schism; a minority, the Shi'a, who remained faithful to the memory and claim of 'Ali (and to the 'house' or family of Muhammad as represented by his descendants), and who dedicated to this legitimism a fanatical devotion and a capacity for intrigue and trouble-making which might have been more useful to 'Ali while he was alive; and finally the numerically insignificant but politically extremely active Kharijite dissidents, opposed to any form of legitimism and to any dynastic or racial privilege. They proclaimed the equal right to the Caliphate of any Muslim possessing the right qualifications, 'even an Abyssinian slave'; and were as ready to shed the blood of fellow Muslims as that of infidels, and to throw away their own lives in rebellion and guerilla fighting. This grave crisis, and the division of hearts which it entailed, in the centre of the Muslim state, had its repercussions in the most distant provinces; it slowed down and complicated the momentum of conquest, but never entirely halted it, and when under Mu'awiya the helm of the state once again had a firm hand upon it, the Arab expansion began again in several directions, and the Arab Empire enjoyed a new period of splendour.

The Umayyad century

It fell to Mu'awiya, the skilful politician and one of the most gifted statesmen the Arabs ever produced, to transform the Caliphate from an elective institution, as it had been hitherto, to a hereditary one, thereby founding the Umayyad dynasty. In its ninety years of existence, this dynasty saw the boundaries of the Arab-Muslim state reach their widest extent, while within it the Arabs themselves consolidated their position of leadership over the conquered peoples. But the underlying contradiction, between this *de facto* hegemony and the increasingly explicit universalism of the religion which constituted its theoretical basis, tormented the whole Umayyad century, and in the end led to the fall of the dynasty and the Arab hegemony together. Arab historiography as it has come down to us, having developed during the period of the rival Abbasid dynasty, is generally hostile to the Umayyads, representing them – with the single exception of 'Umar II – as impious and wordly kings (*muluk*) rather than true Imams of the Muslim community, as the Abbasids later claimed to be. In spite of this, however, Muslim orthodoxy has never seriously disputed the legitimacy of their rule, and various explanations have been devised to reconcile this recognition with their hostile evaluation. From the point of view of Western historiography, the Umayyad period is that in which Arabism was at its strongest, certainly, but the very complaints of certain historians that these sovereigns did not aim at the foundation of a national Arab state on a purely ethnic basis instead of a religious one, is the best proof that these Arab Caliphs felt themselves to be Muslims as much as Arabs, and could not dissociate the *de facto* supremacy of their race from the religious heritage of the Prophet, of which they considered themselves the representatives and guardians.

The twenty years (661–80) of Mu'awiya's reign passed peacefully as far as internal affairs went, thanks to the prudence and energy of the Caliph. But when his son Yazid died, after a reign of barely three years, the centrifugal forces which had until then been held in check exploded violently once more, threatening to bring the recently founded dynasty tumbling in ruins. Already, on Yazid's accession in 680, an incident had occurred which was destined to have enormous repercussions in the history of Islam; the death of 'Ali's son al-Husain at Kerbela. This latter, unlike his brother al-Hasan who had let Mu'awiya buy from his his renunciation of all claims to the Caliphate, raised a revolt against his ill-famed successor and fell in battle as a rebel. The shedding of the blood of the Prophet's grandson inaugurated the Shi'ite martyrology, and reacted on the 'impious' Umayyad line like a curse. From then on, throughout the whole reign of the dynasty, in Arabia, in Syria, and above all in Iraq, Shi'ite and Kharijite revolts alternated, opposed in the principles they supported but at one in their hatred of the 'usurpers', and were suppressed with greater or lesser degrees of difficulty by the Caliphs' governors. This unrest broke into outright civil war, the second that Islam had known, after Yazid's death in 683, and that of his young son, Mu'awiya II, which followed soon after. Already, immediately after Kerbela, the son of one of the Prophet's early Companions, 'Abdallah ibn az-Zubair, had proclaimed himself as a rival Caliph in the Hijaz, and an Umayyad army sent against him had occupied Medina by force, but had then retired on the death of Yazid. In Syria, which under the great Mu'awiya had become the centre of the Caliphate, a part of the Arab tribes declared for Ibn az-Zubair, but the winning in June 684 of the battle of Marj Rahit, near Damascus, by supporters of the Umayyads, kept the throne for the latter, in the person of Marwan ibn al-Hakam, of a junior branch of the dynasty. It fell to the son and successor of Marwan, 'Abd al-Malik (685–705), to reconstruct, not without labour, the unity of the state (victory over the Zubayrites in Iraq, 691; siege and capture of Mecca, and death of the anti-Caliph, 692), and to inaugurate the dynasty's most brilliant period, with the assistance of the faithful governor of Iraq, Hajjaj, on whom depended all the Eastern half of the Empire. The twenty years of 'Abd al-Malik's reign, and the decade of that of his son, Walid I (705–15), marked the apogee of the Umayyad power. Under them the conquests reached their widest extent, the central authority was recognised and respected everywhere, and the Caliph of Damascus controlled a territory that no other Caliph would equal. From this culminating point the Umayyad Caliphate gradually declined, torn from then on by disputes and opposed dynastic policies (the succession of Walid's brother Sulaiman, 715–7, led to a sudden general replacement of the ruling ranks of the Empire, whose repercussions in the provinces we shall examine); by social and fiscal problems, which the piety and goodwill of 'Umar II (717–20) were powerless to solve; and above all by the incurable particularism of the Arab tribes, who were still the social and military backbone of the Empire. The Umayyads enjoyed their last great and prolonged period of power with Hisham, the fourth of 'Abd al-Malik's sons to mount the throne (724–43). Cautious in preserving, if not increasing, his father's political heritage, under him Iraq knew the third of its great Umayyad governors, Khalid al-Qasri (the first two were Ziyad ibn-Abihi under Mu'awiya and Hajjaj under 'Abd al-Malik); the Shi'ite and Kharijite revolts were put down everywhere; the state treasuries were filled by means of a policy of severe taxation and exploitation of the subject peoples. But in this last power and prosperity of the Umayyads were hidden already the germs of their destruction, and in the Eastern provinces of the Empire the subversive propaganda of the Abbasids was already at work, shortly to overthrow the dynasty.

The crisis began with the death of Hisham, with the revolt against and the killing by the Umayyads themselves of his grandson and successor, Walid II (744). Months of anarchy followed, a couple of ephemeral Caliphs succeeded one another on the throne; then one ascended it who was worthy of a happier destiny, fated to be the last of his line – the valiant Marwan II (744–50). He fought strenuously against the resurgent Shi'a and Kharijites, and re-established the Umayyad power in Syria and Mesopotamia, but succumbed in his turn to the Abbasid revolution, which had broken out three years previously in Khorasan and spread victoriously from the East towards the centre of the Caliphate. The battle of the Zab (January 750) marked the end of the Umayyad Caliphate and of everything it had stood for; of the supremacy of Arabs over non-Arabs in the Islamic community, and of Syria over the rest of the Empire; and of the 'Mediterranean', and up to a point Hellenicising phase in Muslim art and culture. Under the Abbasids, the Islamic Empire became de-arabicised and internationalised, looking to the ancient East, and especially to Iran, for its political, social and cultural models. We shall return later to this change.

This very brief sketch of the history of the Muslim community has attempted to give no more than the essential plot of the internal vicissitudes through which the Arab state passed in the hundred and twenty years after the death of its Prophet and founder. In terms of world history, however, the most striking effect of Muhammad's life's work is its expansion in those conquests which form the subject of the next chapters.

6 The making of the Empire

Accident or design?

The Arab conquests of the seventh to eighth centuries AD, present one of the most interesting and perplexing problems of history. Their speed and permanence, the immense size of the lands they covered, and most of all, the contrast between the methods used and the results produced have always been a source of wonder to historians, and it has taxed all their powers to find adequate explanation of them. The conquests have been described so frequently that they might seem a straightforward commonplace event, and yet some inexplicable and mysterious quality still underlies them. We see a horde of nomads with no military experience beyond that of desert skirmishes and bandit raids, who, at a given moment, embark on a phase of rapid expansion, confront and defeat the regular armies of great empires, advance irresistibly for thousands of miles from their native land and establish lasting control over the territories they have conquered. The medieval theological explanations presented from the Christian angle on the one hand and the Muslim on the other (seeing them as some direct work of Satanic malice or divine will) attempted to make a systematic evaluation of the chief causes of this phenomenon. They tried to wrest a meaning from the military, political, religious, economic and social facts known to them, and to discover the secret of this rapid and far-reaching revolution. We shall now attempt a similar evaluation, revising the most important interpretations, emphasising those factors which seem to provide the most convincing explanation, and reducing as far as possible but never wholly eliminating the mystery which surrounds this event – an element of mystery which seems to overshadow almost any great historical event, stigmatising it in such a way that even the most historically sophisticated are forced to contemplate the prospect of a transcendent Providence.

One interpretation which won wide acceptance for a considerable time but has now been superseded by others, places a heavy emphasis on *religion* as the principal factor underlying and motivating the Arab conquests following the death of Muhammad. Such a view immediately poses the problem of whether the Prophet himself either desired or foresaw the fantastic expansion of his faith beyond the borders of his fatherland. In other words: did Muhammad give his teaching the universal significance it in fact assumed after his death, or did he really mean it to be valid only for his own people? Islamic orthodoxy, and with it a section of Western historical opinion, does not doubt that Muhammad's religious vision was of universalist character from an early stage, and both invest it, even in its early period, with what was certainly a subsequent development of the Muslim faith. They base their arguments on those expressions in the Koran which point to the Prophet as one sent by God:

as an act of mercy for the whole world (*rahmatan li – l – 'alamin*) to all men.
(XXI, 107)

Other modern historians such as Caetani hold the contrary view that the Prophet never broadened his horizons beyond those of his own people and his own land, and that such expressions should be taken as general exaggerations, without specifically universalist meaning, and that the Founder of Islam neither intended nor commanded the fantastic expansion of his faith outside Arabia. It is most likely that the truth lies between the two extremes: that Muhammad started out with a mission for his own people, first for his fellow-citizens of Mecca, then gradually for all Arabs, and only towards the end of his life did he come round to the view that his faith might stretch to yet wider horizons. This final stage of the evolution of his views is not explicitly stated in the Koran. It is rather in the history of the final years of the Prophet's life and actions that his slowly growing ambitions can best be seen. The delegations and messages to oriental sovereigns, and the military expeditions to northern Arabia (to Mu'ta and Tabuk) illustrate his desire for the further expansion of both the faith and state of Islam (a single unit for him, as for his successors). At this point in history the Koran's laws on holy war, intended at first to apply only to the inhabitants of the Arabian Peninsula, may already have assumed a wider geographical significance in the Prophet's mind; the duty to fight pagans, Christians and Jews (the first to be slain without mercy, the others to be allowed the alternative of submission and tribute) might then have been extended beyond the Hijaz and beyond the Peninsula. However, neither in the Revelation, nor in any section of the *hadith* or canonical sayings which have any degree of authenticity, did Muhammad ever give his followers an explicit order 'Go and conquer the world to Islam'. For example, the much-quoted words 'Constantinople will be conquered. Blessed are those who will conquer it' were almost certainly put into the Prophet's mouth by young Islam when it was on the crest of its ambition, when it had already embarked on the Mediterranean conquests, and was reaching out towards that splendid goal which the Arabs were never to achieve. The achievement of this goal was reserved for another Muslim people centuries later. To sum up, it can be said that the main works of the Founder of Islam do not express a universality for the new faith; even less do they contain a definite programme for expansion. There are, however, signposts towards a probable evolution in that direction at least in the last part of his career; a number of his later actions, to us apparently isolated, indicate a tendency that the conquering movement, once begun, was quick to follow. The documents at our disposal allow us to say no more on the subject.

Thus, since the Prophet left the scene without giving his community any instructions for the future, we have ruled out any explicit order or programme on his part. This still leaves the possibility that the external conquests could have been an interpretation or continuation of some of his precepts, and that the Arabs, more or less recent converts to Islam, swarmed out of Arabia to spread the new faith. Such is the traditional theory of the conquests: fired by religious fervour, the bedouin neophytes of Islam rushed from their desert birthplace to convert other nations with the sword. Let us say straightaway that modern historiography has so completely dismissed this idea that it could even be tempting to try a partial revaluation of it. Yet the concept of the dissemination of Islam by

the sword must really be abandoned (that is, for the earliest era of
the Arab diaspora), since a critical study of sources has shown that
the victorious Arabs never presented the people they had conquered with the choice between death and the acceptance of their
faith. When the Muslims had dealings with the 'people of the Book'
(Christians and Jews) they did not offer them this choice, but
simply made them subject peoples and exacted tribute money from
them, following the instructions of the Revelation. In the practice
of war, the Zoroastrians of Persia, and later the Indian Brahmans
and Buddhists of the Punjab – among whom the Arabs appeared
victorious – were soon assimilated into the category of the Jews and
Christians of Syria, Palestine, Egypt and Africa. The alternative
between Islam and death was only given to pagan idolaters, with
whom the Arabs had dealings very rarely in that early period of
their activities outside Arabia. Thus, the straight indoctrination
of their defeated enemies never seems to have been the major concern of the Arab conquerors. They sought rather to establish
political hegemony, and to organise the payment of corresponding
tribute money. The members of defeated nations who joined the
faith of their conquerors in ever-increasing numbers were probably
prompted by the sense of moral and material inferiority of a subject
tribute-paying people. The conquerors, however, received their
flocks of converts with mixed feelings. They were well aware, on the
one hand, that this rapid conversion to Islam would threaten their
supremacy as conquerors and their unscrupulous financial exploitation: but on the other hand they were unable to oppose the
propagation of the faith which they held to be the true one. In
addition, the work of fervent Muslims such as the early Caliphs –
committed to the triumph of the faith beyond all material considerations – must undoubtedly have further encouraged the process.
It seems that we should not completely dismiss the old theory of the
religious motive behind the early conquests but make the following
modification to it: while realising that the majority of Arab combatants had other more material and selfish motives, we should not
forget that at least an *élite* among the first generation of Muslims was

inspired by sincere religious ardour. This *élite* would have included many of the Companions of the Prophet, who fought and lost their lives in the wars, and, above all, the Caliphs of Medina. Despite their early hesitation, verging at times on open hostility to the movement, the Caliphs grew gradually firmer of purpose, and preached, strengthened and became a principal driving force behind the conquests. Above all, those who deny all religious interest and motivation in the entire movement should not forget the presence of the great and austere 'Umar at the head of the Muslim state when the first miraculous expansion of the Arabs outside Arabia took place. 'Umar certainly called the Arabs 'the raw material of Islam' and played a decisive part in establishing the principle of Arab hegemony and the relationship between the Arabs and their subject peoples. However, the seed of universalism in Islam, though hardly touched on by the Prophet himself, must have been so firmly rooted in the mind of his second successor that he could not remain indifferent to the propagation of the faith in the wake of the conquerors.

Material motives for expansion

The majority of the Arab empire-builders certainly did not see themselves as propagandists or missionaries, but as conquerors, and practical exploiters of their conquests. Religious motives may have had some importance, but were not the mainspring of their armed migration. We should now examine other motives, which modern historians consider more convincing. These can be summarised as the need for food, pastureland and booty – the age-old needs which had long been goading the nomads to leave their life of hardship, to look for a better dwelling place than their desert, and to try to conquer and settle more fertile lands, which would give a better yield for them and their flocks. This economic incentive is closely connected with the problem of climate: in their reconstructions of ancient Semitic history, Winckler and Caetani emphasise the central importance of the fact that Arabia was gradually drying up. This theory no longer seems acceptable in the terms in which they phrased it, since no radical change has apparently taken place in the climate or geological aspect of the Peninsula in historic times. However the variability of climatic conditions – such as the alternation of long droughts with periods of relatively greater humidity, and correspondingly variable conditions in pastureland and food supply – may certainly have led to hardship. It may have been one factor encouraging the Arab migration away from the desert towards the Fertile Crescent – a migration of which the wave of conquests would be the final episode. It seems to be generally accepted that, after a mainly propitious period in the first centuries after Christ, climatic conditions began to change for the worse at the end of the sixth and in the first half of the seventh centuries. This was precisely the time of Muhammad and the birth of Islam. However, if we attributed the great Arab diaspora of this period solely to the worsening of climatic conditions we would be over-simplifying the situation as much as those who consider it the effect of religious proselytism. Certainly, we may note the climatic factor as one reason for the economic and spiritual hardship overwhelming the Arabs at the beginning of the seventh century, but let us not regard it as the one single direct explanation of their expansion.

It is important to remember that these events took place at the end of a whole process of slow migration which had lasted for centuries, even for millennia: a process by which the nomads had gradually been moving from the unfriendly interior of the Peninsula to more favourable dwelling places. Whether or not the Peninsula was the original home of the Semitic race, great waves of Semites certainly came from there, as if from some human breeding-ground or population reserve, and spread out into near Asia, moulding and modifying its history as they went. This movement had hitherto been curbed by the presence of powerful empires on the borders of the Fertile Crescent, such as Rome, Byzantium and Persia; but, precisely at the time of Muhammad, they were all going through a period of either temporary or chronic decadence. Rome had disappeared; the second Rome of

the Bosphorus, seriously harassed by political, economic and religious crises, could barely maintain control over her Eastern subjects
in Syria and Egypt, hated as she was for her unacceptable dogmas,
and for her grasping system of taxation. Sasanid Persia was in
complete anarchy, weakened by dynastic conflicts and an iniquitous
and unstable feudal system. The Ghassanid and Lakhmid buffer
states, colonies of the Byzantine and Persian empires respectively,
had by now disappeared. For centuries the two states had held the
nomads in check, and prevented them from making a mass movement against the civilised Eastern empires. The weakening or
diminishing of these barriers is another factor to take into account
in seeking an explanation of the Arab onslaughts against the
ancient empires. We will consider purely military factors at a later
stage. Here, we want to make a synthesis of all the incentives which
seem to have combined together to produce the last migration – the
exodus which left the Peninsula, exhausted of ethnic vitality, to
degenerate into little more than a great expanse of barren sand,
distinguished now only by the holy memory of having been the
cradle of Islam.

A significant event, little emphasised in historical writings, preceded
the outbreak of the external Arab conquests; it had some influence
on the diaspora, and in a sense prepared the way for it. Immediately
after the death of Muhammad, the new Muslim state had to resist
a dangerous rebellion, or rather defection, of various bedouin
tribes who refused obedience to Medina. In Muslim tradition, this
defection is described as religious apostasy (*ridda*), but it probably
had some political meaning and content. The tribes were barely
converts to Islam even in name, since what they really felt was a
personal attachment to the Prophet. Once he had died, they meant
to reestablish their freedom of action, and, above all, to stop
paying the religious tax (*zakat*) to the Islamic treasury. Religious
factors were certainly involved, as local 'prophets' set themselves
up to compete against and imitate the Prophet of Medina. Medina
responded vigorously, under the direction of the first Caliph Abu

Bakr. Khalid ibn al-Walid, who had won the battle of Uhud when he was a pagan and of Hunain after he became a Muslim, had command of the anti-revolutionary measures. His pitiless campaigns lasted from the end of 632 AD, to the first half of 633 AD. The rebel tribes, Asad, Tamim, Ghatafan, and above all Hanifa, were crushed in a series of bloody clashes, which came to a head at the battle of 'Aqraba in Yamama (eastern Arabia) where Musailima, the main 'false prophet' met his death. Thus, about a year after Muhammad's death, his new community had won its first struggle for survival, quashing secession with armed reprisal. Even so, Arabia was seething with arms and armed men: the victors, no less than the vanquished, needed an outlet for their surplus energies, and felt a strong drive for action which would provide a diversion from fratricidal war (for this had been a real war, of far greater magnitude than the endemic guerrilla warfare of the period). Certainly one of the major incentives for external conquest may have lain in this explosive internal situation, with its unchained passions, and in the desperate need for plunder and 'living space'. The wise Abu Bakr understood the situation. To alleviate internal tension, to employ the unruly elements in the state, and also perhaps to follow up some plan of the Prophet's for expansion (for us, one that was implied, rather than clearly stated) he gave his consent to the first campaigns in Iraq and Syria.

In addition, the rallying call of the Arab tribes on the frontier of the Byzantine and Persian empires helped to spark off the first campaigns – whose very protagonists would have been hard put to specify the aims and final extent of their field of operations. The Ghassanids and Lakhmids, who had helped to insulate the great states from the desert nomads in the previous century, had now grown weaker. The nomads therefore felt a stronger desire than ever to raid and plunder the foreign settlements, and to this end, they summoned help from their fellow Arabs in the interior. From their foothold at the north eastern border on the Euphrates, the Bakr ibn Wa'il asked the other Arab tribes to join an attack on al-Hira, the former Lakhmid capital, and from there to make a foray on Iraq. The Judham and Quda'a, south of the Dead Sea, were urged to start operations against Palestine and Syria. The former tribes were mainly pagan, the latter Christian. It is obvious, therefore, that most of them had no intention of involving Medina in the campaigns in order to glorify the Muslim faith. The chief factors they had in common were rather desire for plunder, hatred of foreign states (Syrian Arabs in particular were still resentful that Byzantium had withheld payment for their past services as mercenaries) and a vague sense of pan-Arabian solidarity which was to grow in strength and importance with future successes. In the early stages, there must have been some Arab elements among the Byzantine troops facing the invaders, and others in smaller numbers on the Iraqi front, but they soon deserted, prompted by their common racial stock, as at the Yarmuk. Apart from Arab solidarity, another factor helping the invaders must have been the neutrality or even goodwill of the local Semitic (Aramaic) populations, both in Iraq and Syria. They helped to bring about the downfall of their respective Byzantine and Persian masters by their indifference towards or actual enthusiasm for the Arab invasion. At the risk of making one of those dangerous, but in this case reasonable generalisations, we can see the resurgence of the Semitic people in the shining success of the conquests: the Arabs formed the spearhead of attack, with the more or less active encouragement of the Arameans, who joined cause with them to cast off the long oppression that the Greeks and Persians had imposed on them in Near Asia.

Thus the first conquests did not mean a religious triumph for Islam, in its deepest universalist sense, but rather the affirmation of Arab political sovereignty in Near Asia and the Mediterranean basin. The former mercenaries and tribute-paying subjects of the ancient empires at first fought simply to satisfy their land-hunger and to win those material goods which were in ever shorter supply in their exhausted Peninsula; they then became increasingly influenced by a growing sense of racial pride, as the founders of an empire in their turn. The greatest modern historian of the Arab empire has rightly called 'das Arabische Reich' the state which gradually built itself on the conquests of its earliest phase. For at least a century, it was the Arabs who laid down the law to the Turks and Persians, the Arameans and Greeks, the Copts and Berbers, the Visigoths and Iberians, enjoying a brief hour of glory and world power which, in a political sense, Arabism would never know again. It is one of the paradoxes of history which defeat rational analysis that this process began with disorganised forays for plunder from the heart of Arabia, immediately after a bloody civil war.

It is possible, indeed necessary, to qualify this economic nationalistic interpretation of the conquests – as Becker, one of the most perceptive students of the Arab expansion, implies by asking whether 'the whole movement would also be conceivable without Islam.' He seems inclined to answer 'yes' to this question, but we, on the contrary, feel that it calls for a clear 'no'. Even if Muhammad's religion was not the essential and decisive main force behind the diaspora, it was the cement which bound its disorderly centrifugal energies together. To a certain extent it checked the conquerors' chronic anarchy and tribal particularism, far more effectively than their national pride or consciousness could have done. 'Umar, Mu'awiya, 'Abd al-Malik and Hisham (to name some of the greatest sovereigns of the 'Arabisches Reich') succeeded in making themselves obeyed and feared from one end of the vast empire to the other not because they were Arabs, but by virtue of the religious dignity attached to the Commanders of the Faithful, the Prophet's successors and deputies. Without the cement of religion (important at least as a social factor, even if of little significance to the individual) and without a state which had religion as its basis, the Arab impetus would soon have played itself out, or have become fragmented into a number of independent principalities. Such individual local kingdoms (*muluk at-tawa'if*) were non-existent in the first centuries, though they became notorious in later Arab-Islamic history. The Arabs' unity in the early stages allowed a gigantic unitary empire to arise in which the Arab race was the ruling class, its dominant role justified by its incontestable religious supremacy and privilege. Let us therefore say in conclusion that if religious incentives played no part, or only a minor part in instigating the conquests, we should recognize their real and effective function in the preservation and direction of the conquered territories. Islam preserved the empire until such time as the universalism implicit in the faith came to maturity, and other foreign hegemonies emerged from within the heart of the Muslim state, undoing the original Arab empire. Arabism and Islam, distinctive and even opposite if taken separately, complemented and supported each other at the time of the conquests: perhaps the secret of their miraculous success is to be found precisely in this collaboration.

Military morale and strategy

Perhaps one of the most difficult and vexing aspects of the whole problem of the Arab expansion is the purely military one. Once the material and ideological incentives (aptly summarised in the binomial *al-ghanima wa' l-jihad*, plunder and holy war, which sources frequently link together) which sparked off the conquest have been analysed, the secret of all the sweeping victories on the battlefield still calls for further explanation. As we shall see, the history of the Arab conquests is not only one of victories; they also met with more or less serious reverses, but none that had any long-lasting effect, or caused a more than temporary delay in the Arab advance. Even if many of the recorded clashes were minor combats or little more than skirmishes, Ajnadain and the Yarmuk, Qadisiyya, Nihawend, Sbeitla, Wadi Bakka and many others were real pitched battles in which the Arabs and their opponents fought fiercely and long. What was the factor ensuring that victory always went to the Arabs? The question is frequently asked, since the Arabs were superior neither in numbers, arms, nor (it seems) in military skill. The traditional figures of combatants should be somewhat reduced, even for the major encounters, which would leave something in the order of a few tens of thousands, with the Arabs always in inferior numbers. For example, there would have been about twenty five thousand Arabs at the Yarmuk against forty thousand Byzantines; and scarcely six or seven thousand at Qadisiyya against twenty or thirty thousand Persians. Even if the desert nomads could to some extent have improved the efficiency of their extremely rudimentary arms – a sword and shield, a lance and bow, with light coats of mail – they would always have been far inferior to those of the experienced Byzantines, and even more so to those of the Persian army with its long and distinguished military tradition. Furthermore, the Arabs seem to have learned methods of siege and fortification at astonishing speed, since a few years earlier they knew only the crude 'little fortresses' of the desert (*atam*), and had shown themselves unable to overcome the obstacle of a simple ditch in the futile siege of Medina. Finally, as regards tactics, there is no doubt that the Arab campaigns produced some outstanding strategists. Foremost was Khalid ibn al-Walid, 'the sword of Allah', victorious on every front. He was a real military genius, who was nonetheless aware that he must submit to the Caliph's authority at the time of his disgrace, and become once again a private soldier. Other great military leaders included Yazid ibn Abi Sufyan, Abu 'Ubaida, 'Amr ibn al-'As and 'Uqba ibn Nafi': and later at the two opposite ends of the diaspora, Qutaiba ibn Muslim in the east, and Tariq in the west, led the Arabs to victory in the farthest outposts of the empire. In these men, the war produced a whole staff of military leaders of exceptional brilliance and unusual flexibility. We know little about the leaders of the opposing armies, branded as they are with the mark of the defeated; but one can hardly suppose that they were either fools or cowards, and so the problem of explaining Arab military superiority remains unsolved. Recently Canard, one of the most competent students of the subject, surveying all of these factors, noted once again that there is no straightforward explanation of the conquerors' superiority in the campaigns. He had to conclude that the Arab conquests must still baffle the historian, thus apparently lending support to the two principal interpretations we have outlined – the one maintaining that the Arab success was the result of uncontrollable religious fervour, the other, that the motive force was the irresistible goad of famine. Surely in practice the soldiers must have felt a confused mixture of both incentives at once. They must have confused the idea that they were the bearers of a new history, the champions of a young untamed race, with the equally inspiring belief that they were the propagators of a new rule of life, a new faith they were to spread and reveal to the world.

Thus the Arabs suddenly emerged from the obscurity of the *Jahiliyya* and became the major figures in events of world-wide importance, the founders of an empire. We will discuss this process in greater detail, stage by stage, in the following chapters. Here, as a conclusion to the general considerations of the phenomenon, and as an introduction to further analysis, we want to choose and examine a number of important characteristics of the Arab empire in its early formative period. The terms 'Arab empire' and 'formation of a Muslim state' are virtually synonymous, since the empire kept its specifically Arab character for as long as the early conquering movement lasted, and both ended half way through the eighth century, giving way to a different political structure and society. Throughout the first, most clearly Arab period, the conquerors' method of government can be characterised as crudely *ad hoc* and empirical, calling for a minimum of bureaucratic and administrative structure. It allowed constant improvisation, and most important of all it very largely retained the pre-existing economic and social systems. Rather than trying to interfere in any profound way in the life of their conquered peoples, the Arabs seem to have kept aloof at first: they were satisfied with having them relegated to the status of subject and 'protected' (*dhimmi*) peoples, as laid down in the new system of public legislation, and with collecting the tribute money either imposed or settled by negotiation. After the initial stage of occupation, the large districts conquered became provinces of the empire under a military and

The Battle of Uhud. Muslim warriors lie dead, among them the Prophet's uncle, Hamza. The pagan women of Mecca, led by Hind, wife of Abn Sufyan, mutilate the Muslim corpses and devour Hamza's liver. Miniature painting from a Turkish manuscript. Museum of Turkish and Islamic Art, Istanbul.

civil governor appointed by the Caliph. The governors were aided from time to time by a financial superintendent who had the delicate task of collecting taxes and handing them over to the central treasury. Once the taxes had been paid, the local populations could carry on their religion and trade in peace, always referring their internal affairs to their own religious and civil authorities while remaining formally subordinate to the aristocracy of the conquerors. Islam's egalitarianism did not by any means eliminate the Arab's ancestral tribal system: it survived in full force, as the basis of the conquerors' social structure, bringing with it all the elements of discord and unrest implicit in tribal particularism. The native populations, who were gradually won over to Islam either by genuine conversion, or more often by self-interest, came to group themselves as clients (*mawali*) within the tribal system, extending and further complicating it with their new juridical and social problems. Though sometimes disturbed by excesses of Muslim arrogance, a climate of practical tolerance and patriarchal simplicity seems to have prevailed under the early Arab empire. It always kept up its connections with its desert origin, in spite of its contacts with the ancient civilisations of Near Asia and Egypt, with what was left of Roman and Byzantine Africa, and with Spain. The impetuous dynamic of the diaspora was complemented by the conquerors' capacity for easy adjustment to widely varying religious, social and cultural environments. The Arabs brought only their new religion and their ancient national tradition of language and poetry to the lands and peoples they conquered. However, this meeting and blending of cultures produced the composite rich and fertile Muslim civilisation which transcended the Arabism in which some of its deepest roots are buried. We will come back to this theme at the end of the book. Now the amazing chain of historic events, often attaining a truly epic stature, must be examined.

بورنك ايكي قولاغنن كسديلر ايله ديزديلر بيون باغى ايلديلر انلديلر
قحان مكه شهرينه وايربجق قريش قرنقلربكوزبوينه بيون باغى

7 The Eastern conquests: Iraq and Persia

Defeat of the Persians at Qadisiyya

The conquering movement began in 633, as soon as the Arabs had crushed the internal secession. Iraq and Syria were the two first, almost simultaneous objectives. We shall deal with Iraq first, as it takes precedence in both geographical and chronological order: the first engagements against Iraq mark the beginning of the Arab conquests in the East, coming just a few months before those on the Syrio-Palestinian front. The march of the three columns which opened the invasion of Palestine took place in the autumn of 633, whereas the first open hostilities on the Iraqi front occurred in the spring, or at latest the summer, of the same year. This movement, which was to destroy the ancient power of Persia, and in a few years to take the Arabs to the very threshold of Central Asia, began with simple border forays.

As we have already shown, the initiative came not from the centre but from the outskirts of Arabia. After the fall of the Lakhmid kingdom of al-Hira at the beginning of the seventh century, the unruly nomadic Arab tribes of the Euphrates area found an increased temptation to raid and plunder the neighbouring Iraqi settlements. These settlements had been under Sasanid domination for centuries, and though the Persian empire had known periods of power and glory, reaching a climax in the sixth century with the reign of Chosroes Anusharwan, it was now visibly crumbling and seemed to be on the verge of internal anarchy. However, al-Muthanna ibn Haritha, the brave ambitious chief of the Banu Shaiban (a branch of the Bakr tribe which had defeated the Persians at Dhu Qar) can certainly have had no idea of the historical consequences of his act when he invited Khalid ibn al-Walid, the vanquisher of the *ridda*, to join him in an invasion of the fertile Iraqi lands. Together with some of his tribesmen, he had, it is true, just been converted to Islam, and Islam was a convenient password for the new alliance: but he and his followers certainly had plunder as their principal goal when they went to war. The case of Khalid is different: he had dedicated himself body and soul to the new order founded by the Prophet and confirmed by his successor at Medina; indeed he had himself just imposed it by force of arms on the reluctant tribes of central-eastern Arabia. But did Caliph Abu Bakr really give his advance approval to this private war on the Euphrates which was to set so much history in motion? We will never find a certain answer to this question, and it is anyway of only minor importance. As in so many other cases, *fata traxerunt*. historical processes take their course, with or without the clear understanding of even their leading actors.

Thus, in the spring or summer of 633, Khalid ibn al-Walid came to join Muthanna on the Euphrates with part of the forces he had led against the *ridda;* the two allies with their few thousand men then embarked on a series of raids into the territory around al-Hira. Initially, it seems that there were no efficient Persian troops to defend the frontier, and the old Lakhmid city fell after a few weeks, paying a modest indemnity of sixty thousand dirhams. Though the town was spared, it disappeared from history as it was supplanted by the new Arab town of Kufa which the conquerors built a few years later.

The war which developed between the Arabs and the Persian frontier troops – who had slowly been reinforced – took the form of a guerilla conflict more than an open military campaign. The fighting took place between the Euphrates and the Tigris, the area where Arab-Muslim civilisation would one day blossom under the Abbasids. The Arabs suffered a severe loss early in the campaign, when Abu Bakr transferred Khalid, an energetic and versatile military genius, to the Syrian front in 634. The force remained without a leader for a time, until al-Muthanna was appointed to replace Khalid. The new commander withstood the attempted Persian counter-offensive with varying fortunes: after being beaten at the 'battle of the bridge' in 634, he was victorious the following year at Buwaib, but died of wounds soon after. Modern Iraq regards him almost as her founding hero, and not without good reason: he is a prototype of the courageous bedouin guerilla soldier, and seems to live again in Abu Tayy, whom Lawrence immortalised

The desert fortress of Ukhaidir in Iraq, some 120 miles south west of Baghdad. It was erected in early Abbasid times, probably during the third quarter of the eighth century.

in *Revolt in the Desert*. Al-Muthanna did not live to see the decisive encounter which ended the first stage of the war, giving Iraq to the Arabs for ever, but without his initiative and aggressive energy in the first years the Arabs could hardly have gained such a firm footing between the Two Rivers.

In spring 636, or more probably 637 (the chronology of the conquests in Iraq and Persia is exceptionally confused and contradictory), the conflict on the Euphrates finally developed into a frontal military war. Under the pressure of the Arab menace, the Persian empire had made a final effort to overcome her internal differences, and Rustam, the powerful marshal of the court, had at last been given recognition under the wing of the young king Yazdagird. He marched from Ctesiphon to meet the invaders with an army certainly two or three times the size of the meagre Arab forces, even if not so vast as some chroniclers make out. The Arabs had about ten thousand soldiers, later joined by a reinforcement of six thousand men from Syria. They were under the command of Sa'd ibn Abi Waqqas, a former Companion of the Prophet whom 'Umar had sent to Iraq to sustain the wavering fortunes of the Arab army. The two armies met at Qadisiyya, between the Euphrates and the Syrian desert, about twenty miles south-west of al-Hira. The Arabs were now at a turning-point, and had either to make a definitive breakthrough or retreat into their native desert. We have very detailed and vivid accounts of this historic battle presented from the Arab angle (there is no contemporary Persian historiography, and the Arab sources are only supplemented by Syrian and Armenian chronicles); they nonetheless give us many graphic and dramatic details, providing a clear and coherent overall perspective of the fighting. The combat raged fiercely for three days and nights; the Arabs matched the elephants and heavy armaments of the Persians with the vigour and fearlessness of their own attacks. They charged Rustam's army in tribal groups, showing a heroic contempt for death. Rustam himself fell in battle, and the imperial standard, the sacred Palladium of the Sasanid empire, fell into the hands of the starving plunderers from the desert. After an earlier engagement the Persian leader had said contemptuously (and by no means wrongly, in the opinion of modern critics) that the Arab rabble – the same rabble that had now destroyed their army – had been inspired mainly by the need for bread and dates. A new religious fervour had transformed this material need; it was shown in the Muslim battle-cry *Allah akbar* which resounded through the Arab ranks on the Euphrates, as it already had (given our date of 637) on the Yarmuk and would again in the hills of the Iranian plateau. In this battle and again later it was the Arabs' greater idealism which seems to have broken down the Persians' resistance, brave and tenacious though it was. The Persians who fell in the war against the Arabs were defending a blood-sodden and unstable monarchy, which was already being torn apart by irresistible centrifugal forces; or else they were acting in obedience to a blind feudal discipline. Many fled or deserted; we may presume that very few sacrificed their lives to defend their native faith or the traditional values of Iranism.

The victory of Qadisiyya gave the Arabs definitive possession of Iraq. Hormuzan, the new Persian commander-in-chief, withdrew to al-Ahwaz, and meanwhile the victorious troops crossed the Euphrates again and started for Ctesiphon, the capital of Persia. King Yazdagird III hastily left the city to start on his long anabasis to the east. Thus the vast treasures of the Sasanid capital fell into the hands of simple bedouin, who mistook camphor for salt and seasoned their provisions with it, also cutting up the wonderful royal carpet ('the spring of Chosroes') to share in little pieces among themselves. So for the time being, the fruits of an ancient sophisticated civilisation were physically dispersed; however, like the Romans in *Graecia capta*, the uncouth conquerors were destined to be subjugated by the superior civilisation they had defeated, and to make it live again in new forms. For the time being, the invaders quickly took Iraq proper or the area around ancient Babylon, and the adjoining country northward, in Mesopotamia, part of which was under Byzantine rule. The local

Three examples of ninth-century pottery. *Below*: tin-glazed cobalt blue painted ware from Mesopotamia. The decoration represents a Zoroastrian fire-altar. British Museum. *Right top:* lead-glazed mottled ware, Mesopotamia. The production of fine pottery in Islam started under Chinese influence. First specimens were excavated in Samarra. Ashmolean Museum, Oxford. *Right below:* lustre-painted ware. The earliest lustre ware, as here, was painted in polychrome using two or more shades of brown, green, yellow and ruby. Bowl from Iraq. British Museum.

Aramean, therefore Semitic, population felt no regrets on seeing the end of Persian oppression and exploitation. In their new masters they recognised a kindred race, which seemed closer and more human. In the years immediately after the conquests, the military encampments at Kufa and Basra grew up into towns, and they set the seal on Arab dominion in Iraq.

Total victory over Persia

The territory of Iran proper, quite different in its geography, climate and ethnic characteristics, still lay untouched before the invaders. It might seem that the Arabs called a halt in the campaign between the occupation of Iraq and the attack on Persia. But their thirst for conquest had been whetted, and any such delay was dictated not by caution but by the need to make reorganisations and wait for reinforcements. The die was cast: Caliph 'Umar of Medina withdrew his ruling that the advancing Muslim armies should not be separated from Arabia by any large tract of water. He now appointed and recalled commanders, and followed the campaigns with anxious interest. Instead of undertaking the attack on the Iranian plateau frontally, from the east, where they had penetrated as far as Hulwan, the Arabs approached from the south-west, invading Khuzistan. In about 640, they pushed on from their new camp at Basra, working their way northward up the Dujail, and forcing Hormuzan, the Persian general, to flee from Ahwaz to Shustar. The Arabs besieged the town and took the general prisoner in 642. He was sent to the Caliph at Medina, and managed to obtain mercy for his life by a trick. He embraced Islam, and stayed at Medina as the Caliph's adviser on Persian affairs until his tragic death after 'Umar's assassination. The year 642 also saw the occupation of Khuzistan, with the capture of Jundaysabur and Sus, but there was still a big battle in store for the Arabs before they could scatter their armies for the final penetration of the tableland.

The battle took place (still in 642) at Nihawand in the Jibal, south-west of Hamadhan. It was the tottering Persian empire's last effort, in military terms, to delay the moment of its collapse. A strong Persian army had taken up position at Nihawand under the command of a general whom Arab sources call Dhu 'l-hajibain ('the man with two Chamberlains'). The Arabs approached from the west and south under the command of Nu'man ibn Muqarrin al-Muzani, an appointee of the Caliph himself. The long exhausting struggle of Qadisiyya was repeated: the Muslim commander, a former Companion of the Prophet, moved to the attack in the afternoon as the sun was beginning to set – the time when Muhammad used to start his attacks – and he was one of the first to fall in the mêlée. His contingents from Kufa and Basra, veterans of the Iraqi campaigns, battled desperately for three days against forces who were again superior in numbers and were inspired by a fierce fighting spirit (some Persian detachments were chained together to stop their members from fleeing). The Arabs finally won the 'victory of victories', as it is called in their tradition. The Persian commander died in battle and the imperial army was utterly dispersed. Persian resistance did not cease altogether from that moment, as one over-simplified view has it, but was no longer under the control of the central authority, now hopelessly weakened by the dissolution of its armies. The later resistance movements, sporadic and sometimes very determined, came from individual military leaders, governors (*marzuban*) and feudal lords, with no unifying body to hold them together. The fugitive king sent money, envoys and instructions, but to no avail: the proud Sasanid army, which had stood up to Rome and Byzantium, had been destroyed, and never again challenged the Arabs in battle.

The Muslims' first fruit of victory was the fall (in 643) of neighbouring Hamadhan, formerly Ecbatana. From there, the conquerors spread out all over the Jibal, gradually occupying the towns of Ispahan, Kashan, Qumm and Qazwin. All four cities were destined to become famous centres of the Faith and the learning, culture and art of Islamic Persia. It is difficult for us to visualise them in pre-Muslim days. North of the Jibal, the Arabs' next immediate objective was Azerbaidjan, which fell in 633–4, to an army of Kufan forces from the south and other Arab units from upper Mesopotamia or Jazira, in the south-west (where the Arabs had taken possession of Mosul in 641). Arab expeditions to the north reached the steppes of Mughan and Derbend on the Caspian. However, at that time and for some time to come, the territories south of the Caspian (Dailam and Mazandaran) proved impossible to conquer and subdue. Between 644 and 645 the Arabs finally took Rayy, formerly Rhages (in the neighbourhood of present-day Teheran), the most important political, economic and cultural centre of Northern Persia.

The simultaneous Arab advance into South Persia was no less energetically pursued and no less vigorously resisted. At an early stage, offensive thrusts and short-term raids had brought the Arabs to the heart of Fars, the birthplace of most of the national dynasties of Persia, from which the name of the country is derived. After Nihawand, the Arabs advanced eastwards in a systematic campaign against southern Khuzistan. Crushing the sometimes significant resistance movements of local chiefs, they overran and occupied Kazrun, Shiraz, Istakhr and Jur (now Firuzabad). From his refuge in Fars, Yazdagird III fled north into the border province of Khurasan. Jiruft, the capital of the adjacent province of Kirman, fell in 650. From there, the Arabs crossed the southern part of the great salt desert, and arrived in Sijistan, proceeding in a north-easterly direction. Then, either making treaties with the local dynasties (*shah* and *zunbil*) or waging war on them, they managed to establish themselves as far as ar-Rukhkhaj, formerly called Arachosia. Meanwhile, in the south, they advanced into the hostile coastal province of Makran, the future base for attack on India; the northern contingents resolutely set about the penetration of Khurasan. In 650, the brave Ahmad ibn Qais moved northwards through Kohistan, invaded Khurasan and occupied Merv. Having reached the most easterly provinces of the Empire, the Arab menace was making itself felt even in the most distant strongholds where the King of Kings had taken shelter.

Yazdagird III's pathetic finale is bound up with the last stage of

Samarra, the minaret of the Great Mosque. During
al-Mu'tasim's caliphate (833–42) the riots of the
Turkish troops caused so many disturbances in Baghdad
that in 836 the Caliph ordered a new capital, Samarra,
to be built farther up the Tigris. The Great Mosque with its
minaret was built by Caliph al-Mutawakkil (847–61).

Samarra, the palace of al-'Ashiq.
It was built by Caliph al-Mu'tamid
between 878 and 882. The palace lies on
the western bank of the Tigris.

Bowl, painted in polychrome over the glaze, from Rayy, Persia, early thirteenth century. The decoration shows the siege of a fortress. Such overglaze-painted vessels reveal the link between potters and miniature painters of the period. Decorations were taken from historical legends, like those of the *Shahnameh* ('Book of Kings'), compiled by the great Persian poet Firdawsi. Freer Gallery of Art, Washington.

the Arab penetration into Persia proper, around the middle of the century. From the two Merv (Merv-i Shahijan and Merv-i Rud) which had been invaded consecutively, the last Sasanid fled beyond the Oxus, and asked help from the Khaqan of the Western Turks, the rulers of Sogdiana and even from the Emperor of China. The Khaqan was the only one who gave him any effective help, returning with him over the Oxus, to make a last attempt at winning back Eastern Khurasan from the invaders by force of arms. This attempt failed, as had all previous ones, and the Arabs reached Balkh and the Oxus, which, for the time being, constituted the farthest boundary of the conquests. With his political eclipse, Yazdagird also met his death: in 651 the last Sasanid king was assassinated near the river Murghab, where he was living abandoned by all. Some versions say he fell victim to a greedy miller, from whom he had asked shelter, and who wanted to rob him of his rich kingly garments. Others say he was betrayed by Mahoe, one of the governors or local petty monarchs of Khurasan, who, like the satrap Bessos a thousand years earlier, did not hesitate to finish off his fugitive king. Firdawsi later sang his melancholy death, and tells how, as a romantic tradition has it, some Christian monks found the remains of the last Chosroes in the river and gave them holy burial. Yazdagird left a son who took refuge in China, and from there sent out vain appeals for help, but for all practical purposes the imperial dynasty of Persia was extinct. In their consolidation of the eastern provinces, the Arabs had no more to fear from legitimist insurrections.

Thus, in about a decade for Iran proper, and scarcely two if we include Iraq, the power which had been the colossal rival of Rome and Byzantium, both the dream and the nightmare of the desert nomads, was lying vanquished at the Arabs' feet. This rapid and complete catastrophe poses the vast number of questions which we outlined in the previous chapter, with their partial and unsatisfactory answers. Persia had been one of the major powers of the Near East for centuries, and, even in the time of the Prophet, had won a victory on the Mediterranean under Chosroes II. The sudden

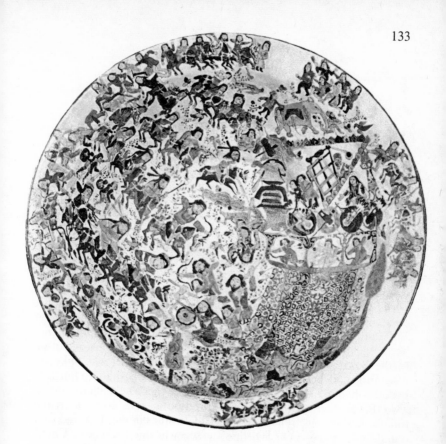

and total military collapse we have described seems inexplicable, particularly so when compared with the fate of Byzantium. The Byzantine empire was also defeated by the Arabs at the same time, and lost some of her provinces, but, by her defences in the Taurus Mountains and by her own political, military and organisational forces, she managed to halt the Arab avalanche and check it for centuries to come. Why were the Persians unable to stop the Arabs at the Zagros Mountains, and to save at least the nucleus of their state from invasion? We must remember that their collapse was more complete: it affected not only the military but also the administrative, social and economic spheres, and struck at the very roots of the empire. This empire was little more than an elegant façade concealing a vacuum left behind by decades of internal conflict. In two or three pitched battles, and then in a relentless irruption forced onwards from behind and inspired by an irresistible national and religious dynamic, the furious Arab onrush dealt that empty façade the blow that brought it down for ever.

The arabisation of Persia

The conquest had various different effects on the lands of the defeated Persian empire. The most important consequence, which developed in a fairly short space of time, though not as short as is commonly believed, was that all the lands were permanently won over to Islam. However, another process developed fully in Iraq only: it was extremely quickly and almost totally arabicised. Before the conquests, the Arabs had only gained a foothold on its borders, with the Lakhmids of al-Hira, and nomadic tribes such as the Bakr, who had first suggested the invasion. Once Persian resistance had been crushed at Qadisiyya, ever greater bands of bedouin had poured out of the Peninsula into the Valley of the Two Rivers, with the conquering armies or following in their wake; they came to live side by side with the local Aramean population and soon overwhelmed it. Some of the Arabs continued their ancestral nomadism in their new lands, but the majority settled and began the new urban life to which they had previously been so hostile. We have already mentioned the two great centres of Basra and Kufa, which developed from the conquerors' military encampments into stable city units, their topography and place names reflecting the original tribal lodging system. They were both to become important as social, political and later cultural centres of the new, vital Iraqi Arabism. Kufa was the capital of the governor-general of Iraq, the representative of the central power of Medina, or (after Caliph 'Ali, who made Kufa his own residence) of Damascus under the Umayyad Caliphs. Kufa was the centre from which Sa'd ibn Waqqas's successors directed the rest of the eastern conquests, and at which the great Umayyad generals, such as Ziyad ibn Abihi and Hajjaj held office and powers of viceroy over all the eastern part of the empire. This office was not an easy one. Apart from dealing with the external wars, the governors had to resist the Iraqi opposition movements to the caliphs of Syria for the whole Umayyad period, and Kufa was the principal hot-bed of rebellion. All the anti-Umayyad movements, both 'Alid legitimism and Kharijite puritanism, found a propitious breeding-ground in Iraq and its capital. We should point out at this stage that Arabs played the dominant role in these subversive movements, though alien elements – Aramean, Kurdish, and above all Iranian – intermingled with the Arabs as *mawali*, and played leading parts in some revolts.

To sum up, it may be said that Arabism, though torn apart by political and religious feuds, was the mainstay of Iraqi social development in this early period. Arabic was the main language, an Arabic culture developed, and a school of fundamentally political and satirical, rather than artistic, poetry emerged and flourished – the beginning of a new tradition, and a new era of secular and religious history. The processes of religious assimilation to Islam and of linguistic and cultural assimilation to Arabism advanced steadily in step, until soon all Iraq became fundamentally Arab-Islamic, and has remained so until the present day.

The intensive process of arabisation which continued throughout of the Umayyad century (mid-seventh to mid-eighth century) paradoxically experienced both its most vulnerable and also its most powerful period with the Abbasid revolution. This upheaval launched its final offensive from the depths of the Persian hinterland, but it certainly drew much of its strength from Iraq's long opposition to the Umayyads. When finally victorious, the Abbasids established the centre of the Muslim empire in Iraq. The Caliphate was transferred from Syria to arabicised Iraq, and a new Abbasid capital was built north of Kufa. This city, Baghdad, was to become the greatest metropolis of the Islamic early Middle Ages, but from then on, Arabism as a political force in Iraq entered a long period of decline. On the one hand, other ethnic influences began to

The Khassaqi *mihrab* in Baghdad, carved
from a single block of marble. (The function
of the *mihrab* is to indicate the direction
of Mecca for the faithful.) Its date is uncertain,
probably either late Umayyad or early Abbasid.

supersede it (Persian and then Turkish); and on the other, in the coming years the Caliphate itself underwent a significant change in form, becoming an absolute, supernational empire, modelled on the ancient oriental monarchies. But such ethnic and political set-backs were to some extent offset by cultural gains. Under the Abbasids, urban Iraq witnessed a rapid growth of literary and cultural activities, written in Arabic, and drawing to a large extent on Arab sources. Kufa, Basra and Baghdad became new centres of Arabic culture and Muslim learning: the art of Arab poetry was lovingly encouraged; the study of Arab grammar and philology flourished in numerous schools; schools of Arab lore attracted the most illustrious scholars to the three towns; and the history of the Arabs and their conquests was the subject of a constant stream of learned classical writings throughout subsequent Muslim culture. Let us emphasise these aspects of the great Abbasid civilisation, as they developed the purely Arab tradition implanted in Iraq by the conquerors, and as they bear witness to the preserved continuity and vitality of Arabism. However, we should not brush aside the other, more essentially Islamic aspects of their culture, the branches of learning which developed under the influence of Hellenistic civilisation – philosophy and science. Always in Arabic translation, these fields of learning were studied intensively in Iraq during its Golden Age.

The cultural aspects of this golden age were to be more enduring than the country's political primacy, which was rapidly eroded by the weakening and disintegration of the Caliphate. While the cultural and scientific life of Iraq continued to flourish unabated, the power of the Caliphate dwindled, until its effective rule extended hardly beyond the frontiers of Iraq itself. When later, in the eleventh century, Iraqi culture in its turn declined, this first great conquest of the Arab empire was reduced to a state of poverty and barbarism. It became no more than a neglected province of the Ottoman empire. Its resurrection as a national state in this century draws heavily on the memories of ancient Arabism, and it dreams of restoring its ancient cultural values.

138

Bronze cauldron, the so-called 'Bobrinsky bucket',
signed by the caster and by the inlayer, and dated
1163. It is the second earliest known Islamic
metalwork with inlay decoration, the earliest being
a pen-box dated 1148. Both objects
are in the Hermitage Museum, Leningrad.

Persia responded differently to the conquest, as would be expected
in a country with its own well-defined ethnic and cultural identity.
Its national status had been destroyed, and it was not for another
thousand years that the lands which had once formed the Sasanid
empire were again united under one rule, and even then the country
was under a dynasty of foreign origin (the Safavids) rather than
under purely Persian rule.

In our period, Persia became part of the Muslim state, and was
ruled by the Arabs, though a number of small local dynasties
survived in some areas, as on the southern shores of the Caspian.
By contrast to Iraq, the Arab conquerors never succeeded in
changing Iran's ethnic structure, nor apparently even tried. They
occupied the country as conquerors, forming a small minority,
whose main concerns were to exploit the country economically,
to set up a base for further conquests to the east, and (with the
reservations stated above) to disseminate the new faith.

Persia's conversion to Islam is of particular interest to the
historian. Here the new faith succeeded in superseding and
almost totally obliterating an old indigenous religion: today, out
of a population of fifteen million, less than twenty thousand are
still followers of the old religion. The decline of Zoroastrianism
has been traced in minute detail through a meticulously thorough
examination of sources. The conclusions of this study confirm the
widely held view that the Persians turned to Islam of their own
choice rather than under duress. Their motives were economic
and social, reflecting the attempt of a subject race to make use of
religion to assimilate itself to its conquerors. However, there is
evidence that the Arabs carried on some missionary work and
attempts at proselytisation, and that the Persians, for their part,
made some resolute attempts to keep their native religion alive,
and with it, its corresponding tradition and culture. Centres of
political, religious and cultural resistance (these words are used in
the narrow sense, meaning the preservation of practices and
customs connected with Zoroastrianism) can be traced in Persia for
almost three centuries, and only begin to diminish in the early

eleventh century. It is only after this date that Persia can be said to have been wholly converted to Islam. Persian Muslims were not Shi'ite from the beginning, and it is important to make a distinction between the nature of Islam in Persia in its earliest period, and that of the modern nation, since the Safavid age. On the contrary, Sunnism, or Islam orthodoxy, took root firmly in the first centuries, and did not finally give way to the Shi'a as the state religion until the

Bronze pen-box, inlaid with silver, made in 1210 for the Grand Vizier Majd al-Mulk al-Muzaffar. Note the vertical strokes of the letters ending in human heads, a type of writing often used in Islamic metalwork during the end of the twelfth and first half of the thirteenth century. The box is signed by a master called al-Shadhi and dated 1210. Freer Gallery of Art, Washington.

time of the Safavids. However, Shi'a, the great Islam heterodoxy, though Arab in origin, acquired a special image and renown in Iran from an early date, as it satisfied some of the country's particular needs and traditions. The concept of religious legitimism – direct inheritance of political and religious dignity from the Prophet – the belief that the *imam* is divinely inspired, and the development of what were fundamentally Shi'a mystic and syncretist ideas in other sects were typical characteristics of Persian Islam, long before the Shi'a gained official recognition in the country. Persian Islam has been extremely prolific in heresiology, from the most ancient sects of the early centuries, to the development of Isma'ilism in the eleventh century, up to the modern heresy of Babism, and Bahaism which is derived from it. When making a judgment between the comparative merits of the heterodoxy of

Persian Islam, and the more moderate and reasonable orthodoxy
– doubtless a closer interpretation and continuation of Muhammad's work – we must not forget, on the one hand, that Persian
Islam was very much influenced by the deep and tortuous beliefs
of Iran's ancient gnostic and dualistic faiths, nor, on the other
hand, should we conceal the fact that, in its extreme cases, Persian
Islam presents a complete contrast to the directness and rationality
of the Muslim faith as history shows it to have been practised by
the majority of its adherents.

However that may be, Shi'ite Islam can be seen as one essential
aspect of Iran's reaction to the Arab conquest. With the conquest,
Persia lost her ancestral religion and national independence, but
still retained her native language and culture, which survived and
flourished under Arab rule, as under the subsequent Iranian,

Turkish and Mongol dynasties which ruled Persia under the banner of Islam. After a few centuries, the small stratum of Arab conquerors vanished among the overwhelming Persian majority. Arabic lived on even in Persia, it is true, as the language of the Holy Book, and of the theological, traditionist and legal literature directly connected with it. Many writers Persian by birth used it for these subjects and some others, thus entering the vast domain of Arab literature, which was open to writers of the most diverse ethnic origins. However, though Arabic was used as the language of learning and religion, the Persian national tongue still lived on as the vernacular, and around the tenth century, again came to be used in high literary and artistic works. Persian literature had its own identity, and developed forms and styles unknown to Arab tradition, for example the epic. Persian-Muslim literature occupies a distinguished position in general world culture: the names of Firdawsi, Attar, Rumi, Khayyam, Sa'di, Hafiz, familiar even to non-orientalists, are Muslim Persia's contribution to world literature. They are at once typically Persian and typically Muslim, the fruits of the cross-fertilisation of Muhammad's religion with Persian tradition, the Arab conquest's most enduring and positive effect on Persia. The Arabs conveyed and propagated their religion but they could do no more: in Persia today Arabic is only understood by *mullas* or Shi'ite theologians. Yet without the Arabs' pervasive influence, Islamic Persia would never have known its ardent spiritual life.

The conquests of Byzantine Syria took place at the same time as those of Iraq and Persia. In this phase of the expansion, the Arabs reached the Mediterranean and the northern limit of their advance, in Mesopotamia and Armenia. As we have already seen, the conquests on the east started with individual initiatives from the outskirts of Arabia, which Abu Bakr was at first reluctant to sanction; the attack on Syria, on the other hand, was worked out and planned at Medina from the very beginning. The Prophet himself had set the young Muslim state an example and precedent for the enterprise with his failed expedition to Mu'ta and his bloodless expedition to Tabuk: he had thus shown aggressive intentions towards the Byzantine border. Whatever Muhammad's exact plans and ambitions may have been, his followers naturally felt tempted to take them up and develop them. For centuries the desert Arabs had been making slow continuous infiltrations into Syria, even more extensively than into Iraq, a process which had been restrained, but never completely checked by the Ghassanid tribal state. For a long time commercial relations and to a lesser extent religious and cultural ones had bound this ancient country with its Mediterranean culture to the very heart of Arabia. It was natural, then, that it should become one of the Arabs' first objectives when their suppressed energies broke loose immediately after the crushing of the *ridda*. Besides, after its brief latter-day resurgence a few years earlier, when it reconquered Palestine from the Persians, the Byzantine empire had once more fallen into serious economic and financial difficulties. These difficulties, aggravated by religious differences, had further alienated the Byzantines' Syrian subjects and the border Arab tribes, who had hitherto been used as auxiliaries, and, at one time, deprived of their wages. Here, as on the Iraqi border, the arrival of the Arab Muslims was joyfully welcomed, or perhaps requested by their co-nationals who lived there.

In autumn 633, three columns each of about three thousand men (or seven thousand, including reinforcements who joined them later) left the Hijaz for the north: two of them, under the command

Dome of the Rock, Jerusalem. Mosaic decoration
on the inner face of the octagon arcade: a vase
decorated with jewels. The mosaics were executed
by local craftsmen who were probably not Muslims.
Western classical elements combine in the patterns
with those of Eastern (Sasanian) origin.

145

of Yazid ibn Abi Sufyan and Shurahbil ibn Hasana, set off for Transjordania by the usual route through Tabuk-Ma'an. The third,
under 'Amr ibn al-'As, took the coast road through Alla, to invade
Palestine from the south. The new armies had perhaps as little
idea of their final objective as the Prophet had had in his expeditions. Their aims were first and foremost war with the infidels and
plunder; then, penetration as far as Allah would wish. Perhaps
none of these soldier-plunderers or even any of their leaders (Abu
Sufyan's brave and wise son Yazid, who brought his younger
brother Mu'awiya with him as standard bearer, and the capable
man of affairs 'Amr ibn al-'As) realised that their march was
opening a new epoch in the history of the Mediterranean peoples.
To start with at any rate, no one general was in charge of all the
expeditionary forces. Guided by his needs for action and plunder
rather than by any ordered strategy, each acted on his own initiative, with only the most tenuous liaison between the different
armies. As in the case of Persia one would have assumed that a
unified well-organised state and an efficient military machine
would easily defeat the small bands of Arab raiders. As also in the
case of Persia, this assumption was to prove false, perhaps because
in both cases the state organisation and the military apparatus
were no more than fragile veneers, unable to withstand the slightest
blow.

The first encounters with the Byzantine forces took place in
southern Palestine in February 634, and it seems that Yazid ibn
Abi Sufyan's army joined battle before that of 'Amr. (From now on
an element of doubt should be understood in all statements of
fact, so uncertain and contradictory are the Arab sources on these
campaigns in Syria; the critical work of modern historians such as
De Goeje, Miednikov and Caetani have only partially clarified
them.) First in the Wadi 'Araba, south of the Dead Sea, and then
at Dathin near Gaza, the Arabs repelled and then destroyed the
Byzantine troops from Caesarea, and killed their leader, Sergius the
patrician. The Arabs then scattered in disorganised bands to lay
waste all of Southern Palestine. Emperor Heraclius hastily took de-

fensive measures, and from his residence at Homs (Emesa) a strong army went to meet the invaders under the command of his brother Theodore. But while Theodore was going south from Syria, a new enemy appeared unexpectedly near Damascus: this was Khalid ibn al-Walid, the brilliant Arab captain, victor of Uhud, the *ridda* and al-Hira, now transferred by Caliph Abu-Bakr from the Iraqi front to help in Syria. His march through the desert in April 634 with a few hundred men – his companions from al-Hira on the Euphrates – and his unexpected arrival at the outskirts of Damascus on Easter Day constitute one of the most memorable enterprises of the military history of the time. There has been much speculation over his exact route, but whatever it may have been, the assistance he brought to his companions on the Syrian front, about to face massive enemy attack, lay more in the weight of his genius, his organisational talents and his moral superiority than in material reinforcements. We do not know for certain whether the Caliph ever appointed him supreme commander of the Syrian campaign, but there is no doubt that once he had joined the southern invading armies, he took charge of the direction and organisation of the operations, and bent the self-seeking insubordination of the other leaders to the common good. We do not know whether he or 'Amr was in command of the united Arab forces which withstood and repelled Byzantine attack the following July in the battle of Ajnadain, south west of Jerusalem. (There is disagreement over the exact location and even the name of the battle.) It would be difficult, however, to visualise this glorious victory with any other general than Khalid himself. From this point, the disorganised Arab campaign becomes a systematic coherent campaign of invasion, penetration and occupation, thus indicating the presence of the will and experience of an organiser and strategic genius: the mind and will of the 'Sword of God'.

Thus, on 30 July 634, the Arabs won a pitched battle at Ajnadain (or, according to another spelling, at Jannabatain, on the road from Gaza to Jerusalem). They defeated a Byzantine army far greater than their own, though not numbering a hundred thousand men,

Dome of the Rock, Jerusalem. The first monument
of Islam. Built by the Umayyad Caliph
'Abd al-Malik (685–705), and completed in 691.
The building was erected around the Holy Rock
where David's altar stood, and from where Muhammad
began his famous night journey to heaven.

as some sources maintain. The commander-in-chief, Heraclius's brother Theodore, was put to ignominious flight, the governor of Palestine died in the battle and Arab versions describe the flight of an *artabun* (perhaps a *tribunus*). This victory had the same effect on Palestine as Qadisiyya was to have on Iraq two or three years later. It inaugurated Arab rule in the Holy Land, a rule which was to last for thirteen centuries – apart from the interval of the Crusades – and has only recently been challenged by the emergence of the new state of Israel. Jerusalem did not immediately fall to the invaders, unpractised as they still were at siege, but in that year Archbishop Sophronius's Christmas sermon deplored the insecurity and devastation the Hagarenes had spread throughout the country, and the fact that the faithful could not make pilgrimages to Bethlehem. Soon after Ajnadain, Abu Bakr died at Medina, and the accession of the energetic 'Umar gave a new decisive impetus to the conquering movement. Wave upon wave of Arab immigrants now started pouring out of the Peninsula into the conquered lands, increasing the numbers of the first contingents; meanwhile, the striking force went northward, invading Syria with Khalid as its active leader. New Byzantine forces, under the command of the Armenian general Vahan (or Baanes in Greek) tried vainly to halt their advance in the two bloody clashes of Fihl (Pella in Palestine) and Marj as-Suffar, both south of Damascus (January to February 635). However, in March of the same year, the invaders reached the walls of Damascus.

For six months the Arabs blockaded rather than attacked the capital of Syria. Then, little disposed to fight, the Byzantine garrison retreated secretly, whereupon a bishop and a Byzantine financial official with the Arab name Mansur negotiated surrender with Khalid on the 10th September 635. Arab tradition is rich in details which modern critics have for the most part rejected. They say that the conquerors made a double onslaught on the city, attacking on the one hand, and making terms for surrender on the other. Some sources say that as a result of the conquerors' double position the Cathedral of Saint John was divided into two parts, one remaining a Christian church and the other becoming a mosque. In fact, it is now maintained that in the first conquest the whole of Damascus was handed over to the Arabs by treaty. A proof of this is a short document attributed to Khalid, which promises the inhabitants their lives, goods and freedom of religion in exchange for tribute money. In the early period, even the Cathedral was kept entirely for the practice of Christianity while Islam came to be practised in a mosque adjacent to it. Only later, in the time of Caliph al-Walid, was the cathedral taken away from the Christians, and the great mosque of the Umayyads raised on both sites. Khalid did not linger in the conquered capital but went straight back to his march towards the north. He took Homs peacefully, and, according to some versions, penetrated as far as Hamat. Meanwhile Yazid and Shurahbil made a complete and thorough conquest of Jaulan, Hauran and eastern Jordan. At the end of 635, the whole of Syria and Palestine can be said to have been largely in the invaders' hands. Some small strongholds of Christian resistance still remained such as Jerusalem, Caesarea and the coastal cities. The Arab rulers now began to try to crush them one by one.

However, the Byzantines could not abandon the birthplace of Christianity and the beautiful province of Syria without making a final attempt at resistance. For some time, a huge Byzantine army had been preparing to launch an attack from the Taurus mountains to recover their lost position. Heraclius had entrusted the command to a *sakellarius* Theodorus, also called Trithurios, with Baanes, by now an experienced soldier, as his second-in-command. As was usual at that time, the Byzantine army consisted of legions of many different nationalities and origins – Greeks, Syrians, Armenians and Caucasians. There was even an Arab unit under the command of the last Ghassanid prince Jabala ibn Aiham – the remains of the former auxiliaries who had by now almost all gone over to the enemy. This impressive punitive expedition went down from the Amanus passes towards the Syrian plain. With his unerring strategic sense, Khalid immediately evacuated Homs and even Damascus, and withdrew his forces to a point from which he could concentrate them together to make a defensive bridge-head. He found a suitable place east of the Sea of Galilee on the banks of the river Yarmuk (which the Byzantines called the Hieromax), a tributary of the Jordan from the left, at the place where the Wadi 'r-Ruqqad flows into it. Protected on the flank by the deep precipices of this river and other tributaries of the Yarmuk, the Muslim army had its back to the desert, its last way of retreat in case of defeat. In summer 636 the two armies faced each other there to fight out the last round to settle the fate of Syria for ever; twenty-five thousand Arabs against double the number of Byzantines.

The battle of the Yarmuk had, without doubt, more important consequences than almost any other in all world history. Between July and August 636 the action was divided into a number of skirmishes; the 20th August, the date generally agreed on for the battle, marks only the final epilogue of the drama of the downfall of Byzantine rule in Syria. Hard pressed by the victorious sons of the desert, their superior commander, and their fanatical will for victory, the Greeks were gradually forced back. They tried to escape towards the west, over the bridges and in the deep river beds of the Ruqqad and the Yarmuk, but most of them either fell to the enemy or died in the steep ravines. Byzantium's last organised attempt to defend the heritage of Rome ended with this disastrous collapse. We can guess how Heraclius, the valiant emperor who had recovered the true Cross from the Persians, responded to the tragedy from the words attributed to him, in Arab tradition, on his departure from the country for ever:

Farewell Syria. What a good country for the enemy!

The victory of the Yarmuk was the summit of Khalid ibn al-Walid's glorious military career. As Khalid broke down the Byzantine counter-offensive, and confirmed his conquest of Syria, he already had the country's new governor-general at his side. 'Umar had appointed a former Companion, the respected Abu 'Ubaida ibn al-Jarrah to succeed him. Either on account of personal antipathy or for political reasons, relations between

'Umar and Khalid had never been good. Ever since the suppression of the *ridda*, 'Umar had shown his disapproval of the great captain's impetuosity and lack of scruple. Khalid thought that 'Umar had influenced Abu Bakr to have him transferred from the Iraqi front to the Syrian, though it was in fact in Syria that he had won his greatest laurels. Now, with the conquest virtually complete, it seemed apposite for the man of war to make way for a peacemaker and organiser, for a man such as the Caliph understood Abu 'Ubaida to be. An influential adviser and collaborator of the two first Caliphs, tradition presents Abu 'Ubaida as a constant companion of the generals in Syria and some say that he had even been working with Khalid during the siege of Damascus, or ever since the battle of Fihl. However, he did not in fact apparently relieve the 'Sword of God' immediately after the decisive victory of the Yarmuk, but kept him on for a time, and thus they began working together towards a rapid and complete occupation of Syria. They took Damascus and Homs again definitively, and, sometime between the end of 636 and 638 – we do not know the time-sequence for certain – Baalbek, Aleppo, Antioch and Qinnasrin. Meanwhile Yazid and Shurahbil made a thorough occupation of Palestine and the Phoenician coastal centres. At the beginning of 638 the conquest could be said to be complete except for Jerusalem and Caesarea, the two main southern centres, both of which were strongly Hellenised. The former was forced to sue for peace in the same year, the latter, a last bastion of hopeless resistance for several more years, was betrayed in 640 and fell to Mu'awiya. Except for these towns, the Arab conquest had, by reaching the foot of the Amanus, now stretched to the permanent boundary of Arabism in this part of the world. Anatolia, which the conquerors attacked from the south and east after they had finished with Syria, was to be overrun by chronic Arab raids for many years to come, but was never definitively occupied. It was not until four centuries later that the Turks began to convert it to Islam.

Acting on the orders given to him, Abu 'Ubaida supervised the organisation of Arab dominion in Syria. He divided it into four

The fortified enclosure of Mshatta, thirty miles
south of 'Amman, an Umayyad building attributed to Caliph
al-Walid (705–15). In the centre was the palace with a
large hall ending in three apsidal recesses, admission to
which was through this three-arched entrance. The arches rest
on square pilasters crowned by acanthus capitals.

'military zones': Palestine, Jordan, Damascus and Homs, to which Qinnasrin in the north was added later. After the Yarmuk, all these districts were subjected to an intensive, if not systematic process of arabisation. Caliph 'Umar gave his sanction to the conquest in 638, while Jerusalem was still resisting 'Amr ibn al-'As's attacks: Muhammad's second successor then came from Medina to hold a solemn general assizes in al-Jabiya, the former Ghassanid residence. Abu 'Ubaida was present, and with him all the military leaders, tribal leaders and other promoters of the conquest. With justifiable pride, traditional sources describe the 'day of al-Jabiya' and the speech 'Umar may have delivered there as among the most distinguished occasions in the history of Muslim Arabism. Apart from the authenticity of the details, modern criticism now casts doubt on the actual substance of some of the decisions traditionally associated with that occasion, holding that they are an arbitrary anticipation of a whole slow process which did not develop till later. However it seems extremely likely that 'Umar's strong personality and the meeting of al-Jabiya would have played a large part in beginning such a process. The problems they dealt with were the organisation of the conquest, the formation of a register (*diwan*) of soldiers, with wages paid by the state, the constitutional position of non-Muslim tribute-paying people (*dhimmi*), and the country's financial system. Declared the undivided property of the Muslim community, Syria was made liable to a land tax or *kharaj*. Together with these great initial problems – and we consider that they were at least touched on at al-Jabiya – 'Umar must have settled endless individual cases, jealous comparisons and conflicts between chiefs, and rulings over minute administrative and religious issues. 'Umar would have treated everything with the qualities generally attributed to him – a rough sense of justice, personal detachment and a lofty awareness of the Prophet's heritage. Once he had set these problems in order, he went down to visit the Holy City of Palestine which had meanwhile surrendered. Archbishop Sophronius and the Greek Christian population of Jerusalem watched the arrival of their conqueror: dressed in coarse simple clothes,

indifferent to any luxury or civilised refinement, 'Umar rode in
on a desert camel.

Accompanied by the archbishop (who could not help murmuring
in Greek to those beside him 'This really is the "abomination of
desolation" mentioned in the Bible'), he visited the site of the
ancient Temple, from which Muslims believe the Prophet ascended
to heaven in a miraculous night journey. The site had been abandoned, but 'Umar had it cleaned, and he built a modest oratory
there. Half a century later, Caliph 'Abd al-Malik replaced it by
the wonderful 'mosque of 'Umar.' These legends and tributes
explain the affective value Jerusalem has always had and still has in
Arab and Muslim hearts. 'Umar returned from there to patriarchal
Medina, capital of the new theocratic state whose area was increased to such a fantastic extent by these conquests, and others in
subsequent years.

The loyal Abu 'Ubaida, whom 'Umar perhaps saw as his
successor to the leadership of the Muslim community, was not
governor-general of Syria for long. Scarcely a year later he died in
the devastating plague which swept the land in 639 (it is called the
plague of Emmaus, after the place in which the disease first
appeared). Invited to return to Medina by 'Umar, he preferred to
remain at his post, dangerous though it was, faithful to a command
attributed to the Prophet not to go into a land infected by plague
nor, once there, to leave it. Yazid and Shurahbil died in the same
epidemic: meanwhile 'Amr ibn al-'As opened a new chapter of the
conquests in Egypt. Yazid had succeeded Abu 'Ubaida as supreme
commander, and was shortly succeeded in his turn by his younger
brother Mu'awiya ibn Abi Sufyan. Mu'awiya was destined to play a
vital part in the future of Syria and the whole Arab empire. With
the help of his own wisdom and of propitious circumstances, this
younger son of the Prophet's old opponent was to rule the province
of Syria for about twenty years. He consolidated and expanded the
conquest with his far-sighted maritime policy. He conquered
Cyprus, and set up a naval force which defeated the Byzantines in
the eastern Mediterranean. When he finally ascended to the

Caliphate he made Syria his centre, and from there organised Arab attacks on places as distant as the Bosphorus.

All of this still belonged to the future. The essential phase of the conquest of Syria lasted for little more than five years, ending in about 640, with the disappearance or departure of its real protagonists. The last to leave the scene, his active role long since over, was Khalid ibn al-Walid, the man to whom, more than any other, Islam owes the conquest. There is something pathetic in his obscure eclipse which has struck biographers of both east and west. After he had obediently yielded his command to Abu 'Ubaida, he went on working with him in the reconquest of Damascus and Homs. He was apparently junior governor for a time, but was demoted because of 'Umar's hostility to him. ''Umar made me governor of Syria when things were difficult: now that it has been pacified, and all is milk and honey, he has taken it away from me,' are reported to have been Khalid's bitter words; however he preserved a dignified silence in the face of the tribulations imposed on him by the Caliph. When called to give a report on his administration, the Caliph (rightly or wrongly) fined him and confiscated some of his property. Now a civilian again, the great veteran captain spent the last years of his life in Homs, and died there, still young, in 641 or 642, leaving his property to the hostile 'Umar. The memorable example of loyalty and obedience he set elevates the moral standing of this violent man of war. Muslim Syria and Islam as a whole recognise him as one of the most brilliant figures of the heroic founding age, and posterity will count him among the greatest military geniuses of all time.

The advance to the Caucasus

Having reached the borders of northern Syria, the Arabs halted at the foot of the Amanus, and then branched off to the north east, invading Mesopotamia. Byzantium and Persia had contested this area fiercely in the preceding centuries: at the time of the invasion, the Greeks held the western part, on the Euphrates, with Edessa, Harran and Raqqa and the Persians the eastern part of the Tigris, with Mosul and Nisibis. However, since the Yarmuk and Qadisiyya, direct control from the central authority had diminished in both sectors; thus when the Arabs arrived the only opposition they met was from local garrisons. In 639, Abu 'Ubaida despatched a body of the army from Homs to the upper Euphrates under the command of 'Iyad ibn Ghanm. The cities of Mesopotamia, by now abandoned by the Byzantines, opened their gates to the invaders one after another, putting up little or no resistance. Between 639 and 641, the Arabs occupied the cities of Edessa, Harran, Raqqa, Sumaisat and Qirqisiyya, and Nisibis and Sinjar in the Persian zone, while other contingents from Iraq occupied Mosul. The country was thus reunified under Arab rule; at first it was dependent on Syria, but later it formed a province on its own, and was named Jazira. It had a distinct identity of its own in the early history of the Caliphate. Arabs had penetrated there in pre-Islamic times (as is shown in some ancient place names, as for example the three zones of Diyar Rabira, Diyar Bakr and Diyar Mudar), and they now intermingled with the Arameans and Kurds, creating problems of racial co-existence which remain unsolved to this day.

Continuing the conquest in a north-north-easterly direction, 'Iyad ibn Ghanm and his lieutenants traced out as it were the flexible boundary which would divide what remained of the Byzantine empire from Arab-Muslim territory for centuries to come: this line went from the Amanus and eastern slopes of the Taurus mountains to Melitene (the city of Malatya, which was to be taken and left many times by the Arabs, later became a key position in the Arab-Byzantine guerilla war), to Erzerum and into Georgia as far as the Caucasus. Mesopotamia thus became a secure direct Arab possession, but Armenia on the other hand was only slowly and partially subjected to the rule of Islam, after being contested by the Arabs and even more strongly by local princes. It is not easy to reconstruct the history of the Arab incursion into this country, owing to considerable divergences over chronology and topography between Arab, Armenian and Byzantine sources. There is little doubt that the Arabs first arrived there in 640 under 'Iyad ibn Ghanm, reaching Bitlis, and perhaps Dvin; several years later (646?) Habib ibn Maslama carried out another far more effective campaign, conquering Erzerum and penetrating as far as Tiflis, and exacting tribute money from its inhabitants. A period of confusion followed, with the Arabs and Byzantines disputing the country, and the Armenian nobles going over from one side to the other and being used by both to further their respective interests. The Arabs finally prevailed in Armenia, and it was ruled by civil governors appointed by the Caliph. However, Armenian sources maintain that it was ruled by princes of the great feudal families, such as the Mamikonian and the Bagratids: a century later, one of these, the Bagratid Ashot, succeeded in founding an almost independent Armenian principality, under the sovereignty of the Caliph of Baghdad.

The Arab penetration towards the north reached the Caucasus not only in Armenia but also in Azerbaijan, beyond the Araxes and the Kura, on the western shores of the Caspian. In the first decades of the eighth century, during Hisham's caliphate, the Umayyad prince Maslama ibn 'Abd al-Malik reached present-day Daghestan in his war with the Khazar Turks, and founded what is now Derbend, then Bab al-Abwab. Arab incursions in that period penetrated some way beyond the Caucasus mountains, and reached the mouth of the Volga, but only in short-term raids, which did not establish Islam. A different people were destined to bring the faith there long after the Arab period.

We will now briefly examine the Arab advance on the Mediterranean; on land, their progress northward halted on the line we have just described, going from south-west to north-east, from the gulf of Alexandretta to the Black Sea and the barrier of the Caucasus. Except for Armenia, which retained her Christian majority, all these countries became lasting though not always immediate converts to Islam. However, Syria constituted the greatest and most permanent acquisition to Islam: the Arabs had

no difficulty in gaining ascendancy over the Aramaic stock of the population and intermingling with it. An Arab historian calls the conquest of Syria the 'easy conquest', in spite of the battles with the Byzantines at Ajnadain and on the Yarmuk. Elsewhere, in general, they were welcomed as friends and liberators: in some places the native populations greeted them with music and songs. When the Arabs evacuated Homs under the threat of Heraclius's counter-offensive, the native people showed their regret openly and said that they preferred the benevolent rule inaugurated by their new masters to the grasping, hated Byzantine regime. On taking office after definitive victory, the Arabs did not persecute the people nor make any forced conversions. They simply demanded tribute-money – poll tax and land tax – from Christians and Jews, and otherwise allowed freedom of religion, language and trade. Islam gained ground in the natural course of events, for the material and ideological reasons already explained. In Syria, as elsewhere, most of the Christian population soon embraced Islam. The assassination of Caliph 'Uthman in Arabia in 656 provoked a political and religious crisis lasting about four years, and Syria reaped its benefits: she found herself suddenly promoted to the centre of the Arab-Muslim empire.

As is well known, it was Mu'awiya ibn Abi Sufyan who effected this change. He had followed his brother Yazid to Syria, and, after the latter's untimely death in the plague of Emmaus, had succeeded him in the governorship. In his fifteen-year rule, Mu'awiya made his province a stable backgound for his personal ambitions. His achievements in this period include establishing Arab naval supremacy in the Mediterranean, and energetically pursuing holy war against Byzantium. In 660 he was recognised Commander of the Faithful, and as Medina was no longer the hub of the empire, he transferred the capital of the Islamic state to Damascus. He ruled the empire from there for twenty years, and succeeded in leaving the Caliphate to his son, by right of inheritance, thus starting the Umayyad dynasty. Arabicised Syria was the first province of the empire for almost a century. All the later conquests between the civil war of 656–60 and 750, which we will discuss later, were dependent on Syria and inspired and controlled from there, and Damascus was the supreme court of appeal. Arabism blossomed in Syria in this period. Without denying its desert origins or its tribal basis, it gradually broadened and its way of life became more advanced and open to the influence of superior cultures. A spirit of great tolerance characterised the relationship between the conquerors and conquered, the Muslims and the tribute-paying Christians, in that early period. The administration, at first with Greek as its official language, remained largely in the hands of Christians such as Mansur ibn Sarjun, who had negotiated the surrender of Damascus and was for a long time a close friend of Mu'awiya, acting as his chancellor and director of finance. An Arab Christian, al-Akhtal was the main panegyrist, almost poet laureate, of the Damascus Caliphs. Hellenism still retained its influence on the arts, imprinting its character on the works produced in Syria, and, from what little we know, the protocol of the Umayyad court, like that of the Ghassanids, seems to have been modelled on Byzantium. The second Rome, driven out of Syria by force, and ceaselessly attacked on land and sea in holy wars (*jihad*), nonetheless represented an ideal, a lofty goal and model, and was an inspiration to the Caliphs of Syria for their projects in both politics and the arts. This phase lasted for less than a century. Half-way through the eighth century the Abbasid revolution overthrew the Umayyads, ending the political primacy of Syria and substituting Iraq as the centre of the empire. The Abbasids looked rather to Sasanid tradition for the political, cultural and artistic models of their civilisation. Syria, the home of their supplanted rivals, dwindled into a neglected secondary province. But because it adjoined the still vigorous Byzantine empire, it was always used as a base for *jihad*, a practice which continued under independent local dynasties even during the decadence and final impotence of the Abbasids. By resisting any attempts at intrusion from the outside world, the Hamdanids of Aleppo in the tenth century, and later, at the time of the Crusades, the Turkish

Quseyr 'Amra, an Umayyad hunting-lodge in Jordan, forty miles south-east of 'Amman. Built 720–40, it has a vaulted audience hall and baths, *Top*: a general view from the south. *Below*: the building contains interesting wall-paintings, one being on the west wall of the hall, showing six kings. Inscriptions in Greek and Arabic identify the first four figures as the Byzantine Emperor, the Visigothic King of Spain, the Sasanian Emperor, and the Negus of Abyssinia.

dynasties descended from the Seljukids, came to represent what was left in Syria of the vitality of Arabism in particular and Islam in general. The implacable conflict between the Arab states and Israel shows that this spirit is still alive today. In the early history of Arabism, the conquest and arabisation of Syria can be regarded as one of the happiest and most productive phases of the diaspora.

9 The Western conquests: Egypt and North Africa

Scarcely was the conquest of Syria over, when the Arabs started off on the long road to the west. The fertile valley of the Nile south of Palestine, rich in grain, and governed, like so many other countries, by the weak Byzantine empire, could not fail to attract the hitherto victorious spirit of conquest. Always insistent on the reluctance with which the conquests were undertaken – a theory which is certainly valid for the first campaigns in Iraq – a traditional source lays emphasis on the fact that 'Amr ibn al-'As had great difficulty in persuading 'Umar to give his authorisation to the Egyptian adventure. However, modern critics consider that the Caliph gave his full consent to the project, and that it was the starting-point for a fully developed plan of expansion. The authoritative Companion 'Amr ibn al-'As was the main instigator of the new conquest and his name recurs frequently throughout its history. 'Amr ibn al-'As did not have Khalid ibn al-Walid's exceptional military qualities. He was more a man of affairs, a good negotiator and diplomat. He had been to Egypt on trade while still a pagan, and perhaps this journey gave him the direct knowledge of people and places which later enabled him to suggest and organise the invasion. The invasion began with active soldiers in numbers which seem paltry to us: 'Amr probably first arrived in Egypt with barely four thousand horsemen. Nevertheless, he conquered and pacified the country in a fairly short space of time, and fewer lives and less effort were lost than in any previous Arab campaign.

This can, to a large extent, be explained by Egypt's internal affairs and the men whom the Arabs found in command there. Ten years earlier, Byzantium had reconquered Egypt from Persia, but religious differences and an oppressive fiscal policy had done much to sever connections between the two countries. The Coptic clergy and people had remained ardent believers in the Monophysite doctrine after the Council of Chalcedon, and they hated the official Byzantine Christology and the doctrine of monothelitism. Heraclius had tried to reconcile these opposing theological attitudes, but in vain. Moreover, the exhausted empire had

Africa and Western Europe

→	680-683 'Uqba Ibn Nafi'
→	711 Tariq Ibn Ziyad
→	712 Musa Ibn Nusair and Tariq Ibn Ziyad
→	713 'Abd Al-'Aziz
→	716-732 Later campaigns

SAVOY
Lyon
• St Bernard Pass
DAUPHINE
PIEDMONT
• Genoa
Avignon
• Marseilles
• St Tropez

CORSICA

Tyrrhenian Sea

• Rome
• Ostia

Bari •
Taranto •

SARDINIA

Palermo •
• Mazara
• Messina
Taormina

SICILY

Carthage •

Mediterranean Sea

• Baghaya
• Qairawan
IFRIQIYA
• Tehuda
• Biskra
Sbeitla •

Tripoli •

TRIPOLI

increased the already extortionate levy of tribute it exacted from its fertile agricultural province. The man sent by Heraclius to implement the Empire's religious and financial policies was one of those equivocal, elusive characters, so numerous in Byzantine history: an ambitious intriguer, traditionally presented as lacking in any sense of loyalty or nobility. This man was Cyrus, patriarch of Alexandria since 631, and civil governor of Egypt. He had formerly been bishop of Phasis in the Caucasus, and this is perhaps why he had the contemptuous nickname 'the Caucasian'; at least this is the most plausible explanation for the strange name 'Muqawqis' used in Arab tradition to refer to the Byzantine chief of Egypt at the time of the conquest; but perhaps other minor characters have been confused with Cyrus.

Thanks to Muqawqis-Cyrus's religious persecutions and excessive financial levies, Egypt was ready to fall into the arms of a new master. Thus, when 'Amr ibn al-'As appeared at the Delta at the end of 639, with a small invasionary force (later reinforced by a further five thousand men under the command of the Companion az-Zubair), the military resistance he met was incomparably smaller than that which the Arabs had had to contend with in Iraq and Syria. He occupied al-Farama (*Pelusium*) early in 640; then, avoiding a direct attack on Alexandria, he pushed on through Bilbais towards the Greek fortress of Babylon at the top of the Delta, near present-day Cairo. At Heliopolis near Babylon, the Byzantines contested Arab possession of Egypt in the only important land encounter of the campaign. The emperor's general Theodore (one of the many Theodores who figure so frequently in the history of the Byzantine disasters of this period) was defeated by 'Amr, in July 640. He retreated to Babylon and it was at this stage, as the general Arab version has it, that Muqawqis began his defeatist or frankly treacherous policy. However this version is not generally accepted, and some modern historians, such as Caetani, consider that Muqawqis took no part in this local surrender. Still, the most popular theory is that the governor made terms with the invaders at this point, arranging to give the country, or perhaps only the town, over to them with a payment of tribute. Recalled to Constantinople to give a report on his negotiations he asked for a ratification of his so advantageous treaty, whereupon Heraclius, outraged, disowned and banished him. However the emperor died soon after, broken and embittered by seeing his desperate attempts to recreate and defend the empire destroyed by a series of disasters. Now that there was no hope of help from Byzantium in the foreseeable future, Babylon fell in the April of the same year, and 'Amr began to move on slowly towards Alexandria.

The capital of Egypt, defended both by the sea and its own strong fortifications, was certainly no easy prize. At first the invaders merely ransomed the outlying areas, but then Muqawqis came back on the scene and acted on their behalf: the peace party under Empress Martina had recalled him to Byzantium and sent him to Egypt as a negotiator in September 641. Clearly Cyrus had no interest in making Egypt a province of the Muslim empire, but rightly or wrongly he was convinced that the Arabs were superior in military strength, and he must have planned to make himself head of the Alexandrian church under Arab sovreignty, freeing himself from any subjection to Byzantium. This is the only explanation of his new conciliatory policy towards the Egyptian clergy whom he had previously harshly persecuted in the name of orthodoxy, and of his project for the surrender of Alexandria, formulated with 'Amr in the November of the same year. They planned that the Greek garrison would evacuate the city in September 642, and the inhabitants would then pay the invaders tribute in return for their lives, goods and freedom of religion. When the Alexandrians first heard of the treaty, riots and general uproar broke out, but the cunning negotiator finally persuaded the people to accept his terms. He never reaped the benefits of his hard-headed dealings, as he died in March 642; that September, the desert Arabs made their entry into Alexander's capital as arranged. We need hardly mention that the Arabs did not burn down the Alexandrine library, as has erroneously been maintained. It had already been destroyed centuries earlier, in the disturbances that the famous capital of

Hellenism had suffered long before the Arab invasion.

'Amr's work in Egypt was at once military, diplomatic and administrative. While he defeated the Byzantines on the battlefield or held them in check, he won far more by treaties than he could have by arms (we have seen the best example of his tactics in the surrender of Alexandria), and his expansion of Arab occupation through the country was mainly peaceful. His overtures to the Pentapolis were equally peaceful; this enterprise was the prelude to the Arabs' western advance; Barca then surrendered without resisting. Instead of making Alexandria his capital and the main place of residence of the governor and the invaders, 'Amr chose the military camp from which he had attacked the fortress of Babylon on the Nile; he developed it as a permanent urban centre and gave it the Arab name of al-Fustat, derived from the Latin-Byzantine φοσσατον. It was the capital of the Arab province of Egypt until the Fatimids founded the city of Cairo north of it. The name of the Nile Valley's conqueror and first disseminator of Arabism is recalled by the 'Mosque of 'Amir,' though little of the original building is still standing today.

In 644, orders from Medina suddenly curtailed 'Amr's leadership of the province he had conquered: 'Umar had appointed 'Abdallah ibn Sa'd ibn Abi Sarh, another man destined to have a lasting effect on the arabisation of the west, to govern Upper Egypt (little is known of the times or methods of Arab penetration here), and 'Uthman, 'Umar's successor, extended 'Abdallah's governorship to include the whole of Egypt. Like Khalid, 'Amr obeyed and withdrew, but his role in the country he had conquered was not completely over. In the following year, 'Uthman had to send him back to Egypt to meet a Byzantine counter-offensive: a Greek fleet had taken Alexandria with the help of the rebel population (which proves that it was only very superficially arabised during the early period). The new governor was more of an administrator than a man of war. 'Amr, as much the one as the other, returned and reestablished Arab supremacy, putting the Byzantines to flight and taking Alexandria by storm in 646. As he refused to be

The Mosque of Ahmad Ibn Tulun, Cairo,
with the outer walls and the spiral minaret.
Ibn Tulun became governor of Egypt in 869
and later founded the independent
dynasty of the Tulunids.

Cairo, the Mosque of Ibn Tulun:
a stucco flat *mihrab* in the sanctuary
which was installed by al-Afdal in
the late eleventh century. There are
five stucco flat *mihrabs* in the mosque.

only the military commander, with 'Abdallah ibn Abi Sarh as civil governor, he had to withdraw once more. He was to reappear in Egypt about ten years later, when civil war broke out in the Islamic state. The civil wars actually began in Egypt: from there an army of rebels set off for the march on Medina which ended with the assassination of Caliph 'Uthman in 656. 'Amr supported Mu'awiya in the ensuring war between him and 'Ali: he was his counsellor at Siffin, and proved an able negotiator at the arbitration of Adhruh; in 658 he finally succeeded in winning Egypt over to Mu'awiya's cause, and he stayed there as governor for the third and last time, until his death in very old age in about 663. His fame as a *dahiya*, or invincible political manoeuvrer far exceeds his fame as a military leader. His work was by no means all self-interested: it produced permanent results in history, winning for the Arabs and for Islam a land where both were to remain deeply rooted.

Though a far less brilliant man, 'Abdallah ibn Abi Sarh, the governor of the Nile Valley during 'Uthman's Caliphate, displayed similarly outstanding organisational and administrative qualities. Among his other achievements, he established supremacy over the southern borders of Egypt, attacking the Christian province of Nubia, and making a political and commercial treaty with it, the record of which is still extant. However, this governor's activities in Egypt have another important aspect, which, matched by a similar venture in Syria, did much to increase Arab power in the Mediterranean basin. 'Abdallah and Mu'awiya created the first Muslim fleet, sometime after 646, at Alexandria and in the ports of the Syrian coast: the original desert plunderers could then embark on ventures at sea. Dissatisfied with the conquests they had already made, the Arabs wanted to pursue their conflict with the Byzantines with the ultimate goal of taking Constantinople. They could only further their chances by challenging the Byzantines' supremacy at sea: due solely to their maritime supremacy, the Byzantines had been able to take temporary repossession of Alexandria in 645, and could put up some resistance to Arab penetration in Africa.

With their well-built fleets manned in part by native crews, the Muslim governors of Syria and Egypt now began to challenge Byzantine maritime supremacy. Mu'awiya took Cyprus in 649, and the Arabs began their raids on the coasts of the Mediterranean in the following years. The new Muslim fleet won its first glorious victory in 655, in the battle of Phoenix on the Lician coast, or Dhat as-Sawari as it is called in Arab historiography. A Syrio-Egyptian squadron under the command of 'Abdallah, according to some sources, or under some less famous admiral according to others, completely defeated the Byzantine fleet under Emperor Constans himself. The outbreak of civil war soon after this battle called a halt to the Arabs' nascent dominion at sea, which in any case never developed into unrivalled supremacy over the Mediterranean. We will follow its subsequent annals in the Arab invasions of Spain, France and Italy, but we should mention its beginnings in the newly conquered Syrian and Egyptian provinces. We do not intend to study the individual histories of these provinces after Arab dominion had been established. However, the conquests and later histories of the Arabs in Egypt and North Africa are so different from each other that we would do well to give some consideration to the Arab regime in the Nile Valley at this stage.

Unlike Iraq and Syria, which were both Semitic by race, and had had large Arab populations even before the conquest, the country, race and language of Egypt were wholly alien to the invaders. However, with the course of centuries, the two-fold process of assimilation, ethnic and racial on the one hand and religious and cultural on the other, has made so profound an impact on Egypt that both west and east have long regarded it as completely arabicised and almost completely islamised. The process of arabisation was carried out by the various contingents of immigrants, mainly southern Arabs, who came to swell the small numbers of the first invaders. The nomads gradually settled on the land, and mixed with the Egyptians, modifying their ethnic make-up, but also assuming some Egyptian physical characteristics, which are still recognisable today. Arabic gained ground quickly, and came to be used even by Christians, making Coptic an almost exclusively religious language. At first both Greek and Arabic were used as official languages, but Greek finally gave way. After a couple of centuries, the ethnic and cultural arabisation of the country had become an accomplished fact, though, of all the various Muslim dynasties who ruled Egypt after the collapse of the Caliphate, only the Fatimids can be regarded as purely Arab from an ethnic point of view. At first a Persian and then a more Turkish flavour – according to the nationality of the ruling class – prevailed over the purely Arab race and language implanted by the conquerors. All in all, Egyptian Arabism has retained some aspects and characteristics *sui generis*, and modern Egyptians either emphasise or reject them, according to the ideological climate of the moment. For example, 'pharaohism' has emphasised the country's indigenous aspects, in its attempt to prove that the Nile Valley has a continuous native race, history and civilisation. Supporters of Panarabism, however, deny the continued existence of a pre-Arab tradition, as they wish to make Egypt the leading state in the Arab resurgence.

Related to but distinct from the process of ethnic and linguistic assimilation is the process of religious and cultural assimilation. Islam was not imposed by force, but grew in strength automatically in time with the irruption, and for the economic and social reasons already examined. It did not immediately reach its present-day overwhelming majority (over ninety per cent of the population) over the Christian minority. Apart from questions of language, the Copts stubbornly defended their religious and to a certain extent their national characteristics in the first centuries. They retained their place in the administration, which often caused protests and riots among the Muslim population. Hard pressed by the burden of taxation, the Copts staged some bloody revolts, as in the time of Caliph al-Ma'mun (early ninth century); but they never succeeded in making their struggle for survival part of an anti-Arab or anti-Islam movement. Moreover, the conquerors'

tolerance, quite generous to start with, gradually diminished, reaching a limit of extreme severity under the Ayyubites and Mamelukes. From that time, Muslim Egypt took on a decidedly hostile, suspicious attitude towards its Christian minority, an attitude which still persists today in less overt forms.

Finally, on the cultural side, Islamic Egypt made almost no contributions to the first flowering of Arab literary civilisation, which had its focal points in Syria and Iraq. It only began to assume its own original form under the Fatimids, and historians are now studying its part in the general framework of medieval Islamic culture. Its contribution became pre-eminent in subsequent periods of history, when the Nile Valley became the centre of Arab-Islam culture, with the decadence and eventual collapse of Abbasid civilisation. ‘Amr ibn al-‘As's far-off conquest has left

Early textiles, silk tapestry woven on single linen
warps in linen cloth. *Left*: part of a garment, from
al-'Azam, Upper Egypt, Tulunid, l te ninth century.
Below: fragment with inscription referring to the Abbasid
Caliph al-Muti' (946–74), probably Egyptian, dated 968.
Victoria and Albert Museum, London.

a permanent fruitful legacy in Egypt's cultural supremacy, which
has lasted from the time of the Ayyubites and Mamelukes until
the present day.

As is well known, many Egyptian papyrus documents have been
preserved, and, supplemented by literary sources, they provide
material for modern scholars to investigate the country's history,
including that of the early Arab period. We can form a reconstruction of the economic and administrative history of the first Arab
period from papyrus documents in Arabic and Greek: they present
a first-hand picture, unique in the countries conquered by the Arabs,
of the relationship between the conquerors and their subjects and
of the system of taxation and social patterns. As in other countries,
the Arabs apparently preserved the general structure of the previous
Byzantine administration, and its terminology was only partly

translated or transliterated into Arabic (Ar. *kura* for Greek
pagarchia, *qarya* for *kome*, *mawazit* for *meizoteroi* or *meizones*, and
so on). They clarified the nature and mechanism of the numerous
different taxes, the conquerors' main preoccupation in the early
period. The whole tributary mechanism, as seen at its original
source, differs on many points from the theory of the classic
system of Muslim law, which shows how chary we should be
of generalising this theory and applying it to the whole ancient Arab
empire.

Uqba's ride to the Atlantic

As we have seen, the conquest of Egypt did not cost the Arabs
much time or much effort. The conquest of North Africa is a very
different story, owing to the vastness of the country, the paucity
of the conquerors' forces, and the violent resistance the native
population offered before finally submitting to Arab rule and
Islam. The Berbers, Libyans and Numids, who had given Carthage
and Rome so much trouble in earlier history, were the main par-
ticipants in the conflict which lasted for over a century in spite of the
successful large-scale raids and reconnoitres which preceded
definitive conquest. In the mid-sixth century Belisarius had re-
gained imperial sovereignty from the Vandals, but in many
areas the Byzantines were only masters in name, and their resistance was in general weak, sporadic and ineffectual. Had the Arabs
not encountered stubborn resistance from the natives, they would
have gained possession of the Maghrib in a considerably shorter
time.

As we have seen, even before the definitive conquest of Alexandria, 'Amr started operations in the west, effecting the surrender of
Barca in 643. All of the Greek Pentapolis fell peacefully to the Arabs
at the same time or soon after, and it became Muslim Egypt's
bastion for defence against the west. At about the same time the
Arabs began making small-scale forays in the area beyond Syrte,
penetrating as far as Tripoli on the coast, and to Waddan, Fezzan

and Zawila in the interior. 'Uqba ibn Nafi', the future conqueror and saint of North Africa fought his first battles in these campaigns. However it was not until after the conquest of Egypt had been completed that 'Abdallah ibn Abi Sarh organised a full-scale expedition. An Arab army moved through Tripolitania in 647 without meeting any serious resistance, and reached the Roman province of Africa (which the Arabs called Ifriqiya), present-day Tunisia. At Sbeitla (formerly Suffetula), they encountered Byzantine forces under Gregory the Patrician. (Gregory had staged a rebellion at Byzantium shortly before, and was thinking of founding an independent power of his own.) The Arabs won the battle and Gregory was killed, but the expedition withdrew for the time being, satisfied with a large payment of tribute.

A new phase, the basis for regular occupation, began more than ten years later when Caliph Mu'awiya appointed 'Amr governor of Egypt for the last time. 'Amr's nephew, 'Uqba ibn Nafi' was the hero and leader of the Arab advance: he had already shown signs of his bold independent qualities in the earlier forays. Acting first under his uncle, and then under one of the first autonomous governors of Africa, whom he eventually succeeded, 'Uqba began the real conquest of Tripolitania and Ifriqiya between 663 and 670. In 670 he founded the city-camp of Qairawan in Ifriqiya, which later became the capital of the Maghrib. However, his bold proud character made him more suited to active service than to the task of careful consolidation after conquest. A more suitable man for such work was his successor Abu 'l-Muhajir, who was sent from Egypt to replace him for some years. Unlike 'Uqba, Abu 'l-Muhajir was able to conciliate the rebellious Berbers of Ifriqiya and their leader Kusaila: he did this so successfully that they joined the Arab cause and went to battle against the Byzantines of Carthage for the first time. Though he had not yet subdued the capital of the province, he continued the penetration towards the north, reaching Tlemcen, in present-day western Algeria (675). But 'Uqba reappeared on the scene in 680: again appointed commander of Africa by the new Caliph Yazid, the great guerilla soldier began his epic incursion from Qairawan to the west, dragging his hated predecessor behind him in chains. 'Uqba's famous 'march to the sea' did not only follow the coastline, but went through Baghaya and Tahert into the Algerian interior, and then to the Rif and Tangier. From there he went into the southern interior through Volubilis (Walila) crossing the Atlas ridge, and reached the ocean north of Agadir. There he rode into the sea, exclaiming 'My God, I call you to witness that if my advance were not stopped by the sea I would go still further.' He then returned, going north-east. Naturally, the country he had left behind was not really conquered, only raided, a breeding-ground for rebellion which soon broke out under the Berber leader Kusaila. On his way back to Ifriqiya through the African interior, 'Uqba divided his army – anyway a small one – into detachments, and he was surrounded at Tahuda near Biskra by overwhelming rebel troops. 'Uqba ended there his fantastic ride with a hero's death in 683. He fell in battle, and all his men and his prisoner-rival died with him. Abu 'l-Muhajir refused to be released from his chains at the last moment: 'I will come into the sight of God in my chains,' he may have said, though in another version he died fighting. In the eyes of posterity, 'Uqba is given sole credit for the Muslim conquest of the Maghrib: he was really only an impetuous raider and outrider, and other men, such as the obscure Abu 'l-Muhajir and the worthy and cautious Hassan ibn an-Nu'man played a less spectacular but more valuable part in the systematic penetration and pacification of the country.

Now that the brilliant Arab leader was dead, every conquest west of Syrte was thrown into the balance. Berbers and Byzantines made common cause and forced the Arabs to evacuate Qairawan. For the next few years, Kusaila and his Berbers made raids through the interior of Ifriqiya, and the urban centres which still had Byzantine populations and governors ruled themselves in what really amounted to total autonomy. In the east, the distant Caliphate of Damascus was engaged in the civil wars, but even before defeating the anti-Caliph Ibn az-Zubair, the Umayyad 'Abd al-Malik saw to the restoration of Muslim dominion in Africa. A

Syrian governor Zuhair led an attack on the Berbers, and Kusaila was killed in a battle near Qairawan in 688, or even 685. The city was recaptured, and soon the energetic and wise Hassan ibn an-Nu'man arrived there with reinforcements from Damascus; as governor, he to some extent consolidated the Arab presence in Africa. Like Abu 'l-Muhajir, Hassan aimed at separating the Berbers from the Byzantines, at subjecting the cities held by the latter, and winning the natives over to the Arab cause, through Islam. In 697, Carthage, the hitherto impregnable capital of the province, finally fell to the Arabs. It was taken back briefly by a Byzantine fleet, but the Arabs definitively reoccupied it, reaffirming their superiority at sea, in summer 698. The next serious danger the conquerors encountered was the revolt of the Berber '*Kahina*', a brave and heroic 'prophetess' who managed to unite her co-nationals under her, routing Hassan's Arabs on the river Nini on the slopes of the Awras. However in 701 she was finally defeated and put to death. Throughout the extremely uncertain chronology of these wars, we are made to realise beyond all doubt what a valuable contribution the Arab governor made to the pacification of the country. He succeeded in bringing the previously hostile masses into the orbit of Islam, and he made an alliance with them against the remaining Greek resistance movements and their own pagan co-nationals. 'Uqba's ride had passed like a tornado through the centre and west of the Maghrib, and only at this time under Hassan ibn an Nu'man's new policy did they begin to be won over to Arabism and Islam. Musa ibn Nusair carried on Hassan's policy from 705; he is principally famous for the conquest of Spain, but no less deserving for his peaceful governorship of Africa.

However, even after these first steps towards order at the beginning of the eighth century, serious trials still beset Arab dominion of the Maghrib, particularly in the westernmost regions of Ifriqiya proper. After Spain had been conquered and annexed to the gigantic complex of the Muslim Empire, more furious Berber revolts broke out in Morocco, threatening Arab supremacy on the whole coast of the Maghrib, during Hisham's caliphate (724–743). The disastrous rout of Sebu was a blow from which direct rule over the far Maghrib of the Damascus Caliphate was apparently unable to recover. The following year by a supreme effort the Arabs defeated the Berber offensive in the victories of al-Qarn and al-Asnam, and though they saved Ifriqiya for Damascus, they do not seem to have re-established the central authority as far as the Atlantic. The Syrian Caliphate held effective dominion over the whole of the Maghrib only for a few decades: however, though the Maghrib soon seceded in political terms and branched off to make her own history separately from the rest of the Muslim world, North Africa as a whole had been included in the religious, social and cultural horizon of Islam.

North Africa: bridgehead of Islam

Historians have estimated that about a hundred and fifty thousand Arab soldiers went to Africa in the various different stages of the conquest. If we include their families, and what may be termed the civil elements (officials, merchants, missionaries) the total number of Arabs is still something in the order of a few hundred thousand men. The Arab population was not increased until the invasion or immigration of the Banu Sulaim and Banu Hilal in the eleventh century, which anyway had disastrous effects on North Africa's economic and social life. Thus a relatively small stratum of Arabs gained ascendancy over the Berber race, and succeeded in effecting a radical change in the language and culture, the religion and civilisation of those enormous lands. The Latin and to a lesser extent Greek flavours which had characterised the north African coast for centuries quickly vanished from the country. African Latinism had been falling into decadence since the time of the Vandals, and the Arab invasion dealt it a mortal blow. Only the most tenuous corrupt traces of it survived, and can be found in coins and tomb epigraphs and in geographers' and travellers' stories until the tenth or eleventh centuries. The Arab invaders' language, culture and faith replaced the Latin in the country of Tertullian and Augustine. As we have seen, the Berbers at first fought back proudly: but after their initial violent resistance they finally submitted, and accepted Islam and the accompanying Arab language and culture. They had no alternative of their own to oppose to them, beyond their rough dialects and the undeveloped seeds of a popular literature. As has rightly been pointed out, the arabisation of North Africa was not a racial phenomenon so much as a cultural one. At the approach of the invaders, most of the Latin Christian population migrated from the urban centres, leaving the field to the Arabs, who were numerically inferior, but intellectually and technically superior to the vast primitive native population. The superiority of the few gained ascendancy over the barbarity of the many. Historians have examined the early history of the Muslim Maghrib in the hopes of finding the key to the process by which the Berbers were assimilated to the faith and culture of their conquerors. It has been noted that the native Africans provided a fertile breeding-ground for some of ancient Islam's heretical doctrines, such as the Kharijite movement, traces of which still exist today in Tunisia and Tripolitania. It has also been noted that the Shi'a was very successful among the Idrisids of Morocco in the ninth century, and the Fatimids of Ifriqiya (who subsequently came to power in Egypt) in the tenth. However, at a fairly early stage, these heterodoxical troubles gave way to a rigid orthodoxy and a fanatically scrupulous attachment to the more formal aspects of Islamic Law, as is shown principally in Africa west of Egypt by the Malikite school of law and ritual.

Arabic soon became the first language of the Maghrib, and so the people were ready for the influence of superior Arab culture. The conquerors' new urban centres, such as Qairawan in Tunisia and later Fez in Morocco played an important role in this process. The Maghrib brought Arab civilisation a rich harvest in literary, legal, historical and artistic spheres, but it made few innovations in its eastern intellectual heritage, and never participated in the seminal philosophical arguments which arose in eastern Islam

The Great Mosque, Qairawan, Tunisia, general view
with the minaret. The original mosque was built
during the Umayyad period but several times
demolished and rebuilt; its present form dates from
the time of Ziyadat Allah in 836.

under the influence of the heritage of the Greeks, with thinkers
venturing into the realms of Hellenistic and Isma'ili gnosis and the
speculations and ecstasies of mysticism. Religious life in Muslim
Africa was very intense, and confraternities took root there to an
even greater extent than they did in the east; but piety, asceticism
and even thaumaturgy were far more prevalent than speculative
thought. In the twelfth century, the Almohad movement founded
by Ibn Tumart attempted to break down and reinvigorate the
Maghrib's religious formalism by bringing it into contact with the
theological ideas of Eastern Islam. However this movement's
success was political rather than religious, which defeated its
original purpose. After Spain had been conquered by the Arabs,
it developed a brilliant school of philosophy, but its connections
with the African coast were purely extrinsic. In conclusion, with
the exception of its one genius Ibn Khaldun, the Maghrib made
only secondary, peripheral contributions to the main line of
Islam's philosophical and scientific thought. Africa's conversion
to Arabism and Islam had much more important results in the
political, religious, economic and social spheres. Even though
Africa soon lost any direct ties with the eastern Caliphate (in the
first half of the eighth century for the far Maghrib, in the ninth
century for Ifriqiya), the ever-present sense of Islamic solidarity
transcended physical distance and political divergences, making
Africa, once Latin and Christian, an active, sometimes even
aggressive and fanatical member of the Muslim community, and
an enemy of Christianity. The attack on Spain and Sicily in the
Early Middle Ages was launched from Africa, and in modern
times the Barbary piracy was sympathetic with and in a sense
dependent on the Ottoman Empire's struggle against Europe and
Christianity. The west responded with the expeditions from the
Italian seafaring republics, the Norman adventure in Africa, and,
in recent history, the short-lived colonisation of all of North
Africa. In the present phase of de-colonialisation, the series of
Arab-Islam states along the African coast testify – in spite of their
regional disputes and rivalries – the permanent value of Islam's

conquest of the country between the seventh and eighth centuries. Destroying the heritage of Rome, Islam directed Africa towards a wholly different destiny. Whatever the qualitative difference between the two civilisations may be, it is significant that Roman civilisation, like the Greek and Punic before it, had only a superficial effect on Africa, on a limited élite and on a limited coastal area. Only Arab Islam plumbed the depth of the country and its people: this is perhaps the secret of its success.

10 Islam in Europe: Spain, France and Italy

The conquest of Spain

The Arab conquest of Spain, which was to make such a valuable contribution to the history of civilisation, was an accidental by-product of the conquest of North Africa. Even its leaders did not really mean it to happen, and had little control over its progress. The distant Damascus Caliph had certainly given no orders for the new venture, and at first regarded it with a rather apprehensive eye, though he subsequently legitimised the conquest and placed the new territory under his supreme authority as far as it lay in his power to do so. The conquests in Central Asia and the Andalusian enterprise were the high tide of Arab power and expansion under the Umayyad caliphate. A few decades later, the huge unitary empire was to crumble and collapse, and, after their downfall in the east, the Umayyads were to take refuge in the most distant province of Spain, and revive their glory there.

Two Muslim conquerors were principally responsible for the invasion and rapid conquest of Visigoth Spain. One, Musa ibn Nusair, was a pure Arab, and the other, Tariq ibn Ziyad, came from a Berber family converted to Islam several generations previously. Musa had come from the east, and as governor of Africa for the first decade of the eighth century had carried on Hassan ibn an-Nu'man's work of subjugating and pacifying the far Maghrib. The expedition of 'Uqba ibn Nafi' had provided a background for consolidation of the Maghrib by these men as a secure Arab possession. Once Musa had secured Tangier, he had left Tariq (a *mawla* or freed slave) there as his lieutenant, and he himself had gone back to Qairawan in Ifriqiya, then the capital of all Muslim North Africa. Tariq felt that the Iberian coast opposite Tangier was inviting him to continue the conquests by sea, as 'Uqba had wished to do on reaching the Atlantic. The Berber general received further encouragement from 'Count Julian' of nearby Ceuta on the coast of Africa. Julian is a character of whom much is told in legend but little in history. Even his name appears to be in doubt (though it does seem to have been Julian and not

Expansion under the Umayyads

GALICIA

PORTUGAL

LEON

CASTILE

Poitiers

Bordeaux

Autun

Nîmes

Carcassonne

Aix

Narbonne

Saragossa

Genoa

St Tropez

Barcelona

CORSICA

BALEARIC ISL.

SARDINIA

Palermo

Carthage

SICILY Messina

Qairawan

CRETE

CYPRUS

Mediterranean Sea

Black

Constantinople

Islam before 656

Acquired by 750

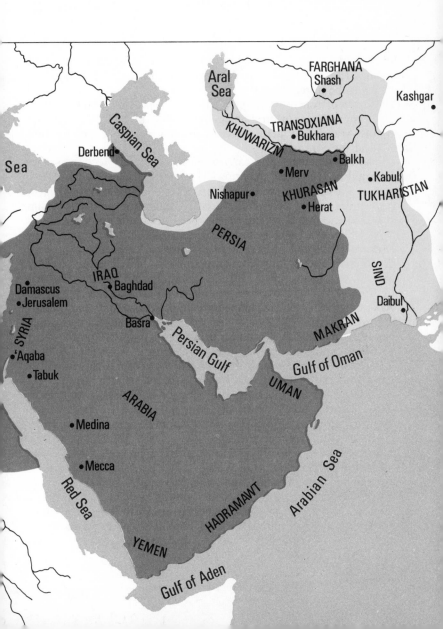

Urban, as has been suggested), as also his race (Berber, Visigoth or Byzantine) and his relationship with the Visigoth kingdom of Spain. The story of King Rodrigo's seduction of his daughter seems to be purely legendary; it is more likely that some political grievance or scheme prompted this man – possibly the Byzantine governor of Ceuta (a surviving Greek enclave in the land conquered by the Arabs) – to incite and abet the conquerors in their venture beyond the Straits.

The Berber chief Tariq carried out a preliminary reconnaissance in a raid of 710. Then, in spring 711, Tariq himself took the fateful step of crossing the straits with an army of seven thousand men, mostly his fellow Berber converts to Islam. He landed in Spain near the mountain which was to bear his name for ever (Jebel Tariq, Gibraltar). According to certain sources, Tariq's superior Musa had worked out the plan of invasion with Julian, and we do not know exactly what instructions he had received. In any case, Musa authorised the invasion, and obtained an unenthusiastic approval from Caliph al-Walid. As in so many of the other Arab conquests, the first immediate objectives were raid and plunder, which could lead to conquest and occupation if circumstances were favourable. Circumstances proved even more favourable than predicted, and took the bold Berber lieutenant much further than his superior had envisaged – which explains the subsequent clash between the two men responsible for Islam's entry into Europe.

Once again, the invaders' fiery energy was directed against a state in crisis: the Visigoth kingdom was weakened by dynastic disputes, economic difficulties and discontent among its subjects. Rodrigo, who had become king the previous year, was widely considered to have usurped his throne from the pretender Akhila, the son of Witiza, the last legitimate king. Legitimist intrigues are thought to have favoured and perhaps even instigated the Arab invasion. On hearing news of the landing, Rodrigo came down from the north, and mobilised troops from Cordoba and Medina Sidonia to drive the invaders back into the sea. After receiving reinforcements, Tariq left Julian at Algeciras, the base for eventual re-embarkation and marched north-north-westwards to meet the enemy. The decisive battle took place on 19 July, 711, near the Lake of Janda on the banks of the River Barbate (the Wadi Bakka or Lakko as Arab sources call it) south of Medina Sidonia; the defection of Akhila's relations and supporters meant disaster for Rodrigo; his defeat is described and embroidered with pathetic imaginative touches in Spanish *romances* of many centuries later. The Visigoth kingdom's effective organised resistance collapsed with the defeat. Rodrigo narrowly escaped capture and disappeared from the political scene to die in obscurity soon after. Some years later his effigy was included among those of conquered kings doing homage to the Caliph in an Umayyad castle in Jordania. After the battle of Lake Janda, as in Persia after Nihawand, the Arabs only had to deal with the resistance of individual cities and individual minor leaders. From a practical point of view the enemy dynasty and state no longer existed.

Encouraged by the victory, Tariq rushed forward on the now open road to the north: having forced his way over the Genil at Ecija, dispersing what was left of the Visigoth army, he besieged Cordoba (which held out against his lieutenant Mughith until October) and set off directly for the capital Toledo. What with reinforcements from Spanish troops who had rebelled against the Visigoths, the support and help of the Jews, and the collapse of any organised enemy power, civil or ecclesiastical, this was a triumphal march. Deserted by the Primate, and most of its Christian population, the Visigoth capital on the Tagus opened its gates without resistance. Swept along by the impetus of his success, Tariq pressed farther north from Toledo, perhaps to Guadalajara, and later to Amaya in the province of Burgos: in these first lightning campaigns he touched what would later be the northern boundary of Muslim Spain's established territory.

When news of his lieutenant's amazing success reached Musa in Africa, he decided to go to Spain himself. His motive was probably not mere petty jealousy, as tradition too strongly implies; he probably felt that his help was necessary for military and political reasons in the extension and completion of the conquest. In June 712, at the head of eighteen thousand men, this time mostly Arabs, the old governor of Africa disembarked at Algeciras and began his own campaigns: his task was to consolidate the Arab position, leaving garrisons in individual cities, following in the wake of Tariq's lightning incursion as he had done in the Maghrib after 'Uqba. Musa's advance followed a more westerly route than Tariq's: he occupied Medina Sidonia, Carmona, Alcala de Guadaira and Seville without much difficulty, and then attacked Merida. Here he met stubborn resistance, the town only falling in June 713 after several months of siege. From there he went towards Toledo, and met his lieutenant at Talavera. He reprimanded him severely for having conquered too much without orders.

Musa spent the winter of 713–4 in the occupied city of Toledo. He had coins struck there and some have been preserved to this day in Spain and Africa. They bear the inscription '*amir Muse filius Nusir*' – the conqueror's name in Latin – and the Muslim statement of faith. The spring and summer of 714 saw the surrender of Saragossa, and a joint expedition of the two captains. Musa went through the Ebro Valley to the Asturias, Oviedo and Gijon, and Tariq, following a roughly parallel but more northerly route, went to Laon and Astorga. In these incursions to the foot of the Cantabrian Mountains and even beyond, the leaders reached lands which were never to be subjugated under regular Muslim dominion but would rather become bases for the future Christian 'Reconquista'. However, for the time being and for some time to come – for as long as Islam was on the offensive in Andalusia – these areas were laid waste by irregular raids, as had happened in Anatolia. But Musa and Tariq were now at the end of their work. The Caliph had sent messages ordering them both to return east, to report on the new conquest. In September 714, Musa left Spain for ever, entrusting the governorship of the country to his son 'Abd al-'Aziz. He set out on the long journey, which according to some he had dreamed of making entirely overland leading his victorious army home through a conquered Islamic Europe. In fact he returned the way he had come, through Africa and Egypt, with Tariq and a huge convoy of Berber chiefs and Spanish prisoners and a large booty of slave-girls and treasure. When Musa finally reached Syria (February 715) Caliph al-Walid was dying, and his successor gave the hero of the Spanish campaigns the same kind of welcome as Musa himself had given his victorious lieutenant. Deprived of their rank, and subjected to more or less well-founded financial impositions, the two conquerors of Andalusia ended their days in the east in complete obscurity. Unlike Khalid and Tariq, Musa's end has inspired various poets: a modern example is 'L`Apothéose de Mouça al-Kebyr' in Leconte de Lisle's Poèmes Tragiques. Popular Arab tradition (as in the City of Bronze in the Thousand and One Nights) records the conqueror of Spain rather as a character of magical adventure, a finder of talismans and treasures.

'Abd al-'Aziz, who had been left in charge of Spain by his father Musa, was only governor for a year and a half, from September 714 to March 716. It seems that Caliph Sulaiman doubted his loyalty and had him assassinated in Seville. However, we know that in this short period, he extended and consolidated the conquest, with offensive expeditions either led by him in person, or assigned to his captains: one of the first expeditions went into present-day Portugal, taking Evora, Santarem and Coimbra, and another went into eastern Andalusia, taking Malaga and Elvira, future Granada. 'Abd al-'Aziz (or his father, if the date 713 is correct) made a treaty with Theodomir the Visigoth lord of Murcia, guaranteeing him protection and friendship. The text of the treaty has been preserved: it grants the Christians of Murcia peace and freedom of religion in return for the surrender of seven cities, and a payment of tribute in money and goods. The little tributary state did not long remain autonomous: it was soon incorporated into Islamic territory, and given the name Tudmir in memory of its former lord. 'Abd al-'Aziz continued the Arab offensive northward to the Pyrenees, conquering Pamplona on the west, and Tarragona, Barcelona, Gerona and other places on the east. Musa's son's internal policy seems to have been one of tolerance and reconciliation towards the conquered people of Spain. He is thought to have married Rodrigo's widow, Aila or Egilona, which is perhaps how he aroused the suspicions of the Caliph and his own companions. His violent death closed the initial phase of the conquest, the phase associated with his father Musa and Tariq. The next forty years saw an agitated period of adjustment for Arab Spain, and the situation was not stabilised until the founding of the Umayyad Emirate.

As a conclusion to the history of the completion of the conquest we should now summarise the salient characteristics of the first European country to be converted to Islam. Spain was always regarded as a dependency of Africa, and theoretically its governors were simply the envoys of the governor of Qairawan. Owing to the dramatic turn of events on both sides of the straits in the first half of the eighth century, the emissaries in Spain often actually ruled in total autonomy, even showing signs of open hostility to their lawful superiors in Africa. Moreover, radical disagreements often arose between the Arab and the Berber groups who had gone to Spain from Africa with the first two leaders, subsequently to be joined by other immigrants. They quarrelled over the manner of continuing the conquest and the division and exploitation of booty: the antagonism between the two ethnic groups, which had made the conquest of Africa so difficult, and was to cause its downfall in about 740, had violent repercussions in Spain. The Spanish Berbers were dissatisfied with the inferior status given them in the assignation of official posts after the conquest, and in 740, in response to the great anti-Arab Berber insurrection in Africa in the same year, they rose up in their turn, massacred the Arabs and threatened Cordoba, the capital of the province, with a march converging on it. Ever since the rout of Sebu, Syrian Arab contingents had been stationed in Ceuta, and they had previously offered their services to the governor of Spain but had always been refused. 'Abd al-Malik ibn Qatan was now forced to accept their help to ward off the Berber menace, and the forces crossed the straits and defeated the rebels on the Wadi Salit near Toledo. Thus they saved Arab supremacy in Spain, but introduced a new element of discord between the old and new immigrants to Andalusia, derived from the ancient genealogical hostility between the north and southern groups of Arab tribes (Qais and Yemenites). The original group of Arab invaders who had arrived with Musa and now considered themselves 'natives' (*baladiyyun*) were mainly southern Arabs, whereas the newly-arrived 'Syrians' (*Shamiyyun*) with their leader Balj were Qaisites: thus even the Arabs were divided among themselves. This situation produced fierce struggles and bloody battles (at Aqua Portora in 742, and Secunda in 747, both victories for the Qaisites) between the two parties. Governors alternated in chaotic succession, sometimes nominated from Africa but more frequently chosen on the spot by the winning party of the moment. The Qaisite Yusuf al-Fihri, aided by his fellow tribesman and *éminence grise* Sumail, was the last of the twenty or so who succeeded each other between 'Abd al-Aziz and the arrival of the Umayyad 'Abd ar-Rahman. After ruling for some years in the turbulent period which saw the collapse of the Umayyads in the east and the outbreak of anarchy in Africa, Yusuf was defied by the strong, capable young prince of Syria, who had fled to the far west to avoid sharing the extermination of his family. In Spring 756, this 'Abd ar-Rahman ad-Dakhil ('the immigrant') defeated Yusuf in battle at Cordoba, having cleverly won the support of the southern Arabs in spite of being himself a Qaisite. He gained unquestioned supremacy and inaugurated the Emirate, later the Caliphate of Spain, the most glorious chapter of Arab dominion in the Peninsula.

During this troubled period, in spite of the fierce internal conflicts and vendettas, the Spanish Arabs succeeded in carrying on the holy war with the infidels on the flexible boundaries of Muslim territory. They pressed northwards into the regions of Old Castile and the Asturias, already reached in Tariq's and Musa's lightning raids, and they overran the Pyrenees to both east and west. However they never succeeded in occupying the whole peninsula, and perhaps they never even tried to. The territory under firm Arab rule was enclosed on the west by the Douro as far as about Osma, and the boundary then swerved north to the upper course of the Ebro in the zone of Alava; from here it went through Calahorra and Tudela, Huesca and Barbastro and Lerida (all these towns were in Arab hands) and in the Umayyad period reached the sea south of Barcelona. The Arabs only held Barcelona for about ninety years (714–801). They reached these boundaries half way through the eighth century at the height of their internal crisis, when the Christian resurgence later to destroy their frontier was already taking its first timid steps down from the north. The Christians' final resistance to the invasion became the starting point for the resurgence movement. Its beginnings are conventionally dated from the semi-legendary episode of Covadonga in 718, when Pelayo checked the Arabs from his refuge in the Asturias. This episode belongs to mythology, almost one might say to hagiography, but we know more of the achievements of Pelayo's second successor Alfonso I (739–57). When the Berbers had been defeated in the civil war and starved out of the regions north of the Douro, he took advantage of their departure and pressed forward to occupy the area they had evacuated, unchallenged. Thus Galicia and present-day northern Portugal, the southern slopes of the Cantabrian mountains, and Old Castile as far as Alava were withdrawn from the Muslim area and came to swell the nucleus of re-emergent Christian Spain.

On these beginnings the Reconquest made no further progress for some time: after the period of anarchy, the unitary Umayyad state emerged in Arab Spain, and for another two centuries it was to constitute a bulwark preventing the Christians from making any further headway to the south. Until soon after the year 1000 it was still the Arabs' turn to take the offensive beyond the boundaries, raising the victorious flag of Islam well within Christian territory (as in Almansor's sack of the shrine of Santiago de Compostela in 997) but these plundering raids did not 'hold' the country and the kingdoms of Castilia and Leon, Navarre and

Aragon still remained as an expandable firm crescent around the north and north-eastern frontiers of Muslim Andalusia. The theme of our study does not include the history of the Christian counter-offensive which undid the work of Tariq and Musa, gradually pushing the Arabs back southward to the final stronghold of Granada. In the period of Muslim ascendancy, we should note that no further conquests were made after the astonishingly rapid initial successes – the Arabs spread from Gibraltar to the Pyrenees and the Atlantic in three years, and Islam later made no further permanent land gains here. But though occupation and its accompanying civilisation and culture halted on the boundaries we have described above, the Islamic military advance continued unabated to threaten other European Christian countries, matching the gigantic tide of *jihad* in the east. After Spain, France tasted the last waves of the turbulent diaspora which had been born in the heart of Arabia less than a hundred years before.

France, Italy and Sicily

The Spanish Arabs in no way regarded the Pyrenees as an insurmountable obstacle. Even before consolidating the conquest of Spain they had made raids across territories which they were never to occupy, such as Navarre and Aragon, and soon penetrated into what is now France. An Arab historian puts 714 as the date at which Tariq first started sending columns of outriders beyond Catalonia, through Roussillon and Septimania as far as Avignon and even Lyons. Arabs from Barcelona and Gerona may have taken, indeed retaken. Narbonne under 'Abd al-'Aziz. However they did not make a secure lasting occupation of this city until 720, under governor al-Samh ibn Malik – he also attempted to take Toulouse but failed – and it was then that the Arabs began their twenty or thirty-year rule of the capital of Septimania. Ruins of what is presumed to be a mosque have recently been found in Narbonne, which would be evidence of Arab rule in the area. Narbonne then became a base for subsequent incursions into the Rhône Valley, and only in 759 (751, as some modern critics believe) did Pippin win it back from the Arabs. One of the most important forays of the period took place in 725, under al-Samh's successor, 'Anbasa ibn Suhaim. He took Carcassonne and Nîmes and went up the Rhône and Saone into Bourgogne, reaching as far as Autun.

The Arabs came up against local resistance in all of these forays, but only on a couple of occasions did they encounter the regular armies of feudal lords subject to the declining Merovingian monarchy. The first they met was Duke Eudes of Aquitaine, who saved Toulouse from invasion in 721. Eudes and Charles Martel, the Merovingian *maire de palais* to whom he appealed for help, were the leading figures in the halt of the Muslim advance at the Battle of Poitiers in 732, the most famous episode of all these campaigns. The initiative for this incursion came from the western Pyrenees, under the command of 'Abd ar-Rahman al-Ghafiqi, governor of Spain. The invaders defeated Eudes near the confluence of the Dordogne and the Garonne, and sacked Bordeaux. They then went on northward, through Angoulême and Poitiers, making for Tours, whose rich churches and monasteries must have been a tempting bait. But before they arrived, they were confronted by Charles's forces. The famous encounter took place at the end of October 732, by a Roman road about twelve miles north-east of Poitiers (perhaps near present-day Moussais-la-Bataille). The importance of this encounter has been exaggerated beyond its due proportions to make it a symbol of the halt of the Arabs in the west. From the Christian angle it was really no more than a successful suppression of a raid for pillage and plunder, itself no different from any other raid of the period. But, with the advantage of hindsight, posterity has pinpointed the defeat of the Muslims on the Roman 'Way of Martyrs' (*balat ash-shuhada* as the Arabs call it) as the turning-point of the floodtide which seemed to be threatening to encroach on and submerge all Christian Europe. In fact, the tide of Arab power ebbed of its own accord, because the people who had scattered out into such an enormous diaspora had exhausted their capacities for demographic expansion and stable conquest. However, their capacities for destruction and pillage were by no means exhausted, as the later history of Saracen incursions into France can prove. Even after the battle of Poitiers (as soon as 734 they were attacking Saint Remi and Avignon from Narbonne in Provence) and after the epic Roncesvalles (in which, as is well known, the Saracens had really no part), they went on harrying Provence and the Delphinate, between the end of the ninth and tenth centuries.

Muslim Spain was not the instigator or organiser of the second phase of the Arab forays into France, as she had been in the eighth century. As in the incursions into Italy, which were carried out at the same time, the initiative came spontaneously from individual and collective Muslim groups, beyond the control of any 'state initiative'. Inspired both by the religious duty of *jihad* and the lure of booty, and confident in their newly-acquired naval experience and the long-familiar practice of guerilla war, random bands of pirates and plunderers (Arabs, Berbers and some renegade Europeans) mustered and acted on their own initiative, usually without showing what authority they were obeying, or of which Islamic state they were agents. Thus in 890 the first nucleus of the Saracen bands came by sea (either from Spain, Africa or Sicily, we do not know which) and settled at Saint Tropez on the coast of Provence, and on the near-by rock of Fraxinetum (possibly present-day Garde Frainet). They stayed there for almost a century, making raids on places such as Aix and Marseilles, in one direction, and over the Alpine passes into the Dauphiné and Savoy, Switzerland (Coira, San Gallo) and Piedmont in the other: the monasteries of Novalesa, Acqui and even Genoa suffered their deadly attacks, but were never able to discover exactly where they came from. In Arab historical sources there are almost no details on the scourge of the Muslim raids into France and Italy, as such activities were included in the normal practice of *bellum perpetuum* against the infidels, as laid down in the Koran, and only more permanent conquests are specified. It is rather among the lamentations of contemporary Latin chronicles and annals and in the records of abbeys and monasteries that we can distinguish some precise facts on the activities of the exile plunderers with their religious fanaticism and their greed for booty. In France they were not driven from their Alpine strongholds, such as the St Bernard, or their coastal centres, such as Fraxinetum, until the second half of the tenth century. Their activities in Italy are bound up with the Sicilian adventure, the last Arab conquest in the west.

Ever since the Arabs had first established their naval power in the Mediterranean under Mu'awiya and 'Abdallah ibn Abi Sarh, and had tested it in the conquest of North Africa, they had been making short-term raids into Sicily and Byzantine Southern Italy. But the idea of embarking on a systematic occupation of the island either had not occurred to them, or did not seem possible. They did not attempt such a venture until much later, by which time Ifriqiya was no longer a direct subject-province of the Caliphate but had become an independent emirate only nominally dependent on the Abbasids of Baghdad. The Aghlabid emir at Qairawan, Ziyadat Allah, took the decision for the Sicilian expedition, seeing it as a religious duty and perhaps as a diversion from internal difficulties. The Byzantine patrician Euphemius played a role comparable to Julian's in Spain, and Tariq's equivalent was Asad ibn al-Furat, no ordinary soldier, but a learned student of tradition, a jurist and religious fanatic. At the head of a small fleet, he disembarked at Mazara in June 827, with scarcely more than ten thousand Arabs and Berbers: he easily defeated a Byzantine commander, and advanced into the interior of eastern Sicily. In the next few years some of the principal towns of the island fell to the invaders (Palermo in 831, and Messina in 842), but they did not gain possession of the strongly defended Syracuse until 878, after a long siege. As usual, the Byzantines put up a poor defence, but the native Christian population resisted more energetically in some places, as in Taormina, which was not taken until 902. However, by the end of the ninth century virtually the whole of Sicily was in Arab possession. They transferred the capital to Palermo and had the island, which was soon converted to Islam, ruled first by Aghlabid governors, and then in the following century by the Fatimids, who had supplanted the Aghlabids in Africa. The Kalbid dynasty became Sicily's ruling family half way through the tenth century, and the governors became the virtually independent emirs of Sicily, though they were nominally subject first to Ifriqiya and later to Egypt, and sometimes co-operated with these countries in military ventures. Arab Sicily lasted until the Norman Reconquest in 1060, but little is known of its internal history. More is known of the emirs who alternated in the course of the conflicts and civil disorders at Palermo, and of the general anarchy which broke out half-way through the eleventh century, dividing the island among petty local princes and thereby facilitating the Norman invasion.

However, the Sicilian Arabs did not see the Straits of Messina as an obstacle to their advance, and they soon began to penetrate into Southern Italy, as the Spanish Arabs had into France a century earlier. They overran Calabria several times, on their way from Reggio (where they built a mosque, but like the one at Narbonne, it was soon destroyed), to Basilicata, Campania and Puglia. However, we must not imagine that all the Islamic forays into southern and central Italy came from Sicily; Africa, Crete, Spain, the coast of Provence and perhaps even Syria were embarkation points for raiding parties. When in 849 a Neapolitan fleet, summoned to defend Rome by Pope Leo IV, won a naval battle at Ostia, the Saracens defeated and taken prisoner there must have been of the most diverse origins – a fine example of Muslim solidarity. The Muslims succeeding in establishing two short-lived dominions on the Italian mainland, one in Bari (about 847–71) and the other in Taranto (850–80), and according to an Arab historian the former of these at least did not apply to the Emir of Sicily, nor to his overlord in Ifriqiya, but to the Abbasid Caliph of Baghdad for legitimisation of the conquest.

We know the names and something of the characters of the

leaders of this Barian emirate. They were firstly the Berber Khalfun, then a Mufarraj ibn Sallam, and lastly the brave wise Sawdan, who was taken prisoner by the prince of Benevento Arechi, when Emperor Louis' expedition put an end to Arab rule in Bari. However, we have virtually no information on the other emirate of Taranto. A third temporary Muslim foothold in Italy was the Saracen colony of Garigliano. A worthy sister of the colonies of Fraxinetum and Saint Tropez, her activity consisted entirely of raids and plunder until she was destroyed in 915. Raids and plunderings were particularly prevalent in the ninth century, but even in the tenth they touched virtually every part of Italy. From records and local chronicles we can reconstruct the full extent of the Islamic scourge from Arab Sicily in the south, and from the Alps down to Liguria in the north, while the vehement onslaughts of pirate fleets attacked the coastline of the whole Peninsula. In the eleventh century Mugetto (Mujahid in Arabic), the Muslim Lord of Denia and the Balearic Islands, sponsored an expedition against Sardinia. The island had already been raided several times but, contrary to general belief, never occupied by the Muslims. Then an energetic reaction started among the Italian maritime republics, who took offensive action as far as Africa, while the Normans reconquered Sicily, and thus the maritime raids were gradually checked. As is well known, the last remaining Arabs in Italy were those who went from Norman Sicily to Lucera: they were no longer conquerors but the last survivors of a conquered people, at first tolerated and then cruelly exterminated in 1300. By the time the Angevins, moved by arrogance and intolerance, destroyed the colony of Lucera, the 'Arab' hour in Italy had long been over and the Islamic scourge long since vanished from both land and sea.

The Islamic legacy in Europe

Although we should not credit the people of the Early Middle Ages with the sophistication and national awareness of much more advanced peoples, we are nonetheless tempted to ask whether any particular results ensued from this encounter between the Arabs and the European heirs of Roman culture. In North Africa the question does not arise, because, as we saw, the weak superficial Latin culture quickly disappeared, leaving the field to the Arabs and Islam and the uncivilised Berbers. The situation in Spain, France and Italy was quite different: here the Arab invaders came up against a deep-rooted civilisation, quite different from their own, which they could not overlook. No contact was made between the Arab and Latin civilisations in France or Gaul, since the Arabs were only there as raiders and were driven out before they could bring in the seeds of their own culture or way of life. But the seven-century Arab rule in Spain, and their two and a half centuries in Sicily (or three, including the Norman period) allowed time for a lasting investiture, an implantation of Arabism which was total in neither case but important in both, and permitted the development of a local Islamic civilisation influenced by the indigenous culture.

The two cultures merged for the longest time and to the greatest extent and depth in Spain, where Arab domination, far from being a temporary adventure, was an important ineradicable phase in the nation's history. The process of arabisation reached deepest in Spain, even though the African Berber ethnic group constituted a large proportion of the invading element. Conversions to Islam kept pace with the growth of Arabism: both Visigoths and Ibero-Romans became Muslims in large numbers (the Arabs called Spanish Muslims '*muwalladun*' and Christians who were arabicised in culture were '*musta'riba*' or '*mozarabs*'). But neither the process of arabisation or that of conversion to Islam succeeded in eliminating the country's previous faith, language or culture. Christianity survived the period of Arab rule, as did the Romance language or languages and to a lesser extent sacred and secular Latin culture. Christianity and its culture gradually gained strength and eventually triumphed with the Reconquest. The existence of two cultures within the one country, far from creating a rigid separation between the two, made for a rich cross-fertilisation of both. We now know that bilingualism in Arabic and the Romance language was common throughout the Arab age in Spain, not only in everyday life but even in literature, as recent discoveries have confirmed. A certain type of Arab verse poetry, characteristic of and fairly fashionable in the Peninsula, often had its last lines (*kharja*) written wholly or partly in the Romance language. Classical Arabic, in its turn eagerly studied by the Mozarabs, was translated into Latin, and similarly there are some fragments of Latin translations from the Arabic. This composite side of Andalusian Arabism's culture (which in other fields adhered strictly to eastern literary models, showing a marked tendency towards archaism and purism) prepared the way for the extremely fertile cultural symbiosis of the twelfth and thirteenth centuries: in that period, western scholars went to Spain almost as pilgrims of knowledge and Arab and Jewish interpreters introduced them to Greek and Arabic scientific and philosophical works, thus allowing them to be made known to Europe. The charming aspects of Moorish culture and art, so beloved of Romanticism, developed out of this intermingling of different languages and cultural traditions, a process which was more intense in Spain than anywhere else. If the value of Spanish Arabism is weighted heavily on the positive side in science and culture, both in the works it produced itself and in the intellectual heritage from other countries it preserved, opinion is divided on its religious and political worth both in respect of Islam and of Roman and European Spain. From the political point of view, it was a united independent state under the Umayyad Emirate and Caliphate, which embraced the whole of al-Andalus for two and a half centuries, and evolved its own active part in Mediterranean policy. Both before and after this glorious period, either anarchy reigned in Muslim Spain or the central rule was broken down into a number of small kingdoms (the Reinos de Taifas), and it finally came under foreign domination, not Arab-Spanish, but Berber-African (the Almoravids and Almohads). All this was finally brushed aside by the Christian Reconquest: fanatically intolerant, it drove out even those remaining Muslims (the Moriscos) who constituted a positive element in the economy, and with them vanished their high medieval civilisation. But the issue of intolerance brings us back to the question of a value-judgment on Arab dominion in Spain. In its best centuries, its internal policy was fairly tolerant, but it nonetheless lit the torch of religious discord and strife in the Peninsula, and according to some theories is responsible for the outbreaks of fanaticism and integralism which have dominated the subsequent history of Spain. According to some historians, the centuries-long war for unity and the Faith occasioned by the Arab invasion is still to blame for the delay in the political and social progress of modern Spain: a negative factor which would offset the important positive cultural aspect of the foreign régime. Even when this has been taken into consideration, the impartial observer cannot fail to realise that the long centuries of Arab dominion were a time of long-lasting glory for Arabism, and made a positive contribution to the general history of civilisation.

We cannot say as much for Arab dominion in Sicily, on account of its shorter duration and more restricted field. It is also because we have many fewer direct sources of information on the period of Arab dominion proper in Sicily than in Spain. Outside the main line of the conquest, and then not even under the governorship of Palermo, its economic, social and cultural history is to a large extent unknown to us. Amari, the greatest modern historian of the subject has collected and used every fragment of documentation available, but many problems still remain unsolved. In Amari's opinion, Muslim dominion in Sicily was on the whole productive, since it brought new blood to the island's crumbling Roman Byzantine society, improved its land system, and introduced new arts and cultures; but the fruits of these measures were not realised (or are not apparent to us), until the Norman period. In the broad framework of Islam the history of Arab Sicily remains, all in all, somewhat secondary and provincial, and it was considered as such by the Arabs themselves. Like France, the mainland of

Italy knew only the disasters and destructions wrought by the Arabs. Only some slight artistic influences from the world of Islam filtered through to southern Italy to compensate for all the devastations. However, as far as we can tell, Sicily enjoyed some of the material and spiritual advantages of the conquerors' civilisation, among them an intense religious and literary life (in these, as far as we can see, the island was influenced by the Maghrib and Spain), and a greater sophistication in court life. However, Latinism and Hellenism survived throughout the Arab period and, influenced by what was left of Arabism, blossomed in the brilliant culture of the Norman period. In their ethnic make-up, in their names and place-names, in some aspects of their agricultural system, and in their mentality and social customs the Sicilians reveal a lasting though not always wholesome legacy from the Arabs.

11 Frontiers to the East

The Arabs' hard-fought incursion into the Maghrib and invasion of Spain belong to the Umayyad period (660–750) after the close of the initial phase of the great conquests under Muhammad's first four successors. During the century of the Umayyad caliphate the Arabs extended their conquests in both east and west, and reached the final confines of the diaspora, propagating Islam as they went. Having followed their western advance until their arrival in Europe, we should now look to the opposite eastern border and trace the fortunes of the closing phase of Arab imperialism.

Their last advance eastward had two spearheads of attack, one towards Central Asia, the other towards India. The Indian conquest remained an isolated episode for the time being, but the former was a systematic follow-up to the previous eastern penetration and will therefore be the main topic of this chapter. In Chapter 7 we saw the Arabs achieve an almost total occupation of Persia in about 650, omitting only its coastal provinces south of the Caspian, and its eastern border-provinces of far Khurasan, Tukharistan and Bamiyan along the Oxus. The Arabs gradually occupied these areas in the second half of the seventh century (soon after 670 they reached the left bank of the Oxus and to the south occupied Balkh, the former religious and cultural capital of Tukharistan, present-day Afghanistan). In the same period the conquerors' vanguard even touched on Kabul and the Gandhara, but for some decades regular occupation did not go beyond the Oxus, the great river which Iranian tradition uses to mark the boundary between Iran and Turan; in fact, even the area east of the Oxus, Transoxiana ('*Ma wara an-nahr* or 'beyond the river' in Arabic, former Sogdiana, and present-day Uzbekistan between the Oxus and the Jaxartes) was Iranian in its population and culture at this time, although the ruling classes in its little states were more Turkish. Transoxiana and Farghana were the objectives of the later Arab campaigns launched from bases in Khurasan: both districts were flourishing commercial and agricultural centres; the Silk Road went through them, linking them to distant China.

Under the Umayyads, Khurasan, the large north-eastern province of Iran (its territory is now divided between Persia and Soviet Turkmenistan) had become the border between the Muslim empire and the east. Sometimes dependent on the governor of Iraq, and ruled by his envoys, sometimes autonomous with its own governor appointed by the Caliph, it was a secure Arab possession. Ever since the earliest period of the conquest, large contingents of Arabs had been living there, their numbers reinforced by subsequent expeditions and immigrations. These first Arab nuclei initially kept themselves aloof from the native population. They came from different Peninsula tribes, both northern and southern (Mudar, Rabi'a and Yemen), and as at the western end of the empire they brought their tribal divisions and conflicts to their new dwelling place in the distant east. The conquerors' internal disputes form an essential part of the history of Arab dominion in Khurasan and the campaigns undertaken in our period: their inveterate tribal particularism eventually caused the downfall of their national hegemony. Most of the governors – either ruling the province from Merv, or leading expeditions to consolidate and extend its boundaries – undermined their own authority by giving their fellow-tribesmen preference over other Arabs: absolute devotion to the Caliph (in the case of Ziyad and Hajjaj, great viceroys of Iraq), or relatively weak tribal loyalties, as in the case of Qutaiba, enabled a few of the governors to overcome such wasting conflicts, and concentrate on the common interests of the Arab empire and its guiding spirit, the Islamic Faith. Arabism's turbulent history and final sterile fate on its eastern frontier (on which, unlike other areas, our documentation is full, with a wealth of detail and colourful touches) is the most eloquent proof of its inability to overcome its own inner conflicts and establish lasting power. Superhuman courage, energy and sacrifice offered in the Arab cause were wasted by the Arabs' own short-sighted sectarianism, the benefits of which were reaped by others. Their efforts furthered the cause of Islam, however, which began to be clearly differentiated from that of Arabism in Persia.

The Arab conquest of Transoxiana at the beginning of the eighth century was carried out under Qutaiba ibn Muslim. In 705 he was appointed governor of Khurasan by al-Hajjaj, viceroy of Iraq. Even before he was appointed, his predecessors had crossed the Oxus many times, bearing the arms of Islam into Sogdiana, they had only made raids there – the usual prelude to actions of broader implication. Now Hajjaj, the controlling mind behind Arab imperialism in the east, meant to establish Muslim dominion in Central Asia beyond the Oxus; a few years later he made a parallel plan for the south beyond the Indus, with his project for the conquest of Sind. Qutaiba was his protégé: a member of the obscure tribe of the Bahila – therefore little involved in tribal disputes – and blindly devoted to his superior and patron, he really acted in the sole interest of Arab hegemony, proving himself an able diplomat where diplomacy would be effective but capable of pitiless severity and treachery when he judged them necessary. With these methods, the Arab conquest reached its furthest limits in Central Asia in less than ten years. After a few decades of struggling to stay in power, the Arabs finally lost their hold in Central Asia but left behind the faith they had propagated.

Qutaiba now prepared to commence operations against the territories east and south-east of the Oxus. These lands did not form a single unitary state, but were ruled by a number of Iranian or Turkish petty princes or rulers. Arab tradition, and the relevant parts óf Chinese tradition, refer to them in some cases with the name of their ruler, in others with the name of the kingdom. Though in practice independent, the rulers nominally recognised the sovereignty of distant China, and, nearer, that of the Khaqan of the Western Turks, who was himself dependent on the Celestial Empire. A grandson of the last Sasanid king Yazdagird had sought refuge in this Turkish state, but his attempts to gain support among anti-Arab resistance movements is a virtually irrelevant detail: Transoxiana and Tukharistan were now gravitating towards the eastern orbit, and were hoping that Turkey and China would help them in their resistance against the invaders. Although the inhabitants of the two provinces were mainly Iranian by race, their

The mausoleum of Isma'il the Samanid, Bukhara. This small building has the perfection of a jewel-box; its decoration is achieved by a brick technique known as *hazarbaf* in Persian, which was later perfected by the Seljuks during the eleventh and twelfth centuries.

culture and society had a Central Asian flavour, as is attested by the presence of Buddhism among the local religions along with Zoroastrianism (there was a famous Buddhist sanctuary, the Nav-bahar in Balkh).

Immediately after his nomination, Qutaiba opened operations against Tukharistan. He marched on the rebellious town of Balkh and cowed Nizak the Iranian prince of Sijistan into temporary obedience. Thus protected on the flank in 705, the Arab general crossed the Oxus at Amul the following year and started his Transoxianan campaigns. Paikand was the first city to fall. It was given lenient treatment at first, but as rebellion soon broke out, the city was sacked, and its population either put to death or deported. The campaign against Bukhara took the next two years: it was defended by a coalition of local troops with ones from other Sogdian principalities, and, after desperate fighting in which the Tamim horsemen distinguished themselves among the desert soldiers, it fell to the Arabs in 709. Action in Transoxiana had to be held in abeyance for a time, while the Arabs decisively crushed Nizak's revolt in Tukharistan: the brave Iranian ruler was taken prisoner and put to death, perhaps by Hajjaj's orders, although Qutaiba had promised him his life. Like that of his predecessors, Qutaiba's policy in the conquered provinces was to keep the petty local dynasties in their official positions, allowing them a semblance of power, by these means exploiting the prestige they held in the eyes of their subjects to ensure their obedience and payment of tribute to the Arabs. The actual power was of course in the hands of the Arab garrisons. Thus, Tughshad, a local prince stayed in power in Bukhara. The local Khwarizm Shah remained under Arab protection in Khwarizm on the lower Oxus, where the Arabs intervened by taking sides in a dynastic dispute. And even in Samarqand, the capital of Sogdiana – which the Arabs had then occupied without delay – the local sovereign was kept in office as a go-between or guarantor of obedience to the conquerors. The native lord of Samarqand with whom Qutaiba and some of his successors had dealings, is called Ghurak in Arab sources and

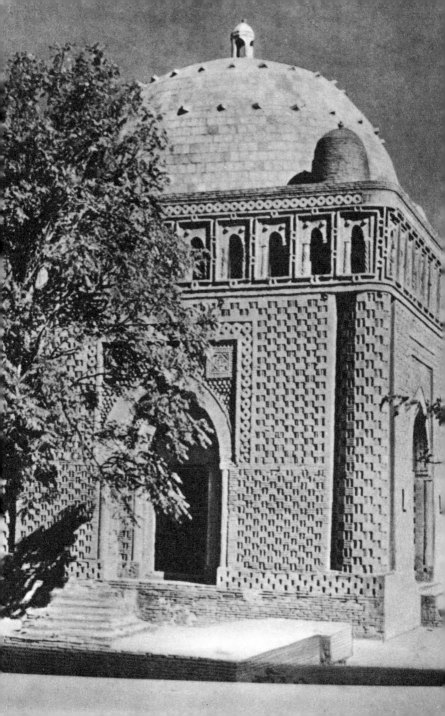

U-le-ka in Chinese. Having ascended to the throne to defend his people from the Arab menace, he met the invasion with a flexible policy of concessions and agreements, saving his country from devastation and carnage and preserving what he could of his autonomy. In fact when Qutaiba first entered the city by treaty, he broke his word to Ghurak and established regular military occupation; this forced Ghurak to leave his capital and found a new city in its environs. Nevertheless, until his death in 737, the determined Sogdian ruler managed to defend his countrymen by a successful policy of hindering, countering or moderating direct Arab dominion.

The conquest of Transoxiana can be considered complete with the capture of Samarqand, the other minor towns of Kish and Nasaf already being under Arab occupation. The victorious armies reached the Jaxartes (now called the Sir Darya), the boundary of Iranism in the north east. Beyond it stretched the lands of Shash and Turkish Farghana: but the Arabs soon surmounted this final obstacle to their advance and the Bahilite conqueror occupied the capital of Shash in 712. The capital had the same name as the country and was on the same site as modern Tashkent. One tradition says that Qutaiba pushed straight on to Kashgar, which would then be the most easterly point touched by Arab forces, but it is doubtful that he really went so far. Even if he stopped in Shash and Farghana, he would still have reached the heart of Central Asia, China's sphere of political and commercial influence. Arab and Chinese sources record that at about this time (713–4) a Muslim delegation visited the Celestial Court, probably with the aim of establishing Chinese neutrality and setting up profitable commercial relations. Apparently Qutaiba's last offensive operations took place in 714, going towards Turfan as far as Isbijab. However, his work was soon to draw to a close. In the June of that year, his patron died in Iraq: Hajjaj had been the main instigator behind the Arab advance in the east towards China. According to one tradition he had promised the governorship of China to whichever of his two lieutenants, Qutaiba in Central Asia or Muhammad ibn al-Qasim in India, reached it first. Neither of the two in fact did so, as their careers were wrecked by the death of the brilliant viceroy of Iraq.

The Umayyad Caliph al-Walid, under whom the Arab empire had stretched from Samarqand to Toledo, died a few months after Hajjaj. Al-Walid was succeeded by Sulaiman, a bitter enemy of Hajjaj, and all the men who owed their promotion to the latter now felt their positions were in danger. Muhammad ibn al-Qasim, the conqueror of Sind, suffered his disgrace and death with manly dignity, but Qutaiba lost control of himself, and tried to declare war on the new Caliph. Both Arabs and Persians sided against the rebel governor and his attempt failed. The victorious general died in a military riot in Farghana, the furthest point he had reached in his conquest. Perhaps more than being a great general, like Khalid and Tariq, Qutaiba was a capable organiser and diplomat, an intelligent and dynamic executor of Hajjaj's iron will. For example, it has been noted that his national pride did not prevent him from making shrewd use of native auxiliary contingents in his campaigns, or from showing trust and openness towards his conquered peoples, unless Arab interests seemed to demand intransigence and deception. The Arab conquest of Transoxiana is inseparably linked to his name, but the fluctuations of the next thirty years were to reveal the precarious nature of that conquest.

In the following period the enemy whom the Arabs had to contend with were the Central Asian Turks, who had joined the war in response to the Sogdian princes' appeals for help. The fighting took place mainly beyond the Oxus and the Jaxartes but the Arabs sometimes had to defend their bases in Khurasan, west of the Oxus. The Sogdians had also asked the Chinese for help, but received nothing but expressions of goodwill: the man who had actually pledged himself to repelling the Arabs was Su-Lu, the Khaqan of the Turgesh Turks, a western branch of the race (called Tu-Kiu in Chinese sources) who had recently established power in the Ili basin and probably had their capital on the river

Ciu. This campaign was one of the first contacts – and a far from peaceful one – between the Arab bearers of Islam and the Turks, who would later become such important members of the faith though – let us say right away – at Arabism's expense. From now on the Turgesh army, sometimes under the Khaqan in person but more often under a lieutenant whom the Arabs called Kursul (really Kul-Ciur Bagha Tarkan), formed the spearhead of native resistance and counter-offensive movements, the forces of the rebel kings of Sogdiana becoming a minor factor. The Arab governors of Khurasan after Qutaiba, particularly in the period 724–43 under Caliph Hisham, were charged with the task of countering the Turkish menace from the steppes of Central Asia, an area as yet untouched by Arab penetration. The Turks placed the most recent acquisitions in jeopardy and even threatened the earlier ones in eastern Persia. Arab historiography has preserved a vivid and detailed though not always coherent or precise chronicle of these conflicts; unlike most other accounts of the scenes of the conquests, their sources are eye-witness.

We will fill in this general outline by touching briefly on a few major episodes of the wars, in particular the *ayyam* or pitched battles so vividly recorded in Arab tradition. One example is the 'Battle of the Thirst' (*yawm al-'atash*) when the Turks made their first mass armed entry into Farghana, forcing the Arab governor Muslim ibn Sa'id to make a disastrous retreat, first to the Jaxartes and then to the Oxus. Another famous encounter was the battle 'of the Pass' (*yawm ash-shi'b*) in 730, which also caused the Muslims serious losses. Having joined battle in a pass south of Samarqand with Turco-Persian forces under Su-Lu and the Sogdian princes – including Ghurak who had at that time gone over to the enemy – the governor Junaid al-Murri returned to the capital of Transoxiana with only a fragment of his army and had only averted total disaster by the sacrifice of one of his lieutenants. Seven years later, under the otherwise mainly successful governorship of Asad al-Qasri, the Arabs met another severe defeat, this time in the area of the Khuttal north of the middle Oxus. They retreated decimated and disgraced to Balkh, east of the river, bringing their belongings with them (hence its name the 'Battle of the Baggage' *yawm al-athqal*). The two main towns of Sogdiana were lost and retaken many times during these reverses, which involved the usual Arab internal disputes and the dangerous secession of an egalitarian rebel, Harith ibn Suraij of the Tamim tribe, who finally made common cause with the Iranians and Turks The Arabs only succeeded in stabilising their defences (by now it was a question of defence, even though some offensive measures were still attempted) after the *yawm al-athqal* in 737, when they repelled Su-Lu at Kharistan, the Turkish army having crossed the Oxus and occupied eastern Khurasan. We can date Arab reaffirmation of authority in the whole theatre of operations from this, in itself a minor skirmish. The Turkish Khaqan never reappeared in Transoxiana, and was anyway assassinated soon after; his brave lieutenant Kursul, the man most feared by the Arabs, was captured in 738 and crucified on the banks of the Jaxartes. Around 740 Transoxiana can at last be said to be conquered and pacified, thanks to the wisdom and courage of Nasr ibn Sayyar, Khurasan's last Umayyad governor.

The native people's stubborn resistance was not simply animated by their desire for independence and their hatred for foreign rule: their discontent had other deep-reaching moral and economic causes, such as the brutal exploitation that the conquerors perpetrated on their defeated nations here as elsewhere, and (most important of all) the injustices in the system of tribute payment. Only infidels were liable to poll tax (*jizya*), and so converts to Islam should have been automatically exempt from it; however, in practice the Arabs often continued to demand it from new converts (*mawali* or native people who had joined the conquerors' social groupings), giving every reason for vindictiveness. The more scrupulous governors such as Asad al-Qasri and Nasr ibn Sayyar, whom we have already mentioned above, opposed such abuses. They diminished the yield of revenue, thereby laying themselves open to the Caliph's disfavour, but gained the goodwill of the native people, thus making the only possible effective contribution to the pacification of the country. What with discontent and disquiet among the indigenous converts to Islam, let alone unrest among some of the Arabs, the country provided a fertile breeding-ground for Abbasid propaganda. The Abbasid supporters preached an equivocal legitimism on behalf of the Prophet's family, favouring the descendants of Muhammad's uncle al-'Abbas, and questioning the basis of the Umayyad Caliphate. This secret propaganda gained ground in Khurasan throughout this period until in 747 both Arabs and Persians broke out into open rebellion against the Damascus Caliphs and their representatives. Nasr ibn Sayyar, who had fruitlessly pacified Transoxiana and warned his sovereigns in Syria of the rising tide of opposition to them, was overthrown and died fleeing to the west. In Persia, or more precisely Khurasan, the revolution then began which caused upheavals throughout the Arab empire between 748 and 750, overthrowing the Umayyads and bringing their Abbasid rivals to power. No less than the Umayyads, the Abbasids were Arabs by blood, but consciously or unconsciously, their coming effected a profound change in the basis and methods of governorship of the Muslim Empire. From being purely Arab, it became universalistic, echoing the transformation which had already taken place in the deeper spirit of Islam. The Persians, ardent supporters of the new dynasty which they had brought to power, succeeded the Arabs in the leadership of the Muslim empire and were succeeded in their turn by the Turks, who from being pagans and enemies of Islam were to become its principal champions and heirs.

This was of course a very long process of several decades. To return to the more restricted topic of this chapter, the Abbasid revolution immediately provoked a crisis in the very lands in which conquest had just been consolidated. In the messages Nasr ibn Sayyar had sent to the Umayyads and his co-nationals to warn them of their danger, he had said that the real aim of the rebels of Khurasan was the 'murder of the Arabs'. In fact the anti-Umayyad revolution of Khurasan cannot really be called anti-Arab, since the Arabs themselves, goaded by their tribal divisions and resentments, took an active part therein. However, without their realising it, the new order of things was to prove fatal for Arab hegemony, particularly in the eastern regions of the empire. For the moment, the expelled Umayyad governor in Khurasan and its dependency Transoxiana was replaced by the leader of the Abbasid propaganda movement, a previously unknown Persian called Abu Muslim. For his support, Abu Muslim relied essentially on the *mawali*, the new Persian Muslims who had tried to resist the control of the Arab governors and now witnessed the triumph of their nationalist and egalitarian aspirations. However, Arabs and Persians, united by Islam and by deep loyalty to the Abbasids, together had made up the 'Khurasanians' (significantly, the name overrules tribal distinctions), the prop of the Iraqi dynasty of caliphs for at least fifty years. And the Arabs and Persians joined together to withstand external attack for the last time: in July 751 on the River Talas, under the command of the Abbasid governor Ziyad ibn Salih, Arab Persian troops flanked by the Qarluk Turks defeated the Uighur and Chinese contingents who were threatening the Islamised regions beyond the Jaxartes, roughly on the furthest point reached by Qutaiba and his successors. This is the last date we have for Arab military action in Central Asia. Subsequently, any specifically Arab elements disappeared from there, from Khurasan and from the whole of Persia, absorbed as they were among the indigenous Iranian or Turkish and increasingly Muslim population. How were the conquerors absorbed, and to a lesser extent, driven out? It has been calculated that about two hundred thousand Arabs had been in Persia and Transoxiana for more than a century and had been the most powerful social group there. The process by which they disappeared is an almost total mystery. At the time of their emergence as autonomous political units at the beginning of the ninth century, Khurasan and Transoxiana, so arduously won for Islam by the Arabs, seem to be wholly Muslim but still Iranian in their language and culture. Revitalised by the new faith of Islam, the indigenous tradition and the Iranian language and culture took on a new lease of life and blossomed. At first the Arabic language and culture were still preserved as the truest expression of Islam, by then the dominant religion, but the Arabs' ethnic strength had collapsed and their political supremacy was a thing of the past. Then with the course of centuries the Arabs' linguistic and cultural heritage also disappeared and the area's original Iranian character was modified by Turkish influences. Scholars have recently observed and studied traces of Arab dialects in Central Asia, but they probably do not date back to our ancient period, but to some more recent time, perhaps to elements transplanted there from Syria in the time of Tamerlaine. The only lasting heritage the Arabs left was Islam.

At the same time as Qutaiba's advance into Sogdiana, another very young Arab general, Muhammad ibn al-Qasim was organising operations in the Indus Valley. Muhammad was another protege, in fact a co-tribesman and cousin of Hajjaj; they were members of the small tribe of Thaqif, from Ta'if in the Hijaz. The tribe had risen from obscurity to fame (infamy in pious Islamic opinion but fame in the judgment of modern historians) thanks to its most illustrious son, the dynamic governor-general of Iraq. The dearest ambition of Hajjaj, by no means a bad Muslim in his way, was the expansion of the Arab Empire under the Damascus caliphs, to whom he was deeply devoted. Just as he had sent Qutaiba to the north east to invade the country beyond the Oxus, advising and stimulating him in his endeavours, so he entrusted the south-eastern conquest of western India and Sind to his seventeen-year-old cousin. In 710, with a chosen body of six thousand Syrians and various auxiliary contingents, the young general set off from southern Persia through the hostile coastal region of Makran for the mouths of the Indus. The Arabs had already reached this corner of the Indian subcontinent, both by land from Persia and by sea, but with plunder not conquest as their aim. Now the imperialism of the viceroy of Iraq was attracted by the ambitious project of conquest. The basin of the Indus was inhabited by people of many different races and creeds, (the Jat or Zott, of gipsy origin, the Maid corsairs, and Hindu and Buddhist communities). In the preceding century, a large kingdom had been created under the Brahmin Čač (whom the Arabs called Sassa), and it now fell to his son Dahir to contend with the invaders. They first invaded the port of Daibul, in the centre of the Indus Delta (the exact location of the town remains uncertain), which had already been the target of some unsuccessful forays. Probably on the personal instructions of Hajjaj, the besiegers bombarded the city with catapults and took it by storm, perhaps in the autumn of 711. It was then sacked and its inhabitants massacred. The conqueror stationed a thousand Muslims there and a mosque was built, the first on Indian soil, dedicating the conquest to Islam.

From his base at Daibul Muhammad ibn al-Qasim extended his field of operations through the lower Indus district, and then began to work his way up the river. The towns of Nirun, Sehwan and Sadusan either surrendered or were taken by storm. In June 712 Dahir was defeated and killed in a pitched battle near Rawar, and the conqueror occupied his capital Brahmanabad (on the site where the Muslim town of Mansura was built later). Brahmanabad had a happier fate than Daibul, as Hajjaj, who was following the progress of the invasion with close attention, advised Muhammad ibn al-Qasim to count Buddhists and Hindus as people of the Book (Jews, Christians and Zoroastrians) and grant them freedom of religion in return for tribute, as laid down in the Koran. The same principle was applied in Rur, the other capital of Sind, which Muhammad reached on his way up the Indus: but here and in other places Muslim nuclei took root beside the tolerated local religions (we know the name of the first qadi of Rur, a fellow-tribesman of the conqueror). According to a rather uncertain tradition, the detailed, and somewhat fanciful chronicles of the first conquest are attributed to these Muslim groups. We know for certain that, still on his way up the Indus Valley, Muhammad ibn al-Qasim crossed the Beas (formerly Hyphasis, where Alexander halted) and invaded Multan, the great sanctuary of the

Punjab which had a famous temple to the sun god. It fell after a long siege, probably in 713, and was the furthest point reached in the first Arab penetration into Sind. At Multan the following year the victorious young general received news of his powerful cousin and master's death in Iraq, soon followed by news of Caliph al-Walid's death. Hajjaj's men could expect no good from the new caliph, and his accession meant the end of Muhammad's career and fortune, as it had for Qutaiba. But unlike Qutaiba, Muhammad ibn al-Qasim resigned himself to his fate. After completing the occupation of the middle and lower Indus Valley, apparently including present-day Cutch, he obediently resigned his command to the new governor, a member of the opposing family of Muhallabites who had come to the fore at Hajjaj's death. He was sent back in chains, with the pretext of financial accounts to render, and was obscurely put to death in Iraq according to an ancient Arab tradition. The romantic version of later Indo-Persian sources is pure legend: it claims that the conqueror of Sind was killed in an affair of honour, the concubines of the dead Indian King Dahir denouncing him to the Caliph.

Muhammad's campaigns did not have a direct development in the history of India. Not all the lands he had conquered were abandoned: Dahir's kingdom was divided into small local kingdoms which accepted a more or less effective vassalage to the Caliph, and the Arab colonies founded in the Indus Valley lasted for several more centuries, in almost total autonomy. However, it was not until a century after the first conquest, at the height of the Abbasid period, that the Islamic centre of Mansura, for long the commercial capital of Sind, was built near ancient Brahmanabad. In any case, the earliest colonies were backwaters cut off from the rest of the empire, and it was not from them that the new, decisive movement to conquer part of India for Islam was launched. The initiative came three centuries later, from the north, when the Ghaznawid sultan Mahmud invaded the Punjab from Afghanistan, and went down the Indus Valley southward, the opposite way from Muhammad ibn al-Qasim, extending the conquest eastwards, as far as the foot of the Himalayas. The new conqueror made a move to strengthen the surviving Muslim nuclei in Sind, and he nominated proper lieutenants to replace the native chiefs and mayors in Multan and some other towns. But under Mahmud, and even more under the Muslim dynasties which succeeded him in India (Ghurides, or Slave Kings of Delhi, Tughluq, and gradually the rest of the country as far as the Mughul), it was Islam not Arabism which took root in the country. The Arabs achieved their moment of greatest glory under Hajjaj's younger conqueror, and under Qutaiba and his successors in Farghana and at the Talas. Hajjaj had perhaps dreamed of making the two prongs of his attacking force meet in the middle of Asia for an attack on the fabulous land of China, but the zest of the Arabs' striking-power dwindled and stagnated without the far-seeing will which had set it in motion. The Arabs had reached the limit of their expansionary potential as conquerors and founders of states. Their tide now started to ebb, and not Arabs but other peoples were to push back the boundaries of the Faith in whose name the first spectacular conquests had been achieved.

12 The achievements of Arab Islam

The establishment of the Arab Empire was the work of a few short decades, an achievement only made possible by the courage and initiative of the Arabs, their lust for booty, their conviction that they were obeying a divine command, and their adaptability and capacity for compromise, together with the military and political skill of some of their leaders. However, the structure only lasted intact for a few more decades. The unity of the empire was lost in the mid-eighth century. In its place there evolved a collection of smaller states, Arab and non-Arab, centring around the Caliphate in the east for another few centuries. Throughout this period continued use of the Arabic language still provided a common bond between the various new states which had arisen within the area once covered by the conquests. These years can still be re-garded as an essentially Arab period of Islamic history, in that great Arab states still survived, albeit at odds with one another. These included the Umayyad Caliphate in Spain, the Fatimid in Egypt and the Abbasid in Baghdad – although in this last case the Arabic influence was fairly soon superseded by that of other nationalities. Despite its internal divisons Arabism remained on the whole an active and expansionary force until about the year 1000.

In traditional Islamic opinion the Arabs have been seen as the propagators of the Faith throughout this period. Some Western historians, whose views have been widely adopted by modern Arab nationalists, see the process more as an affirmation under the banner of Islam of the national identity and hegemony of the Arabs. Ibn Khaldun (1332–1406), the great political and social historian of the Maghrib, was the first Muslim to undertake a thorough exam-ination of the problems of the Arab expansion. He assimilated the phenomenon of the diaspora into his general theory that the rise and fall of states and power groups is determined by the strength or weakness of their *'asabiyya*, or sense of solidarity and unity. The *'asabiyya* of the Quraish, once they were united together behind Muhammad, made possible the foundation and development of the Muslim state and its enormous conquests.

Tombstone with Kufic inscription, Egypt, 860. Arabic
writing was important in the dissemination of Islam.
The two main styles are the angular Kufic and the cursive
Naskhi (*see overleaf*). The Kufic emphasises vertical
strokes, and was extensively used during the first five
centuries of Islam. Museum of Islamic Art, Cairo.

The weakening of this '*asabiyya* contributed to the fall of the caliphal dynasties and the emergence of new leaders within the world of Islam. Ibn Khaldun puts forward this pragmatic and secular interpretation of the Arab expansion, but at the same time upholds the theory of religious motivation and the supernatural facts of the revelation and prophecy; he does not, however, attempt to reconcile the two. As we have already seen, Western historians have tried to synthesise both theories.

At this stage, we need hardly detail again the sweeping changes that the Arab expansion caused throughout the Near East: it completely destroyed one great empire and permanently impaired another – the Muslims put the Byzantine Empire on the defensive and were subsequently to cause its downfall. The Arab onslaught dealt a mortal blow to Zoroastrianism, which had anyway long been a lifeless and over-formalised religion, gradually losing more and more of its adherents and only contributing to the religion and culture which replaced it in that its influence encouraged the growth of heretical and syncretist doctrines within Islam. Christianity also lost its impetus in Asia, its place of origin, with the coming of the Arabs and Islam; like Zoroastrianism, it became a minority religion, and, torn apart by schism and discord, degenerated into ritualism or at best contemplative piety. The vitality of young Islam – not only its expansion and proselytisation but also its internal theological evolution – was accompanied by the stagnation of the religions it replaced in the Near East – a confirmation of the appeal and vitality of the message propagated by the Arab conquests. It has been maintained that foreign non-Arab Muslims were solely responsible for Islam's religious evolution (in theology, ethics and law): the Arabs are credited with only the physical act of conquest; and to the new converts to Islam, the bearers of the knowledge of Greece and the East, is attributed the modification and elaboration of Muhammad's religion. This theory is untenable. These foreign influences were certainly crucially important, but they were welcomed and developed not only by non-Arab Muslims but also by many of the Arab descendants of the conquerors.

Tombstone with Naskhi inscription, Egypt, 1184.
From the eleventh century onwards, the
cursive Naskhi gradually replaced Kufic.
Museum of Islamic Art, Cairo.

The Arabs are responsible not only for the first rising and spreading of the Faith, but also for many of its further elaborations, for many of its intellectual and social developments. We must not replace the erroneous concept of Islam as purely Arab with the equally erroneous one of Islam as non-Arab, and in giving other peoples and cultural traditions due credit for their participation, we should not forget that the first seed of Islam and the important developments of the Faith throughout history (including modern times) have always flourished in a purely Arab environment. The protection of the Faith has always been an undeniable function of Arabism, particularly in the heroic expansionary period we have been studying.

The positive value of the Arab diaspora in the Near East and in the accompanying dissemination of Islam is therefore not in question; however, opinions differ on the value of the Arab presence in the Mediterranean. The Mediterranean world had produced the highest civilisation of ancient times, which, though somewhat modified by the barbarian invasions, survived until the disruptive intrusion of the Arabs and Islam. Such is the theory put forward in the 1920's by the Belgian historian Pirenne, not an orientalist but a learned student of the economic and social history of the medieval west. In his view – indicated by the title of his most famous book on the subject *Mahomet et Charlemagne* – the economic, religious and cultural unity of the Mediterranean survived the barbarian invasions only to be destroyed by the eastern barbarians, that is, by the Arabs. Their eruption in the seventh century placed a wedge between western Europe and the Near East, paralysing freedom of movement and trade on the vital sea-routes.

This theory is at once military, political and economic; the conclusions Pirenne draws from it touch on many important aspects of the history of the medieval west (for example, the interruption of sea trade; the continental policy and economy of the Carolingians, as opposed to the maritime policy and economy of the Merovingians; the decline of the Mediterranean as a means of communication between east and west, when sea power passed into the hands of the Saracens). A study of the times and methods of the Arab expansion in the Mediterranean reveals that this theory is not really acceptable. There is no doubt that with the coming of the Arabs a new element appeared in the former *mare nostrum;* the unchallenged naval power established by Rome had been passed down to the second Rome of the Bosphorus, and then used again in the sixth century to re-establish at least a semblance of empire in Italy and all North Africa. The Arabs put an end to Byzantium's total mastery of the sea, but this does not mean that they replaced it by an equally unchallenged sway of their own, as they sometimes aspired to. The Arabs' bold advance on land, backed up by their growing sea power, had won them the entire coast of North Africa, and not without hard-fought struggles; their makeshift navy gave them easy access to Spain and Sicily. The Arab fleet then began to develop quickly until it came to match itself successfully against that of Byzantium even in major naval encounters (from the Umayyad victory of Phoenix in 655 to the Fatimid and Sicilian victory of the Straits of Messina in 965); the navies of some of the Muslim coastal states reached a high level of efficiency, as for example those of the Fatimids and their rivals the Umayyads in Spain. The joint actions referred to previously between navies and religious-piratical groups (however strange it may seem, religion and piracy appear to be connected throughout Islamic history up to modern times) must undoubtedly have aggravated the uncertainty of communications in the Mediterranean between the eighth and tenth centuries or perhaps for even longer. Yet at no point in history can we find any evidence to support Pirenne's theory of the closure of the Mediterranean. Though gravely tried and deprived of some precious provinces, Byzantium stood firm, showing her usual ability to recover from even the most serious reverses. She may have lost her supremacy over the Mediterranean with the Arab invasions, but the Arabs did not necessarily inherit it. At the same time rivals and partners, the Arabs and Byzantines shared the mastery of the sea throughout the Early Middle Ages, neither side managing to deal the other a fatal blow. Admittedly the Byzantines lost North Africa again and then lost Sicily, but thanks entirely to their naval forces they succeeded in defending the Italian mainland, Greece and the Balkan coast (not to mention Constantinople itself, which we will discuss later). In spite of the enemy fleets and the apparently widespread practice of pirate *jihad*, communications and trade in the Mediterranean between Christianity and Islam were never completely broken off. A much-quoted passage from a text by a ninth-century Arab geographer refers to the regular voyages made by Jewish merchants from Provence to Egypt by sea and then from Egypt to India and China by land. Pilgrims such as Arculf continued to visit the Holy Land after it had fallen to the Arabs, and frequently travelled by sea. Thus traders and pilgrims went on risking the Mediterranean sea routes sometimes even sailing in company with the Saracens. Contemporary documents prove that in the tenth century merchants from Amalfi established a flourishing trading centre at Alexandria in Fatimid Egypt. Naturally all of these travellers were running the risks of interception, forfeiture, robbery and capture implicit in the permanent state of undeclared war between the three worlds (the Arabs, Byzantium and the West) among whom the seas and Mediterranean coasts were divided. Our conclusion is that at no time during the period was the Mediterranean deserted by all but Saracen pirates. Trade and commerce still continued, though in more difficult circumstances and certainly not through any lack of enthusiasm for *jihad* on the Arabs' part. They continued because the Arabs never actually achieved that total mastery of the sea and coasts which would have made the Mediterranean an 'Arab lake'.

The undeniable fact remains: conditions in the Mediterranean were insecure and the Arabs had a wholly adverse effect on those parts of the coast where they never established stable regimes, such as Greece, the Balkans, the whole Italian mainland, Corsica and Sardinia, and southern France. If we had to judge the Arab presence in the Mediterranean on their record here alone, we would have to compare it to such disastrous barbarian invasions as those of the Vandals and Huns; here the Arabs showed only their destructive capacities, as Ibn Khaldun admits in his unbiased analysis. But wherever they came to live and settle, in what they called *dar al-Islam*, that is, the lands where the Muslim faith and civilisation became implanted, a constructive phase followed the destructive phase of conquest: the Arabs mixed with the native peoples and via their religion they introduced their culture, literature and art. Though retaining the indelible Arab imprint, these became blended with the influences of the preceding civilisations and ethnic groups. Examples are the Arabs' encounter with the Berbers in North Africa, with the Ibero-Latins and Visigoths in Spain, and the Latin-Byzantine Christians in Sicily. The austere Islam of the Maghrib and the splendid annals of Arab culture in Spain and Sicily are a lasting monument to the positive side of the Arab venture in the western Mediterranean. Like Peleus's lance, the Arabs could inject new life into the wounds they had opened.

Since pre-Islamic times, the Arabs had come into contact with two great empires, and had attacked them both in the first outbreak of the conquering movement. Of these empires Byzantium exercised a particular fascination over their new imperialism throughout its earliest period. The Arabs were fascinated by it because of their vague belief that it carried on the heritage of Rome (as is shown by its Arab name Rum), because of the Byzantine influences via Ghassanid channels, because of the occasional references to its history in the Holy Book, and because the Prophet's foreign policy, in his last years, showed that he had an interest in that direction. All of these factors combined together made Byzantium a coveted goal as soon as the Arabs became aware of their own strength and fortune. The attraction of Byzantium was further increased when the Umayyads made Syria the centre of the caliphate, and Mu'awiya, by his brilliant construction of a naval fleet, let the Arabs learn the part they could play at sea and in the Mediterranean. When they first reluctantly embarked on 'riding the waves', a complete transformation took place in the mentality and customs of the sons of the desert, once hostile strangers to the sea. We have already seen that their navy supplemented their advance on land, and furthered their progress in the Mediterranean. We should now reconsider the relationship between the Arabs and Byzantium and the offensives launched by the former against the latter.

Once they had reached the Amanus and then the Taurus mountains the Arabs abandoned the idea of occupying any more of the country. They turned instead to making numerous seasonal raids into it (such as the *sawa'if* or summer campaigns in Anatolia). These raids in effect cut a diagonal line across Asia Minor, soon taking the Arabs to the shores of the Bosphorus where they arrived at the same time as their fleets came in by sea. Three times, in three memorable climaxes of their offensive expansion, the Arabs seemed to be within reach of attaining their ambitious goal. In 668, Yazid, Mu'awiya's son and future successor, conducted the first siege of Constantinople, in which the Companion Abu Ayyub al-Ansari, future patron saint of the Ottoman Conquest, met his death. After the Byzantines had repelled this attempt and other maritime offensives, Sulaiman made the most determined effort of the Umayyad period. The Caliph's brother, the great captain Maslama, led an enormous expedition to the Bosphorus by land and sea, but after a full year's siege he was defeated by the energetic and skilful defence of Leo the Isaurian. In 782, during the Caliphate of the Abbasid al-Mahdi, Arab forces appeared on the Bosphorus for the third and last time, under the command of Harun, the future al-Rashid, again a prince of the blood. This time Empress Irene bought their withdrawal by treaties which included a humiliating tribute. The Abbasids carried on with the incursions into Anatolia for almost all of the first century of their Caliphate; al-Mu'tasim's famous conquest of Amorium in Phrygia in 838 took place during this period. However, never again did they attempt to take Constantinople. They must have understood the difficulties involved in attacking the capital without having first established control over the Anatolian hinterland, a step they never achieved and perhaps never even dreamed of. It was the Byzantines who started the second phase of open hostilities, launching attacks from Asia Minor into northern Syria and Mesopotamia. The Arab poet al-Mutanabbi describes these tenth-century frontier wars in his poetry and by this time the Hamdanids of Aleppo had superseded the decadent caliphs of Baghdad as champions of Arabism. However the Byzantines never succeeded in advancing their boundary beyond the Amanus, and the Arabs had lost both the lofty goals of the Umayyad age and the means to achieve them: no fundamental change took place in the balance of power between the Byzantines and the Arabs, who were anyway soon to lose their function of the driving force behind Islam.

Throughout the Umayyad century, Byzantium was the number one enemy of rising Arab imperialism, and at the same time was its guiding light, almost its model. It has recently been discovered that the two countries maintained cultural relations, in spite of being in a chronic state of war, both on land and at sea. Hellenistic influences dominated the art of Syria, Palestine and Transjordan in the Umayyad period, and Byzantine workmen and materials were brought in to decorate the Caliphs' mosques and palaces. Arabism and Islam were both clearly looking towards the West throughout this era. It is futile but nonetheless tempting to imagine how different their histories might have been had the Syrian dynasty survived.

However, after the fall of the Umayyads (or even earlier – in the opinion of some historians in the last decades of their regime) the attraction of Byzantium and the west began to diminish and a new contrary influence came to prevail over Arab-Islamic policy, culture and art. Persia had been the breeding-ground and starting-point for the anti-Umayyad revolution and the Abbasids relied to a large extent on Persian support. One of the effects of the revolution was to accomplish a complete change in the empire's direction, the new Caliphate losing interest in the Mediterranean world, and veering towards the east. Iranism became the model for the Abbasid state and society, taking the place of Hellenism, and

Sasanid tradition, ritual and culture were substituted in place of the Byzantine as formative influence on court life and the empire's ruling classes (it is significant that conversely the Fatimid court in Egypt was strongly influenced by Byzantium). Effectively, the Muslim Empire became orientalised under the Abbasids, in as much as it ceased to be an Arab state, and in the east the Arabs began to decline as a political force after a hundred and fifty years of leadership. Islam no longer needed them for its further development and subsequent conquests. Taha Husein, a modern Egyptian writer, regards the cultural tradition implanted in his country in the ancient Arab period as 'Mediterranean' and western, and as much could be said for Syria. This view is of course exaggerated, but contains an element of truth.

One of the most striking features of the history of the Medieval East is the gradual eclipse of Arabism as supreme political force in the Muslim world. The violent upheaval in the Caliphate in the mid-eighth century and the ensuing change of dynasty were only harbingers of the Arabs' decline, as they still kept an important place in the empire under the early Abbasids. But the Arab tribal system – at once their weakness and their strength – which had worn itself out little by little during the Umayyad period, disappeared altogether under the Abbasids. The power of the new dynasty was not based on the desert tribes but on the absolutism of ancient emperors. Some historians have recently compartmentalised the history of Islam in such a way that the new non-Arab period would date not from the rise of the Abbasids in 750 but from the mid-ninth century, at which time Arabism quite definitely took second place and new elements came to power at the centre of the caliphate and on the eastern periphery.

Iranians only constituted the dominant element for a short time – as the political and religious revolution which had brought the Abbasids to power had only been partly Iranian. In the eighth to tenth centuries Iranism had a brilliant linguistic and cultural revival in which it developed its native traditions, and it succeeded in founding some national Islamic dynasties in Transoxiana and eastern Persia, but it made no further headway in political terms; Persia was not reunified and did not show itself capable of any expansion towards the east. As driving force behind Islam, the Turks were the Arabs' real heirs: the pagans who but a century earlier had been pressing in on the northern and eastern borders of the Arab-Islamic state were converted to Islam astonishingly quickly. Won over by its linear simplicity, they embraced Islam with sincere enthusiasm. Unaware, in the first phase of their conversion at any rate, of any intellectual problems or heretical deviations, they were rigidly orthodox and their religious life was simple and intense. They placed their outstanding military qualities at the service of their new Faith, at first acting as the auxiliaries and merce-nariès of the Muslim state, but gradually becoming the dominant military element with the Arabs and Persians in adminstrative offices. The crisis which developed in the Baghdad Caliphate after its few decades of glorious power is closely connected with the rise of the Turkish influence and with the strength of the military leaders who made and unmade caliphs, eventually undermining the authority of the Abbasids and causing anarchy reminiscent of Rome in the third century and the worst periods of Byzantine history. The Arabs, the conquerors and masters of yesterday, became reconciled to the loss of their former position, showing no signs of apparent resistance apart from some poets' vain laments. Some of them went back to the desert and their ancestral nomad-ism; others became absorbed into urban life, which became more widespread in the Abbasid period. They lost the habit of war.

The Iranians made another bid for supremacy in the tenth century, and for a few decades a branch of the Buwaihid dynasty controlled the Caliphate. However, after the year 1000 Turkish predominance advanced irresistibly: the Seljukids set up a diarchy with the Caliphs of Baghdad, and feudal officials (*atabeg*) established little Turkish dynasties all over near Asia. These dynasties at first formed the backbone of Muslim resistance against the Crusaders. Contemporary propagandist documents in Arabic praise 'Muslim

Mosaic floor in the bath of the Umayyad
palace of Khirbat al-Mafjar, Jericho. The vast
enclosure, which includes not only the bath but also
a palace complex, was excavated by British
archaeologists between 1934 and 1948.

zeal and Turkish courage' as the driving forces behind resistance against the Franks, utterly ignoring the Arabs as a political or military force. Saladin, the greatest champion of the Islamic resurgence, and the dynasty he founded, were Kurdish in racial origin, Arab-Muslim in culture and Turkish in military technique. The Mameluke sultans who took over from the Ayyubites in Egypt and Syria were probably of Turkish origin. The Ottomans were Turks, the heirs of the Seljukids in Asia Minor, destined to write the last great chapter of the Islamic conquests. At the beginning of the thirteenth century the Mongol invasion threw Islam into confusion throughout the east, but the invaders assimilated themselves into the Muslim community, bringing their own adjustments to it. However, the new conquerors' slight ethnic consistency could not halt the gradual irresistible process by which Turkish influence became dominant throughout the part of Asia which the Arabs had once won for Islam. Tamerlaine was a Turk, as was his descendant Babur who carried out Islam's last conquest in India. Of the great potentates who became known to Europe at the time of the Renaissance – the Sultan of Constantinople, the 'Sofi' or safavid Sultan of Persia – not a single one had a drop of Arab blood: thus the Turks had gained complete ascendancy over other nationalities and had become the main representatives and protagonists of Islam. They remained so until the last century.

The dissemination of Turkish influences reached as far as western Islam. Here, the Arab-Berber element always remained dominant, but did not entirely escape the effects of Turkish infiltration: from the thirteenth century, and then increasingly in the Ottoman period, Turkish elements entered into the ethnic make-up of Tripolitania, Tunisia and Algeria, stopping only on the Moroccan border. In the rest of the Maghrib, Arabism managed to hold its own while accepting the influx of Turks, who came to be the political and military backbone of society, relegating the Arabs to second place. In the history of North Africa up to modern times, the Arabs have never shown signs of any consciousness of or pride in the memory of their own past, nor of any determination to reassert themselves in their ethnic purity. The great reawakening of modern Arabism in both east and west can largely be attributed to the influence of European invaders and colonisers. Another lance of Peleus, European colonisation, has inoculated the peoples with a sense of national pride and a craving for liberty by the very act of enslaving them.

Thus the Arabs, the 'raw material of Islam', were only the bearers and propagators of their Faith in its first decisive period of expansion. The vast lands into which Islam has subsequently spread (a large part of black Africa, eastern Europe, Anatolia, India and Indonesia) were untouched by the first Arab penetration. Other conquerors won them for Islam, and if Arabs played any part in the process it was only as peaceful merchants and missionaries. Genuine Arab imperialism spread at lightning speed in the times and manners we have described, but then died an early death. If we were to attempt an explanation of the causes of its decline, as we have for its phase of ascendancy, all we would really be able to do would be to refer to Ibn Khaldun's thesis of the cycle of the *'asabiyya* the sense of unity and race, which flared up briefly among the Arabs when they were first inspired by Islam but then died down. It died down, we should add, on account of the congenital obstacle of particularism, which the Arabs could only overcome for a short space of time, sinking their chronic tribal divisions in a broader national *'asabiyya*. Once their political primacy had collapsed, the lasting fruit of their expansion and contacts with other peoples still lived on in the splendid phenomenon of medieval Muslim culture and civilisation, Arab in origin and with Arabic its main mouthpiece.

After its long humiliating period of lethargy, Arabism has had a resurgence in the present day. Its resurgence has taken place under the stimulus of European culture and thought, and has even perhaps been reinvigorated by European violence. The history of the modern resurrection or renaissance of Arabism is outside the scope of this book, and has been described by the author in other works. We must now give a brief consideration to the link between the past and the present, and establish whether they are comparable in ideology, practical aspirations and possibilities. Unlike the first expansion the resurgence of the modern Arab world was not proclaimed under the banner of Islam, but under that of nationalism. The new nationalist ideology does not deny Islam, but sees it more as a tool, a cement and subsidiary force, and not as it was originally as the principal bond and most effective stimulus to action. However, the memory of the *imbraturiyya 'arabiyya*, as the phenomenon we have described in this book is now called (though the ancient Arabs would scarcely have understood such an expression), the memory of the Arab Empire gives inspiration to the most dynamic forces of Arabism and its two goals of reunification and expansion. In the light of past experience, do these goals seem attainable?

As regards unity, there is no doubt that this ideal is another step in the historical process in which the scattered desert tribes joined together to create a united state and empire, and then separated again and broke their empire down into regional and sectional units. According to the vicissitudes of the diaspora, Arabs of the same tribes were scattered both in Spain and in Central Asia. However, they quickly assimilated themselves to their new surroundings, coming to regard themselves as Andalusians and Khurasanians respectively, while remaining Arabs in language and faith. The Caliphs never held dominion over all the lands won by conquest, as small regional dynasties emerged. Today, many states have arisen in much of that huge expanse of land which call themselves and feel themselves to be Arab, but which are not prepared (or even if they were, would perhaps be unable) to sacrifice their historic regional identity, the precious result of centuries of evolution, in the cause of pan-Arabism. Every attempt to overcome this regionalism and recreate even just a part of the ancient Arab Empire has so far failed. It seems unlikely that any such attempts will succeed in the future, precisely because the regional divisions between the Arab peoples have become too strong, even though they claim a common origin. Those units which were tribes for twelve centuries, the centrifugal forces of the short-lived empire, are now single nation states, ready enough to call themselves 'Arab', but not prepared to renounce their narrow national sovereignty (and present-day Europe hardly sets them an example in such matters). It is difficult to make *e pluribus unum* when the *plures* are unwilling to make any sacrifice for the sake of unity.

As attempts at unity have not gone beyond the stage of setting up a League, and efforts towards partial union have hitherto been abortive, it seems equally unlikely that they should realise their dream of expansion through the united efforts of Arabism. In response to its greatest challenge, which we should regard as an attempt to recover what has been lost rather than to expand, namely in the conflict with Israel, after one first unhappy endeavour, Arabism has dared to take no further action. In conclusion, it seems impossible to go back over the course of history and make an artificial re-creation of something which was achieved in exceptional circumstances in a world completely different from our modern one. Arab neo-imperialism, which is sacrificing internal freedom in order to create a new unity and phase of expansion, has no chances of success in either field.

We are left with the fact – either inspiring or depressing, according to our outlook and opinion – of the contrast between the power and civilisation of the glorious past, and the present of the Arab peoples. Worn out by economic distress and sterile nationalist grievances, they seem unable to make good use of the independence they have won. When the Arabs realise that they have no chance of fulfilling their ambition to renew their old power, they should try eventually to recreate their past in a manner worthy of it, by the peaceful paths of culture and civilisation. In the present state of affairs this is simply a hope, not yet a reality. Faust's motto is a fitting comment on their destiny: 'Weh dir, dass du ein Enkel bist'.

Bibliography

From the vast bibliography on the Arabs, Islam and the conquests, we have selected only the most important works and those which elucidate controversial issues or support specific theories upheld in the text.

1 Muhammad in history

For a thorough examination of the Muslim community's attitudes towards the Prophet, see T. Andrae, *Die Person Muhammeds in Leben und Lehre seiner Gemeinde*, Stockholm, 1918. On the medieval Christian legend of Muhammad, see A. D'Ancona, 'La leggenda di Maometto in occidente', in *Studi di critica e storia letteraria*, II, Bologna 1912, 167–306. Carlyle's assessment of Muhammad is contained in the second chapter of his *On Heroes and Hero-worship*, 1840.

For Lammen's attitudes, see his 'Mahomet fut-il sincère?' in *Recherches de science religieuse*, 1911, and his learned but tendentious *Fatima et les fiilles de Mahomet*, Rome, 1912. For the opposing point of view, two very perceptive modern studies, principally on Muhammad's religious work, are K. Ahrens, 'Muhammad als Religionstifter', in *Abhandlungen für die Kunde des Morgenlandes* XIX, 4, Leipzig, 1935, and G. von Grunebaum's, 'Von Muhammeds Wirkung und Originalität', in *Wiener Zeitschrift für die Kunde des Morgenlandes*, XLIV, 1936, 29–50.

2 Arabia before Muhammad

A. P. Caussin de Perceval, *Essai sur l'histoire des Arabes avant l'Islamisme*, 3 vols., Paris 1847–8, a general work on pre-Islamic Arabia, out of date but not replaced. M. Guidi, *Storia e cultura degli Arabi fino alla morte di Maometto*, Florence, 1951, a fragmentary and unpolished work of modern criticism. I. Guidi *L'Arabie antéislamique*, Paris, 1921, provides a quick synthesis of the subject. On South Arabian civilisation, see C. A. Nallino concentrated and detailed summary in *Enciclopedia italiana*, s.v. *Yemen* reprinted in *Raccolta di scritti editi e inediti*, III, Rome, 1941 (its chronology has provoked violent arguments). On Beduin life and society, see H. Lammens, *Le berceau de l'Islam*, Rome, 1914; *L'antica società beduina* (collected writings edited by F. Gabrieli), Rome, 1959; C. A. Nallino, 'Sulla costituzione delle tribù arabe prima dell'Islamismo', in *Raccolta* (as above), III, 64–86, old (1893) but still important; and G. Jacob, *Altarabisches Beduinenleben*, Berlin, 1897. On tribe and state in ancient Arabia see W.

Caskel, W. Montgomery Watt, F. Gabrieli in the volume *Dalla tribù allo stato* of the Accademia dei Lincei, Rome, 1962. On the Ghassanids, Lakhmids, and Kindites, see respectively T. Noeldeke, 'Die Ghassanischen Fürsten aus dem Hause Gafnas', in *Denkschriften d. Preuss. Akadm. d. Wissenschaften*, Berlin, 1887; G. Rothstein, *Die Dynastie des Lahmiden in al-Hira*, Berlin, 1899; and G. Olinder, *The Kings of Kinda of the family of Akil al-Murar*, Lund, 1927. On ancient Arab paganism, see J. Wellhausen, *Reste arabischen Heidentums*, Berlin, 1897, new edition Berlin, 1961, a fundamental work. On Christians and Jews in pre-Islamic times see Nallino's study of this title in *Raccolta* (as above), II, 97–156; and articles by J. Henninger, J. Ryckmans, F. Gabrieli in the volume *L'oriente cristiano nella storia della civiltà* of the Accademia dei Lincei, Rome, 1964.

3 and 4 Muhammad in Mecca and Triumph in Medina

On Mecca at the time of Muhammad's birth see H. Lammens' valuable and stimulating *La Meque à la veille de l'hérgire*, Beirut, 1924, (Mélanges de l'Université St Joseph, IX, 3, a fuller version of earlier works.) Ibn Ishaq's canonical biography of the Prophet *Sira*, Guillaume, London and New York, 1955. For the most sceptical view of Arab tradition see Lammens, 'Coran et tradition: comment fut composée la vie de Mahomet,' in *Recherches de Science religieuse*, 1910, taken up by R. Blachère in *Le problème de Mahomet. Essai de biographie critique du fondateur de l'Islam*, Paris, 1952, and criticised by T. Noeldeke in *Der Islam* v, 1914, 160–70, and C. Becker in *Islamstudien*, I, Leipzig, 1924, 520–27. (Lammens' views are not generally shared by modern biographers.) The most recent biographical works on the Prophet (for details on some of these and other less recent works see chapter 1 of this book) are F. Buhl, *Das Leben Muhammeds*, Leipzig, 1930 (the original Danish edition was published in 1903); T. Andrae, *Mohammed. Sein Leben und sein Glaube*, Göttingen, 1932 (*Mahomet: the man and his faith*, London 1936, New York 1936, revised ed. New York, 1956); W. Montgomery Watt, *Muhammad at Mecca*, London and New York, 1953; *Muhammad at Medina*, ibid., London and New York, 1956; and his short popularising *Muhammad Prophet and Statesman* (essentially an abridgement of the two previous books), London and New York, 1961; M. Gaudefroy – Demombynes, *Mahomet*, Paris, 1957; M. Hamidullah, *Le Prophète de l'Islam. Sa vie. Son Oeuvre*, Paris, 1959 (the author is a learned orthodox Muslim). See also the chapters on Muhammad by L. Caetani,

244

Annali dell' Islam, i–ii, Milan, 1905–7, *Studi di Storia Orientale*, iii, Milan 1914, and M. Guidi's short work referred to above. On two crucial issues of Muhammad's biography, the so-called 'charter of Medina' and the extermination of the Banu Quraiza, see respectively J. Wellhausen, 'Muhammeds Gemeindeordnung von Medina', in his *Skizzen und Vorarbeiten*, iv, Berlin, 1889, and W. Montgomery Watt, 'The Condemnation of the Jews of Banu Qurayzah', in *Muslim World*, xiii, 1952, 160–71 (according to the all too favourable viewpoint on Muhammed by that author).

5 Islam and the Arab-Muslim state

There are a great number of general text-books on Islam, many of them excellent: in English H. A. R. Gibb, *Mohammedanism*, New York, and London and Toronto, 1949, 2nd ed. 1953, New York and London; in French H. Lammens, *L'Islam. Croyances et institutions*, Beirut, 1926 (English translation by Sir E. Denison Ross, *Islam: Beliefs and Institutions*, London, 1929); in Italian M. M. Moreno, *Islamismo*, Milan, 1947. A work of high scholarly level is I. Goldziher, *Vorlesungen über den Islam*, Heidelberg, 1910 (2nd ed. 1925, Fr. trans. *Le dogme et la loi de l'Islam*, Paris, 1920). On the caliphate, see C. A. Nallino, 'Appunti sulla natura del Califfato in genere, e sul presunto "Califfato ottomano"', in *Raccolta di scritti editi e inediti*, iii, 234–59, Rome, 1939 ('Notes on the nature of the caliphate in general and on the alleged "Ottoman caliphate"', trans. from the 2nd ed., Rome, 1919). E. Tyan, *Institutions du droit public musulman, I, Le califat*, Paris, 1954. On the 'orthodox' caliphs, in addition to general histories of the Arabs and Islam, see E. Sachau, 'Der erste Chalife Abu Bekr', in *Sitzber. d. Preussischen Akad. d. Wiss.*, *1903*, and 'Über den zweiten Chalifen Omar,' ibid. 1902; G. Levi Della Vida, 'Il califfato di Ali secondo il K. Ansab al-Ashraf di al-Baladhuri', in *Rivista Studi Orientali*, vi, 1913. There are also modern biographies in Arabic by A. M. Aqqad and Taha Husein. On the Kharijite schism, see F. Gabrieli, 'Sulle origini del movimento harigita', in *Rend. Accademia d'Italia*, ser. 8, iii (1942) 110–17; M. Guidi, 'Sui Harigiti' in *Riv. St. Orientali*, xxi (1944), 1–14; L. Veccia Vaglieri, 'Il conflitto Ali̧-Muawiya e la secessione kharigita riesaminato alla luce di fonti ibadite', in *Annali Ist. Orientale di Napoli*, n.s. iv (1952), 1–94. A classic general study of the Umayyad caliphate can be found in J. Wellhausen, *Das Arabische Reich und sein Sturz*, Berlin, 1902 (*The Arab Kingdom and its fall*, Mystic, Conn, 1963, and *The Arab Kingdom and its fall*, trans. by Margaret Graham Weir, Calcutta, 1927) and by the same author 'Die religiös-politischen Oppositionsparteien im alten Islam', in *Abhandlungen d. K. Ges. d. Wiss. zu Göttingen*, 1901; on the Abbasid revolution see G. van Vloten, *De Opkomst der Abbasiden in Chorasan*, Leiden, 1890; Cl. Cahen, 'Points de vue sur la révolution abbaside', in *Revue Historique*, 468 (Oct.–Dec. 1963), 295–338.

6 The making of the Empire

The best over-all synthesised exposition of the Arab conquests is C. Becker, *The expansion of the Saracens*, Cambridge Medieval History, 1912, 329–90, and in German 'Die Ausbreitung der Araber im Mittelmeergebiet', in *Islamstudien*, I, Leipzig, 1924, 66–145. A more recent and popular book is J. B. Glubb, *The Great Arab Conquests*, London, 1963. On the climatic interpretation, see L. Caetani, 'La psicologia delle grandi vittorie musulmane', in *Studi di storia orientale*, I, Milan, 1911, 330–400. On military aspects, see M. Canard, 'Le problème militaire', in *L'Occidente e l'Islam nell'Alto Medioevo*, I, Spoleto, 1965, 37–63, and K. W. Butzer, 'Der Umweltfaktor in der grossen arabischen Expansion', in *Saeculum*, VIII, 1957, 357–71, also on climatic factors.

For the most complete analysis from the year 12/633 to 40/660, see L. Caetani, *Annali*, vols. III–X, Milan, 1900–26.

7 The Eastern Conquests: Iraq and Persia

The first critical examination of tradition – as of other topics – is J. Wellhausen, 'Prolegomena zur ältesten Geschichte des Islams', in *Skizzen und Vorarbeiten*, VI, Berlin, 1899, pp. 37–51 and 68–93 (conquest of Iraq), and 93–113 (conquest of Persia). A fuller and more detailed account is in Caetani, *Annali*, vols. III, IV, V, VII. Also Caetani, *Studi di storia orientale*, IV, 78–86, gives a reconstruction of Muthanna and Khalid's first campaign until Khalid was transferred to Syria. On early Islamic Persia, see B. Spuler, *Iran in frühislamischer Zeit*, Wiesbaden, 1952, with particular reference to pp. 5–21 ('Die arabische Eroberung Irans') and 133–145 ('Der Verlauf der Islamisierung Persiens').

8 The Northern Conquests: Syria, Mesopotamia and Armenia

Caetani's *Annali*, III–IV and *Studi di st. or.*, IV, 175–224 were preceded by much intensive critical study: Wellhausen, *Prolegomena* cit. 51–68 (Syria), and 83–9 (Mesopotamia); M.J.De Goeje, *Mémoire sur la conquête de la Syrie*, 2nd ed., Leiden, 1900 (Mémoires d'histoire et de géographie orientales, 2) N.Mednikov, *Palestina* (in Russian), 1, St Petersberg, 1897 (among other things he puts forward the suggestion, not generally accepted, that Ajnadain should be changed to Jannabatain). On the invasion of Armenia, apart from Caetani's *Annali*, vii, see J.Laurent's old study, *L'Arménie entre Byzance et l'Islam*, Paris, 1919 – a modernised version of it is now in preparation. It has been superseded on many points by H.Manadean, in *Byzantion*, xviii, 1946–48 (see also M.Canard in *Encyclopédie de l'Islam*, 2nd ed. 1,657). On Umayyad Syria, the most lively and stimulating picture is presented in H.Lammens' *La Syrie*, *Précis historique*, i, Beirut, 1921.

9 The Western Conquests: Egypt and North Africa

On the conquest of Egypt, Wellhausen's *Prolegomena* cit. 89–94 provides a summary analysis, and the standard reconstruction is A.J.Butler, *The Arab Conquest of Egypt and the last thirty years of Roman dominion*, Oxford, 1902. As indicated in the text, Caetani gives some contrary opinions in *Annali*, iv, viii. On the conquest of Africa some worthwhile information can still be found in H.Fournel's dated work *Les Berbers. Etude sur la conquête de l'Afrique par les Arabes*, Paris, 1875, and M.Caudel's *Les Premières invasions arabes dans l'Afrique du nord et l'Orient au Moyen Age*, Paris, 1900. General histories of North Africa are by E.Mercier (Paris 1889–91) and C.Jullien (Paris 1931). Important for its evaluation of a new source is E.Lévi-Provençal, 'Un Nouveau récit de la conquête de l'Afrique du nord par les Arabes', in *Arabica*, i, 1954, 17–43 (we followed its chronology in the text). On the arabisation of the Maghrib, W.Marçais, 'Comment l'Afrique du nord a été arabisée', in *Annales de l'Institut d'études orientales de l'Université d'Alger*, *17*, 1938, 1–22.

10 Islam in Europe: Spain, France and Italy

On the conquest of Spain, more worthwhile information than that of R.Dozy's *Histoire des Musulmans d'Espagne*, Leiden (1861; nouvelle édition revue et mise à jour par E.Lévi-Provençal, 3 tomes, Leiden, 1932) can be found in the same author's *Recherches sur l'histoire et la littérature de l'Espagne pendant le Moyen Age*, Leiden-Paris, 11, 1881, i, 183.

An admirable but not always reliable detailed study is E. Saavedra *Estudio sobre la invasión de los Árabes en España*, Madrid, 1892, completed by F. Codera's *Conquista de Aragon y Cataluña por los Musulmanes*, 1903; *Limites probables de la conquista arabe en la cordillera Pirenaica*, 1906; and *Narbona, Gerona y Barcelona bajo la dominacion musulmana*, 1909. All three are included in his *Estudios criticos de historia árabe-española*, I, Zaragoza, 1903, 95–110, II, Madrid 1917, 235–76, 277–334. The most modern and authoritative work is E. Lévi-Provençal, *Histoire de l'Espagne musulmane*, 2nd ed., I, Paris, 1950. An early work on the Arabs in France is J. Reinaud, *Invasion des Sarrazins en France*, Paris, 1836 (photographic reprint of the 1836 edition, Paris, 1964). There is also J. Lacam's *Les Sarrazins dans le haut moyen-âge français*, Paris, 1965.

On Switzerland see F. Keller, 'Der Einfall der Sarazenen in die Schweiz', in *Mitteilungen d. Antiquarischen Gesellschaft in Zürich*, XX, 1856. The classic work on Arab Sicily is M. Amari, *Storia dei Musulmani di Sicilia*, 2nd ed. Catania, 1933–38 (the first volume is on the invasion). There is no adequate general study on the incursions into Italy. On the emirate in Bari, G. Musca, *L'emirato di Bari*, Bari, 1964, which places the date of its foundation at 847.

11 Frontiers to the East

On the Arab occupation of Khorasan and the Arabs' internal conflicts, see J. Wellhausen, *Das Arabische Reich und sein Sturz*, Berlin, 1902, 247–306 (Ch. 8, 'Die arabischen Stämme in Churasan'), (see also English editions cited under chapter 5). On the conquest of Transoxiana, see H. A. R. Gibb, *The Arab Conquests in Central Asia*, London, 1923, and 'Chinese records of the Arabs in Central Asia', in *Bulletin of the School of Oriental Studies*, II, 1923, 613–22. On the wars with the Turks under Hisham, see F. Gabrieli, *Il califfato di Hisham*, Alexandria, 1935, 34–70 ('Il Khurasan e le guerre di Transoxiana'). The rich Arab literary documentation has been further increased by a documentary *unicum*, a letter from a local king to the Arab governor al-Jarrah (718–19), discovered in Soviet expeditions to Mugh on the Zarafshan (V. & I. Kračkovsky, *Sogdiisky Sbornik*, Academy of Science of the USSR, Leningrad, 1934, 52–90).

On the conquest of Sind under Hajjaj, see F. Gabrieli, 'Muhammad ibn al-Qasim e la prima penetrazione araba nel Sind' in *Rendiconti Lincei* Rome, 1965, 345–62.

12 The achievement of Arab Islam

There is a bibliography of works written in answer to H. Pirenne, *Mahomet et Charlemagne*, Paris-Brussels, 1937, London, 1940, and New York, 1955. See A. F. Havighurst, *The Pirenne Thesis. Analysis, Criticism and Revision*, Boston, 1958; London (paperbacks), 1958. On Arab sea-power in the Mediterranean, there are various studies, see H. Monès, *Moslems and the Mediterranean*, Cairo, 1956 (in Arabic); W. Hoenerbach, 'La Navegación omeya en el Mediterraneo y sus consecuencias politico-culturales', in *Miscelanea de estudios arabes y hebraicos*, Granada, 1953, II, pp. 77–98; E. Eickhoff, *Seekrieg und Seepolitik zwischen Islam und Abendland*, Berlin, 1966. On the Arabs and Byzantium, J. Wellhausen, 'Die Kämpfe der Araber mit den Romäern in der Zeit der Umaijaden' in *Nachr. Ges. Wiss.*, *Göttingen*, 1901, pp. 414–48; H. A. R. Gibb, 'Arab-Byzantine relations under the Umayyad Caliphate' in *Dumbarton Oaks Papers*, 12, 1958, pp. 219–33 (now incl. in *Studies on the Civilisation of Islam*, London, New York and Toronto, 1962, pp. 47–61); and F. Gabrieli, 'Greeks and Arabs in the Central Mediterranean', ibid., 18, 1964, pp. 59–66. For the Arab expeditions against Constantinople, see M. Canard in *Journal asiatique*, 208, 1926, pp. 61–121. On present-day Arabism, see F. Gabrieli, *Risorgimento arabo*, Turin, 1958; London, 1961, *The Arab revival*. ('The great revolutions'; Tr. by Lovett F. Evans.)

Acknowledgment is due to the following for illustrations (where the item illustrated forms part of a museum collection, this is shown in the caption to the illustration): Elek Books Ltd 28–9, 56–7; Radio Times Hulton Picture Library 66; Librairie Orientaliste Paul Geuthner 96; Dr Geza Fehervari 120–1, 136, 152–3, 165, 175; Ian Graham 129; Professor Arthur Upham Pope 139; Professor Richard Ettinghausen and Editions d'Art Albert Skira 144 and 161; J.E.Dayton 147; A.F.Kersting 156–7 and 173; Dr K.S. McLachlan 187; Dr Edmund de Unger 213; Oxford University Press 236-7.

Particular thanks are due to Dr Geza Fehervari and the School of Oriental and African Studies, London, for facilities made available to the publishers in collecting the illustrations.

The maps were researched and drawn by Design Practitioners Limited, and are the copyright of the publishers.

World University Library

Some books published or in preparation

Economics and Social Studies

The World Cities
Peter Hall, *London*

The Economics of Underdeveloped Countries
Jagdish Bhagwati, *Delhi*

Development Planning
Jan Tinbergen, *Rotterdam*

Leadership in New Nations
T. B. Bottomore, *Vancouver*

Human Communication
J. L. Aranguren, *Madrid*

Education in the Modern World
John Vaizey, *Oxford*

Soviet Economics
Michael Kaser, *Oxford*

Decisive Forces in World Economics
J. L. Sampedro, *Madrid*

Money
Roger Opie, *Oxford*

The Sociology of Africa
Georges Balandier, *Paris*

Science and Anti-Science
T. R. Gerholm, *Stockholm*

Key Issues in Criminology
Roger Hood, *Durham*

Society and Population
E. A. Wrigley, *Cambridge*

History

The Old Stone Age
François Bordes, *Bordeaux*

The Evolution of Ancient Egypt
Werner Kaiser, *Berlin*

The Emergence of Greek Democracy
W. G. Forrest, *Oxford*

The Roman Empire
J. P. V. D. Balsdon, *Oxford*

A History of China
G. F. Hudson, *Oxford*

The Age of Charlemagne
Jacques Boussard, *Poitiers*

The Crusades
Geo Widengren, *Uppsala*

The Medieval Economy
Georges Duby, *Aix-en-Provence*

The Medieval Italian Republics
D. P. Waley, *London*

The Ottoman Empire
Halil Inalcik, *Ankara*

Humanism in the Renaissance
S. Dresden, *Leyden*

The Rise of Toleration
Henry Kamen, *Warwick*

The Left in Europe since 1789
David Caute, *Oxford*

The Rise of the Working Class
Jürgen Kuczynski, *Berlin*

Chinese Communism
Robert North, *Stanford*

Arab Nationalism
Sylvia Haim, *London*

The Culture of Japan
Mifune Okumura, *Kyoto*

The History of Persia
Jean Aubin, *Paris*

Philosophy and Religion

Christianity
W. O. Chadwick, *Cambridge*

Monasticism
David Knowles, *London*

Judaism
J. Soetendorp, *Amsterdam*

The Modern Papacy
K. O. von Aretin, *Göttingen*

Sects
Bryan Wilson, *Oxford*

Language and Literature

A Model of Language
E. M. Uhlenbeck, *Leyden*

French Literature
Raymond Picard, *Paris*

**Russian Writers and Society
1825–1904**
Ronald Hingley, *Oxford*

Satire
Matthew Hodgart, *Sussex*

The Romantic Century
Robert Baldick, *Oxford*

The Arts

The Language of Modern Art
Ulf Linde, *Stockholm*

Architecture since 1945
Bruno Zevi, *Rome*

Twentieth Century Music
H. H. Stuckenschmidt, *Berlin*

Aesthetic Theories since 1850
J. F. Revel, *Paris*

Art Nouveau
S. Tschudi Madsen, *Oslo*

Academic Painting
Gerald Ackerman, *Stanford*

Palaeolithic Cave Art
P. J. Ucko and A. Rosenfeld, *London*

Primitive Art
Eike Haberland, *Mainz*

Romanesque Art
Carlos Cid Priego, *Madrid*

Expressionism
John Willett, *London*

Psychology and Human Biology

The Molecules of Life
Gisela Nass, *Munich*

The Variety of Man
J. P. Garlick, *London*

Eye and Brain
R. L. Gregory, *Cambridge*

The Ear and the Brain
E. C. Carterette, *U.C.L.A.*

The Biology of Work
O. G. Edholm, *London*

The Psychology of Attention
Anne Treisman, *Oxford*

Psychoses
H. J. Bochnik, *Hamburg*

Psychosomatic Medicine
A. Mitscherlich, *Heidelberg*

Child Development
Phillipe Muller, *Neuchâtel*

Man and Disease
Gernot Rath, *Göttingen*

Chinese Medicine
P. Huard and M. Wong, *Paris*

Mind in the Universe
Gösta Ehrensvärd, *Lund*

256

Zoology and Botany

The Age of the Dinosaurs
Björn Kurtén, *Helsingfors*

Animal Communication
J. M. Cullen, *Oxford*

Mimicry
Wolfgang Wickler, *Seewiesen*

Migration
Gustaf Rudebeck, *Stockholm*

Lower Animals
Martin Wells, *Cambridge*

The World of an Insect
Rémy Chauvin, *Strasbourg*

Biological Rhythms
Janet Harker, *Cambridge*

Life in the Sea
Gunnar Thorson, *Helsingore*

Primates
François Bourlière, *Paris*

The Conservation of Nature
C. Delamare Deboutteville, *Paris*

The Variation of Plants
S. M. Walters and D. Briggs,
Cambridge

Earth Sciences and Astronomy

The Structure of the Universe
E. L. Schatzman, *Paris*

Climate and Weather
H. Flohn, *Bonn*

Anatomy of the Earth
Andrè Cailleux, *Paris*

Physical Science and Mathematics

Energy
Etienne Fischhoff, *Paris*

Crystals and Minerals
Hugo Strunz, *Berlin*

The Quest for Absolute Zero
K. Mendelssohn, *Oxford*

Particles and Accelerators
Robert Gouiran, *C.E.R.N., Geneva*

What is Light ?
A. C. S. van Heel and C. H. F. Velzel,
Eindhoven

Waves and Corpuscles
J. A. e Silva and G. Lochak, *Paris*
Introduction by Louis de Broglie

Mathematics Observed
H. Freudenthal, *Utrecht*

Science and Statistics
S. Sagoroff, *Vienna*

Applied Science

Words and Waves
A. H. W. Beck, *Cambridge*

**The Science of
Decision-making**
A. Kaufmann, *Paris*

Bionics
Lucien Gérardin, *Paris*

Metals and Civilisation
R. W. Cahn, *Sussex*

Bioengineering
H. S. Wolff, *London*